ENGLISH PRONUNCIATION
Made Simple

PAULETTE DALE • LILLIAN POMS

Longman

longman.com

D0074143

English Pronunciation Made Simple

Pearson Education, 10 Bank Street, White Plains, NY 10606

Editorial director: Sherry Preiss
Acquisitions editor: Laura LeDréan
Development editor: John Barnes
Senior production editor: Kathleen Silloway
Art director: Tracey Cataldo
Higher education marketing manager: Joe Chapple
Senior manufacturing buyer: Nancy Flaggman
Cover and text design: Tracey Cataldo
Text composition: Laserwords Pvt. Ltd.
Text fonts: New Aster 10/13, Myriad 10/11
Text art: Tracey Cataldo

Reviewers

Judith Cocker, English and French Language Center, Canada
Carole Franklin, University of Houston, TX
Roberta Hodges, Sonoma State University, CA
Hakan Mansuroglu, ZONI Language Center, NJ
Kate Reynolds, University of Wisconsin—Eau Claire, WI
Alison Robertson, Cypress College, CA

Library of Congress Cataloging-in-Publication Data

Dale, Paulette.
  English pronunciation made simple / Paulette Wainless Dale, Lillian Poms.
    p. cm.
  Rev. ed. of: English pronunciation for international students. c1994.
  ISBN 0-13-111596-0
  1. English language–Pronunciation by foreign speakers–Problems, exercises, etc. I. Poms, Lillian. II. Dale,
Paulette. English pronunciation for international students. III. Title.
PE1157.D355 2004
428.3"4—dc22
                                                                          2004044196

Printed in the United States of America
4 5 6 7 8 9 10–BAH–09 08 07 06

Contents

Part 2: Stress, Rhythm, and Intonation

Part 3: Consonants

Appendices

About the Authors

Paulette Dale, Ph.D.

Dr. Paulette Dale is a full professor of Speech Communication/Linguistics at Miami-Dade College and an adjunct professor in the graduate program in Linguistics at Florida International University.

Dr. Dale is an internationally known author and consultant in the area of English Pronunciation and Speech Communication. Her published works include numerous articles, a pronunciation program written for Berlitz International, and five successful texts published by Pearson Education (*English Pronunciation for International Students, English Pronunciation for Spanish Speakers, English Pronunciation for Japanese Speakers, Speech Communication for International Students,* and *Speech Communication Made Simple: A Multicultural Perspective*).

Dr. Dale's pronunciation programs have been featured in newspapers and on radio and TV talk shows. She has conducted workshops in techniques of teaching English pronunciation for professionals and teachers worldwide and has made presentations at a variety of U.S. and international TESOL conferences.

Lillian Poms, M.Ed.

Lillian Poms is the Executive Director of the Hearing and Speech Center of Florida, which serves the speech-, language-, and hearing-impaired. She is also an adjunct professor in the Communication Arts Department at Miami-Dade College, where she has taught accent reduction, voice and diction, and public speaking.

Ms. Poms has co-authored *English Pronunciation for International Students, English Pronunciation for Spanish Speakers, English Pronunciation for Japanese Speakers,* and a pronounciation program for Berlitz International. She is past president of the Miami Association of Communication Specialists, from which she received honors in 1986. In 2002, she was awarded the Clinical Career Award from the Florida Association of Speech-Language Pathologists and Audiologists.

Ms. Poms pioneered the accent-reduction program at the Hearing and Speech Center of Florida and has provided accent-reduction training for many performers. One of her more famous students is Julio Iglesias, who received diction and pronunciation coaching from her.

Preface

English Pronunciation Made Simple is designed to help students develop pronunciation skills and overcome pronunciation problems when speaking English. We understand how frustrating it is to have someone say, "I can't understand you because of your accent." We know that students of English as a second language may be afraid to use certain words because they are difficult to pronounce. Many students avoid words like *rice* and *berry*, for instance. *English Pronunciation Made Simple* gives students the fundamental understanding of pronunciation—and the confidence they need—so they no longer have to avoid certain words and phrases. Most important, students *don't* have to be misunderstood by other people.

English Pronunciation Made Simple can be used either as a classroom textbook or as a comprehensive program for self-study. It is organized so that any academic schedule can be accommodated, making it ideal for use as a course textbook. However, *English Pronunciation Made Simple* may also be used independently, by students who want to be better understood in English. Presented in clear, easy-to-understand terms, the material in this book is accompanied by an audio program that enables students to maximize their learning outside of the classroom.

English Pronunciation Made Simple is divided into three parts—Part 1: Vowels, Part 2: Stress, Rhythm, and Intonation, and Part 3: Consonants. Each part contains a series of brief lessons, and each lesson presents one or two specific pronunciation points.

Vowel Lessons and Consonant Lessons

The vowel and consonant lessons (Parts 1 and 3) follow a consistent format and are designed to provide both clear, accessible presentations of pronunciation points and ample practice. Each lesson includes:

- **Pronouncing the Sound**   A simple explanation of how to pronounce the sound, with mouth drawings that show how to use the articulators (lips, tongue, etc.) for each sound.

- **Possible Pronunciation Problems**   An explanation of how and why the sound may create problems for students.

- **Hints**   Rules to help students remember when to produce the target sound, which emphasize the recognition of English spelling patterns as a guide to pronunciation. (NOTE: Not every lesson includes a hint.)

- **Exercises**   A comprehensive wealth of productive practice opportunities using the sound as it occurs in words, common phrases, and sentences.

- **More Practice**   A variety of listening, reading, and communicative conversational activities that reflect how the sound is heard and used in daily life. At least one activity in this section is productive.

- **Check Yourself**   Additional activities designed to help students recognize and evaluate their progress. Answers to all *Check Yourself* exercises are provided in Appendix II.

Stress, Rhythm, and Intonation Lessons

The lessons in Part 2 expose students to the stress, rhythm, and intonation of American English and focus on helping students hear and produce natural-sounding language beyond the word level. Students work on common phrases, sentences, and pieces of more extended discourse.

The audio CDs that are packaged with this book contain the *Check Yourself* listenings. In addition, a classroom audio program available on both CDs and cassettes includes the listenings for these sections as well as for the exercises for each lesson. This classroom audio program also provides models of correct pronunciation for each sound presented.

To the Student

Welcome to _English Pronunciation Made Simple_! Before we begin, let's look at the term "foreign accent" in general. The _Longman Dictionary of American English_ defines _accent_ as "a way of speaking that someone has because of where s/he was born or lives." So the truth is, we _all_ have accents! In fact, you should be proud that you speak English with an accent. A "foreign" accent tells people that you speak at least two languages. And the world would be very dull if we all sounded the same.

Unfortunately, the disadvantage to having a "foreign" accent is that it may hinder effective communication in your nonnative language and cause you to be misunderstood. Our main goal is to help you improve your pronunciation of North American English. This will enable you to communicate clearly what you want to say. Frequent practice and review is important. We suggest practice sessions at least three or four times a week, even if you can only manage 20 or 30 minutes each session. We know this is hard work. Take breaks when you get tired. Improvement takes time, but little by little, you will succeed.

If you live or work among English speakers, you will quickly find ways to apply what you learn in _English Pronunciation Made Simple_ to situations outside of class. But even if you live in a non-English-speaking environment, you should try to get as much practice as possible in applying the material in the book. Here are some things you can do to reinforce what you are learning.

- Watch English language news on TV as often as you can. Pay careful attention to the newscaster's pronunciation. Notice especially words and phrases that are repeated every time you watch. Practice saying them. Write them down. Compare your pronunciation with the newscaster's.

- Listen to radio news stations for 5 to 10 minutes at a time. Repeat common words and phrases after the announcer.

- When one of your favorite English language TV shows is on, try to understand the dialogue without watching. Or try this with commercials: See if you can tell what is being advertised without looking.

- Whenever you have the opportunity to converse with a North American English speaker, use it! Try to include common expressions presented in this book, such as "See you this evening" or "Pleased to meet you."

- Ask your listener if your pronunciation of a specific word is correct. Most listeners will be glad to help.

Although *English Pronunciation Made Simple* emphasizes pronunciation, it can also help you increase your vocabulary. When you don't understand a word or idiom, look it up in your dictionary. (We recommend the *Longman Dictionary of American English*.) Write the definition down so you won't forget it.

Using *English Pronunciation Made Simple* on Your Own

If you are using these materials for self-study, you will probably want to own the entire set of classroom CDs or cassettes, so you can get the most from the comprehensive program. To get the greatest benefit, follow these simple suggestions:

- **Exercises**   Go to the appropriate exercise in the audio program. Read the directions. Listen. Repeat words or phrases during the pauses. Stop and go back whenever you like. If you have difficulty at any time, stop and reread the directions for pronouncing the sound. Look in a mirror as you say the sound to be sure that your articulators (tongue, lips, and so on) are in the correct position. Use the drawing in the book to check this. Repeat the exercise until you can say the sounds, words, phrases, or sentences easily. When you are able to repeat the material without looking at the book, you are ready to move on.

- **More Practice**   When you are satisfied with your pronunciation of the target sound in the exercises, you are ready to apply what you have learned to content and situations similar to those you might encounter in real life. More Practice provides controlled practice with this. Be aware of situations in your daily life that provide parallel practice. Have fun recognizing and producing the sound in other poems, readings, and conversations, and try to find other ways to incorporate what you have learned in your daily encounters with English.

- **Check Yourself**   Do not be discouraged if you make some mistakes in this section. The purpose of the Check Yourself section is to help you measure your progress and to identify areas that still need work. The instructions for each Check Yourself exercise are different. Read all directions carefully before beginning. When you finish a test, check your answers in Appendix II. If you have difficulty with an exercise, return to the beginning of the lesson and repeat the activities in More Practice. The dialogues and paragraphs are the most difficult activities in each lesson. Review them often as you progress through the book.

You may wonder how long it will take before you see improvement. We believe that improvement depends on practice—and *English Pronunciation Made Simple* provides all the tools you need to practice often. We hope you find it makes a difference in a matter of weeks!

Part 1 Vowels

Lesson 1 Pronouncing the Vowels of American English

You have probably discovered that there is a big difference between the way words are spelled in English and the way they are pronounced. English spelling patterns are inconsistent and are not always a reliable guide to pronunciation. For example, in the following words, the letter *a* is used to represent five different sounds.

hate   father   have   any   saw

Pretty confusing, right? That's why we need a set of symbols in which *each* sound is represented by a *different* symbol. In this book, you will see symbols used. These are the International Phonetic Alphabet (IPA), which is used all over the world. It consists of a set of symbols in which *one symbol* represents *one sound*.

DON'T PANIC! It is not necessary to learn all the symbols at once. Each sound will be introduced and explained one at a time. You will learn the symbols easily as you progress through the book. A pronunciation key to the different vowels and diphthongs of American English with their IPA symbols is presented below. Refer to it as needed.

To help you understand the exact pronunciation of the phonetic symbols and key words, the Key to Pronouncing the Vowels of American English is included in the audio program. You will hear each phonetic symbol introduced and pronounced once. Each English key word will be said once.

Key to Pronouncing the Vowels of American English

INTERNATIONAL PHONETIC ALPHABET SYMBOL		ENGLISH KEY WORDS
SECTION 1	[i]	me, tea, bee
	[ɪ]	it, pin
	[eɪ]	ate, game, they
	[ɛ]	egg, head, pet
	[æ]	at, fat, happy
	[a]	hot, father
SECTION 2	[u]	you, too, rule
	[ʊ]	put, cook
	[ʌ]	up, but, come
	[oʊ]	boat, no, oh
	[ɔ]	all, boss, caught
SECTION 3	[ə]	soda, upon
	[ɝ]	urn, first, serve
	[ɚ]	father, after
	[aʊ]	out, cow, house
	[aɪ]	my, pie, I
	[ɔɪ]	oil, boy, noise

Definitions

As you progress through *English Pronunciation Made Simple*, you will frequently see the terms *articulators*, *vowels*, and *diphthongs*. We will now define these terms for you.

Articulators: The articulators are the different parts of the mouth area that we use when speaking, such as the lips, tongue, teeth, and jaw.

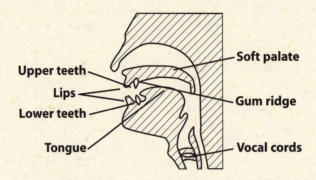

Vowel: A vowel is a speech sound produced with vibrating vocal cords and a continuous unrestricted flow of air coming from the mouth. The most well-known vowels in English are:

A   E   I   O   U

The various vowel sounds are affected by the changing shape and position of your articulators. The different vowels are created by:

1. **The position of your tongue in the mouth.** For example, the tongue is high in the mouth for the vowel [i] as in "see," but is low the mouth for the vowel [a] as in "hot."

2. **The shape of your lips.** For example, the lips are very rounded for the vowel [u] as in "new," but are spread for [i] as in "see."

3. **The size of your jaw opening.** For example, the jaw is open much wider for [a] as in "hot" than it is for the diphthong [eɪ] as in "pay."

Diphthong: A diphthong is a combination of two vowel sounds. It begins as one vowel and ends as another. During the production of a diphthong, your articulators glide from the position of the first vowel to the position of the second. For example, when pronouncing [eɪ] as in "vein," your articulators glide from the vowel [e] to the vowel [ɪ]. In English, the most common diphthongs are [aʊ], [eɪ], [aɪ], [ɔɪ], and [ou].

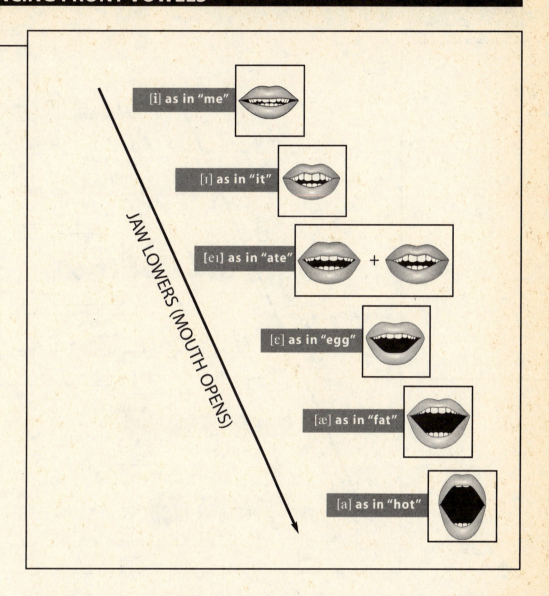

JAW LOWERS (MOUTH OPENS)

[i] as in "me"

[ɪ] as in "it"

[eɪ] as in "ate" +

[ɛ] as in "egg"

[æ] as in "fat"

[a] as in "hot"

You can see in the pictures how the jaw moves from a closed position to an open one during pronunciation of the vowel sequence [i], [ɪ], [eɪ], [ɛ], [æ], [a]. Becoming familiar with this progression and understanding the relationship of one vowel to another will help you with your pronunciation of the vowels.

- The phonetic symbol [ɪ] represents a sound between [i] and [eɪ]. It is pronounced with the jaw and tongue raised more than for [eɪ], but not as much as for [i].

- The symbol [æ] represents a sound between [ɛ] and [a]. [æ] is pronounced with the jaw open more than for [ɛ] but not as much as for [a].

Refer to these pictures whenever you have difficulty pronouncing any of the vowels. Repeat the sequence [i], [ɪ], [eɪ], [ɛ], [æ], [a] several times. Notice the progressive dropping of your tongue and jaw as you pronounce each sound.

PRONOUNCING BACK VOWELS

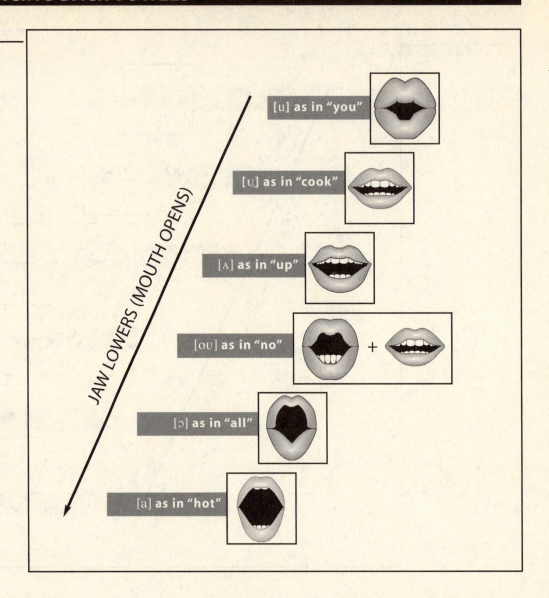

JAW LOWERS (MOUTH OPENS)

[u] as in "you"

[ʊ] as in "cook"

[ʌ] as in "up"

[oʊ] as in "no" +

[ɔ] as in "all"

[a] as in "hot"

Once again you can see how the jaw moves from a closed position to an open one during the pronunciation of a vowel sequence. Practice pronouncing the series several times. Place your hand under your chin and feel your jaw drop with the pronunciation of each vowel.

Refer to these pictures whenever you are confused about the pronunciation of any of the vowels. Repeat the sequence [u], [ʊ], [ʌ], [oʊ], [ɔ], [a] several times. You'll be able to see and feel your jaw lower as you pronounce the vowels in the series. TRY IT NOW! IT REALLY WORKS!

Lesson 2 [i] as in *me*, *tea*, and *bee* and [ɪ] as in *it* and *pin*

PRONOUNCING [i]

Lips: Tense and in a "smile" position

Jaw: Almost completely raised

Tongue: High, near the roof of the mouth

Possible Pronunciation Problems

Pronunciation problems occur because of confusing English spelling patterns and the similarity of [i] and [ɪ] (the sound to be described next).

EXAMPLES If you say [ɪ] instead of [i]:   **sheep** will sound like **ship**.

eat will sound like **it**.

Remember to feel tension in your lips, tongue, and jaw. [i] is a *long* sound; be sure to prolong it.

Smile when you say [i]; we guarant*ee* it's *ea*sy to say [i]!

Practice

EXERCISE A   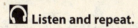 **Listen and repeat.**

[i] At the Beginning of Words

eat	each	eager
eel	even	either
east	equal	
easy	eagle	

[i] In the Middle of Words

mean	seal	please
need	leave	police
keep	reach	
deep	scene	

[i] At the End of Words

he	fee	she
be	tree	agree
key	knee	
tea	free	

[i] Spelled

e	*ee*	*ea*	*ie* or *ie*
he	see	east	niece
we	feel	lean	brief
me	deed	team	piece
scene	heel	cheap	belief
these	need	peach	either

Less frequent spelling patterns for [i] consist of the letters *i* and *eo*.

    police   people

EXERCISE B

Listen and repeat. The vowel [i] is prolonged before consonants. (Consonants are all the sounds that are not vowels.) The dots are there to remind you to lengthen the [i].

fee	fee . . . d
see	see . . . d
pea	pea . . . s
bee	bee . . . s
tea	tea . . . m

EXERCISE C

Listen and repeat. The boldfaced words in the following sentences all include the vowel [i].

1. **See** you at **three**.
2. **See** what I **mean**?
3. **See** you next **week**.
4. **See** you this **evening**.
5. **Pleased** to **meet** you.
6. **Steve eats cream cheese**.
7. **Lee** has a **reason** for **leaving**.
8. **She received** her **teaching degree**.
9. A friend in **need** is a friend **indeed**.
10. They **reached** a **peace agreement**.

CHECK YOURSELF

Listen and repeat. Circle the word in each group that does NOT contain the vowel [i]. (For answers, see Appendix II, page 271.)

EXAMPLE	keep	lean	(fit)	piece
1.	bead	great	leave	tea
2.	eight	piece	believe	niece
3.	scene	women	these	even
4.	need	been	sleep	thirteen
5.	police	thief	machine	vision
6.	pretty	wheat	sweet	cream
7.	people	bread	deal	east
8.	tin	teen	steam	receive
9.	leave	live	leaf	lease
10.	steep	Steve	easy	still

EXERCISE A   📖 **Read aloud the paragraph about the Beatles. All the boldfaced words should be pronounced with the vowel [i].**

The **Beatles**

What is a **Beatle**? **Maybe** you think of a **real creature** who **creeps** and **leaps** about. But most **people** recall four English **teens** called the **Beatles**, who appeared as a rock group in the **nineteen sixties**. **Leaving bebop** behind, the **Beatles** created a **unique beat** that **appealed** to everyone. **Seen** on American **TV**, they were **greeted** by **screams** and cheers. "**Please Please Me**" and "**She** Loves You" were among their **many pieces**. They **even received** an award from the **queen** of England. The **team** broke up as they **reached** their **peak**, but **each** member continued his own career. The world **grieved** the loss of their **leader**, John Lennon, who died in December **1980**. Although only **briefly** on the **scene**, the **Beatles created meaningful** music that will **be** here for an **eternity**.

EXERCISE B   👤 **Think of five things you need to do. Be sure your response contains many [i] words. When you complete your responses, choose any classmate and ask the question, "What do you really need?"**

EXAMPLES   I **really need** to **feed** my **parakeet**.
               I **really need** a new **key**.

PRONOUNCING [ɪ]

Lips: Relaxed and slightly parted
Jaw: Slightly lower than for [i]
Tongue: High, but lower than for [i]

Possible Pronunciation Problems

The vowel [ɪ] may be difficult for you to recognize and say. Some learners substitute the more familiar [i] sound. This can result in miscommunication.

EXAMPLES   If you say [i] instead of [ɪ]:   **hit** will sound like **heat**.
                                        itch will sound like **each**.

As you practice the exercises, remember not to "smile" and tense your lips as you would for [i].

[ɪ] *is a short, qu*i*ck sound; your l*i*ps should barely move as you say* i*t!*

Practice

EXERCISE A

🎧 **Listen and repeat.**

[ɪ] At the Beginning of Words			[ɪ] In the Middle of Words		
is	if	it	pin	lift	give
ill	itch	into	miss	simple	winter
ink	inch	issue	listen	timid	minute
instant			little		

The vowel [ɪ] does not occur at the end of words in English.

[ɪ] Spelled

y	ui	i
gym	build	sin
syrup	quick	lips
symbol	quilt	with
system	guilty	gift
rhythm	guitar	differ

note

The most common spelling pattern for [ɪ] is the letter *i* followed by a final consonant.

win   this   hit   trip   begin

Less frequent spelling patterns for [ɪ] consist of the letters *o, e, u,* and *ee.*

women   pretty   busy   been

EXERCISE B

🎧 **Listen and repeat. The boldfaced words in the following sentences all contain the vowel [ɪ].**

1. **This is it**.
2. What **is this**?
3. **This is** my **sister**.
4. **This is Miss Smith**.
5. **This is big business**.
6. I **will sit in** a **minute**.
7. **Give** the **list** to **Lynn**.
8. My **little sister is timid**.
9. **Is** the **building finished**?
10. **Did** you **give him his gift**?

Listen to the words. Circle the number of the word with the vowel [I].
(For answers, see Appendix II, page 271.)

EXAMPLE   *You hear*   mitt   meat   meat
          You circle   ①   2   3

1. 1   2   3
2. 1   2   3
3. 1   2   3
4. 1   2   3
5. 1   2   3
6. 1   2   3
7. 1   2   3
8. 1   2   3
9. 1   2   3
10. 1   2   3

More Practice

EXERCISE A   **Read aloud the paragraph about the Olympics. All the boldfaced words contain the vowel [I].**

The **Winter Olympics**

Since 1924, the **Winter Olympics** have **been** an **international** event. Now these **activities** are seen by **millions** on **television**. Men and **women** from **distant cities** and countries **participate in this competition**. They all **wish** to be **winners**. They ski **downhill amidst pretty** scenery. **Figure** skaters **spin** to **victory**. **Skill will** make the **difference**. Some **will finish with** a **silver** medal, some **with** a gold. But all **will win** our hearts and **infinite** respect.

EXERCISE B   **Work with a partner. Complete each of the following sentences with a phrase or word that rhymes with the boldfaced [I] words. Think of as many responses as you can for each rhyme. Read the sentences aloud.**

EXAMPLE   My sister **Jill** _____.
          (ran up a **hill**/took a **pill**/felt very **ill**/has a cat named **Bill**/fell off the window**sill**)

1. My friend **Tim** _____.

2. He will **sit** _____.

3. The boy liked to **grin** _____.

4. What do you **think** _____?

5. We went on a **ship** _____.

LESSON REVIEW: [i] AND [ɪ]

Remember to "smile" and feel the tension in your lips when you repeat the words with [i] and to RELAX your muscles as you pronounce the words containing [ɪ].

Practice

EXERCISE   🎧 **Listen and repeat.**

[i]	[ɪ]
1. least	list
2. seat	sit
3. heat	hit
4. feet	fit
5. leave	live
6. Heat it now.	Hit it now.
7. Change the wheel.	Change the will.
8. Did you feel it?	Did you fill it?
9. The meal was big.	The mill was big.
10. He will leave.	He will live.

          [ɪ] [ɪ]   [i]
11. Please sit in the seat.

          [ɪ]   [i]
12. He did a good deed.

          [ɪ]   [i]
13. Phil doesn't feel well.

          [ɪ]   [i]   [i]
14. Lynn ate lean meat.

          [ɪ]   [i]
15. Potato chips are cheap.

CHECK YOURSELF 1   🎧 **Listen. Circle the word that you hear. (For answers to Check Yourself 1–3, see Appendix II, pages 271–272.)**

EXAMPLE   meat   (mitt)

1. field   filled
2. bean   bin
3. neat   knit
4. deal   dill
5. beat   bit

6. team   Tim

7. sleep   slip

8. green   grin

9. heel   hill

10. week   wick

CHECK YOURSELF 2 🎧 **Listen. Circle the word that is used to complete each sentence.**

EXAMPLE   You need a new ((wheel)/will).

1. They cleaned the (ship/sheep).

2. Will he (leave/live)?

3. The boy was (beaten/bitten).

4. His clothes are (neat/knit).

5. She has plump (cheeks/chicks).

6. I like low (heels/hills).

7. The children will (sleep/slip).

8. I heard every (beat/bit).

9. They stored the (beans/bins).

10. Everyone talks about the (heat/hit).

📖 **After checking your answers, read each of the sentences aloud twice. Use the first word the first time you read and the second word the second time.**

CHECK YOURSELF 3 🎧 **Listen and circle all the words pronounced with [i]. Underline all the words with [ɪ].**

Jim: Hi, (Tina!) Do you have a <u>minute</u>?

Tina: Yes, Jim. What is it?

Jim: My sister is in the city on business. We will eat dinner out tonight. Can you recommend a place to eat?

Tina: There is a fine seafood place on Fifth Street. The fish is fresh, and the shrimp is great. But it isn't cheap!

Jim: That's OK. It will be "feast today, famine tomorrow"! I'll just have to eat beans the rest of the week!

👥 **Now practice reading the dialogue aloud with a partner. Remember to "smile" and tense your lips for [i] and to relax them when pronouncing the [ɪ] words.**

EXERCISE A

📖 The words in the following box occur in the poem "The Passionate Shepherd to His Love." Read the words aloud.

	[ɪ]		[i]	
his	sit	me	field
live	rivers	be	yield
with	sing	we	meat
will	silver	see	eat
hills	dishes	feed	each

EXERCISE B

📖 Read the poem aloud. Be sure to pronounce all the boldfaced [i] and [ɪ] words from the box correctly.

The Passionate Shepherd to **His** Love
Christopher Marlowe

Come **live with me** and **be** my love,
And **we will** all the pleasures prove
That **hills** and valleys, dale and **field**,
And all the craggy mountains **yield**.
There **will we sit** upon the rocks
And **see** the shepherds **feed** their flocks,
By shallow **rivers** to whose falls
Melodious birds **sing** madrigals.

Thy **silver dishes** for thy **meat**
As precious as the gods do **eat**,
Shall on an ivory table **be**
Prepared **each** day for you and **me**.

EXERCISE C

👤 These phrases are often used in introductions. Read them, paying attention to the [ɪ] and [i] words. Then work with two other students. Practice using the phrases to introduce each other.

———————, **this is** ————— .
(Name)   OR   (Name)

————————, I'd like you to **meet** ——————— .
(Name)   (Name)

Hi, ——————— ,
(Name)

nice to **meet** you.

Remember to k*ee*p practicing! We guarant*ee* *it*'s *easy* to say [ɪ] and [i]!

Lesson 3   [eɪ] as in *ate*, *game*, and *they*

PRONOUNCING [eɪ]

Lips: Spread and unrounded

Jaw: Rises with the tongue and closes slightly

Tongue: Glides from midlevel to near the roof of the mouth

[eɪ] is a diphthong. A diphthong is a compound vowel sound made by blending two vowels together very quickly. [eɪ] begins with [e] and ends with [ɪ].

Possible Pronunciation Problems

Pronunciation problems occur because of confusing English spelling patterns and the similarity of [eɪ] and [ɛ] (the sound to be described in the next lesson).

EXAMPLES   If you say [ɛ] instead of [eɪ]:   **late** will sound like **let**.

paper will sound like **pepper**.

With practice, you'll *say* [eɪ] the right *way*!

Practice

EXERCISE A   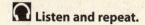 **Listen and repeat.**

[eɪ] At the Beginning of Words

ate	aim	ache
ape	ale	eight
age	able	April
apron		

[eɪ] In the Middle of Words

same	lake	place
rain	date	break
came	table	paint
paper		

[eɪ] At the End of Words

way	lay	obey
say	May	away
day	they	stay
weigh		

[eɪ] Spelled

a	*ai*	*ay*	*eigh*
late	main	day	eight
sane	fail	bay	weigh
safe	wait	hay	sleigh
hate	grain	ray	freight
lady	raise	play	neighbor

note

Less frequent spelling patterns for [eɪ] consist of the letters *ea*, *ey*, and *ei*.

br**ea**k   gr**ea**t   th**ey**   gr**ey**   v**ei**n

hint

When *a* is in a syllable ending in silent *e*, the letter *a* is pronounced [eɪ] (the same as the name of the alphabet letter *a*!).

s**a**me   n**a**me   c**a**se   l**a**ne   b**a**ke

The letters *ay*, *ai*, and *ey* are usually pronounced [eɪ].

pl**ay**   aw**ay**   b**ai**t   **ai**m   th**ey**

The letters *ei* followed by *g* or *n* are usually pronounced [eɪ].

w**ei**gh   n**ei**ghbor   r**ei**gn   v**ei**n

EXERCISE B

🎧 **Listen and repeat the following phrases and sentences. The boldfaced words should all be pronounced with the diphthong [eɪ].**

1. **Wake** up!
2. **gain weight**
3. What's your **name**?
4. **late date**
5. **Take** it **away**!
6. **Make haste**, not **waste**!
7. **April** showers bring **May** flowers.
8. **They played** a **great game**.
9. The **plane** from **Spain came late**.
10. They **made** a **mistake** in **today's paper**.

CHECK YOURSELF 1

📖 **Read the following shopping list. You are going to buy the items with the [eɪ] sound. Circle only the items containing the vowel [eɪ]. (For answers to Check Yourself 1–3, see Appendix II, pages 272–273.)**

1. (steak)	lettuce	(pastry)	cereal
2. bread	raisins	melon	bananas
3. cake	tomatoes	bacon	baking soda
4. potatoes	crackers	peas	ice cream
5. grapes	celery	gravy	carrots
6. toothpaste	peas	squash	paper plates

🎧 **Listen. Circle the one word in each group that is pronounced with the diphthong [eɪ].**

	EXAMPLE	*You hear*	hat	hot	hate
		You circle	1	2	③

1. 1   2   3
2. 1   2   3
3. 1   2   3
4. 1   2   3
5. 1   2   3
6. 1   2   3
7. 1   2   3
8. 1   2   3
9. 1   2   3
10. 1   2   3

CHECK YOURSELF 3 📖 **Read aloud the following newspaper advertisement. Circle all words pronounced with [eɪ].**

JAMESTOWN DAILY NEWSPAPER   MAY 7, 2004

FAMOUS ONE-DAY SALE AT

Ames Ladies Store

(located at 18th Street at the corner of Main and Blake)

Monday, May 8th—*Mark that date*!

Great buys!

Take home famous name brands,
your favorite labels!
Available for ladies of all ages.

Save up to **80%**

Why pay more? Take a train, take the subway, take a plane—but don't wait!
Don't stay away from this major sale.

Head straight to Ames—the place that "aims" to please!

SINCE 1888   NO EXCHANGES OR RETURNS

EXERCISE A

Read aloud the following paragraph about Babe Ruth. Remember that all the boldfaced words should be pronounced with the diphthong [eɪ].

Babe Ruth

Babe Ruth was a **famous baseball player**. He was born in Baltimore and **raised** there as an orphan. He first **played** for the Boston Red Sox but was **later traded** to the New York Yankees. He hit 714 home runs and **became** a **baseball** legend. He was **named** to the **Baseball** Hall of **Fame**. The last team he **played** for was the Boston **Braves**. He died in **1948**. Many **say** he was the **greatest player** of his **day**.

EXERCISE B

Choose an article from the sports section of a newspaper. Circle the words in the article that contain the vowel [eɪ]. Practice reading the article aloud. Bring it to class and read it to your classmates.

Say [eɪ] the right *way*! Practice *makes* perfect!

Lesson 4 — [ɛ] as in *egg*, *pet*, and *head*

PRONOUNCING [ɛ]

Lips: Slightly spread and unrounded

Jaw: Open wider than for [eɪ]

Tongue: High, near the roof of the mouth

Possible Pronunciation Problems

Pronunciation problems occur because of confusing English spelling patterns and the similarity between [ɛ] and other sounds.

EXAMPLES   If you say [eɪ] instead of [ɛ]:   **pen** will sound like **pain**.

If you say [æ] instead of [ɛ]:   **met** will sound like **mat**.

When pronouncing [ɛ], open your mouth wider than for [eɪ] but not as wide as for [æ] (the sound to be discussed in the next lesson).

Practice and reduce your errors on [ɛ]!

Practice

EXERCISE A   **Listen and repeat.**

[ɛ] At the Beginning of Words			[ɛ] In the Middle of Words		
any	edge	effort	bed	rest	bread
end	else	error	next	bent	fence
egg	every	elephant	west	many	present

The vowel [ɛ] does not occur at the end of words in English.

[ɛ] Spelled

e	*ea*
yes	head
red	lead
sell	dead
seven	meant
never	measure

Less frequent spelling patterns for [ɛ] consist of the letters *a, ai, ie, ue*, and *eo*.

any ag**ai**n fr**ie**nd g**ue**st **leo**pard

The most common spelling pattern for [ɛ] is the letter *e* before a consonant in a stressed syllable.

l**e**t am**e**ndment att**e**nded pl**e**nty

The letter *e* before *l* is usually pronounced [ɛ].

w**e**ll t**e**lephone f**e**lt s**e**ldom

The letters *ea* before *d* are usually pronounced [ɛ].

thr**ea**d ah**ea**d r**ea**dy d**ea**d

EXERCISE B

🎧 **Listen and repeat the following pairs of words. When pronouncing the words with [ɛ], be sure to lower your jaw a bit more than for [eɪ].**

[ɛ]	[eɪ]
met	mate
bet	bait
fed	fade
less	lace
pen	pain/pane
let	late
wet	wait/weight
get	gate/gait
red	raid
wed	wade

EXERCISE C

🎧 **Listen and repeat the following phrases and sentences. The boldfaced words should all be pronounced with the vowel [ɛ].**

1. You **said** it!
2. **head** of **lettuce**
3. **best friend**
4. **healthy** and **wealthy**
5. **bent fender**
6. **never better**
7. **Breakfast** is **ready** at **ten**.
8. **Fred left** a **message**.
9. **Let** me **get** some **rest**!
10. Don't **forget** to **send** the **letter**.

🎧 **Listen and repeat each word. Then circle the word in each group that is NOT pronounced with [ɛ]. (For answers to Check Yourself 1 and 2, see Appendix II, pages 273–274.)**

EXAMPLE	Mexico	America	(Egypt)	Texas
1.	any	crazy	anywhere	many
2.	paper	letter	send	pencil
3.	seven	eleven	eight	twenty
4.	health	wreath	breath	wealth
5.	reading	ready	already	head
6.	present	precious	previous	president
7.	November	February	September	April
8.	guess	guest	cruel	question
9.	thread	threat	fresh	theater
10.	mean	meant	mental	met

🎧 **Listen to the sentences. Some words that should be pronounced with [ɛ] will be said incorrectly. Circle C for correct or I for incorrect.**

EXAMPLES	*You hear*	Who fed the fish?	*You circle*	Ⓒ	I
	You hear	I got wait in the rain.	*You circle*	C	Ⓘ

1. C   I
2. C   I
3. C   I
4. C   I
5. C   I
6. C   I
7. C   I
8. C   I
9. C   I
10. C   I

EXERCISE A

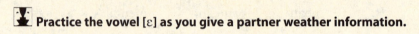 **Read aloud the paragraph about Peter Pan. Pay attention to the [ɛ] sound in the boldfaced words.**

Peter Pan

Do you **remember** the play *Peter Pan*? Who can **forget** the boy who **never ever** wanted to grow up! **When Wendy** and her brothers **met** Peter Pan and the fairy Tinker **Bell**, they flew to **Never-Never** Land. They had **many adventures** with Peter's **friends** and **enemies**, but the play had a happy **ending**. Sir James Barrie, the author, **presented** this play in 1911.

This **sentimental treasure** was his **best** work and made him **very wealthy**. It was an even **better success** on Broadway. It was **set** to music and had **special effects**. It is often **said** that no one can be young **forever**. But with the **legend** of Peter Pan we **get** to **pretend again** and **again**.

EXERCISE B

Practice the vowel [ɛ] as you give a partner weather information.

1. Look at these example sentences:

   It's **twenty**-two degrees and **very** windy.
   The **temperature** on **Wednesday** will be in the upper **seventies**.
   The **weather** for the **weekend** is **expected** to be **wet** and cloudy.

2. Read a weather report in the newspaper, watch a weather report on TV, or listen to a weather report on the radio. Use the information about weather in your area to make new sentences, based on the examples in item 1 above.

3. Tell a partner your weather report.

Practice your [ɛ] ag*ai*n and ag*ai*n, and reduce your *e*rrors wh*e*n you say [ɛ]!

[æ] as in *at*, *fat*, and *happy*

PRONOUNCING [æ]

Lips: Spread

Jaw: Open wider than for [ɛ]

Tongue: Low, near the floor of the mouth

Possible Pronunciation Problems

The vowel [æ] might not exist in your language and may be difficult for you to hear and produce. Also, irregular English spelling patterns are likely to cause confusion.

EXAMPLES   If you say [a] instead of [æ]:   **hat** will sound like **hot**.

If you say [ɛ] instead of [æ]:   **bad** will sound like **bed**.

When producing the vowel [æ], remember to spread your lips and open your mouth. But don't open it too wide, or you will find yourself substituting [a] (the sound to be discussed in the next lesson) instead!

Practice, practice, practice, and you'll have [æ] down pat!

Practice

EXERCISE A   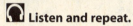 **Listen and repeat.**

[æ] At the Beginning of Words			[æ] In the Middle of Words		
am	apple	angry	cat	back	black
and	after	absent	map	happy	last
ask	actor	animal	have	rapid	classroom

The vowel [æ] does not occur at the end of words in English.

note

A less frequent spelling pattern for [æ] consists of the letters *au*.

laugh   **lau**ghter

🎧 **Listen and repeat. When saying [æ], remember to open your mouth more than for [ɛ].**

[æ]	[ɛ]
had	head
mat	met
pat	pet
land	lend
past/passed	pest
tan	ten
sad	said
and	end
bad	bed
add/ad	Ed

🎧 **Listen and repeat the following phrases and sentences. The boldfaced words all include the vowel [æ].**

1. **last chance**
2. I'll be **back**.
3. **at** a **glance**
4. **wrap** it up
5. Is **that** a **fact**?
6. **Hand** me a **pack** of **matches**.
7. I **have** to **catch** a **taxicab**.
8. **Ralph can't stand carrots**.
9. **Al** is a **happily married man**.
10. He who **laughs last, laughs** best!

🎧 **Listen and circle the number of the word with the [æ] sound. Only one word in each series will be pronounced with the [æ] vowel. (For answers to Check Yourself 1–3, see Appendix II, page 274.)**

EXAMPLE *You hear*   add   Ed   odd

You circle   ①   2   3

1.	1	2	3
2.	1	2	3
3.	1	2	3
4.	1	2	3
5.	1	2	3
6.	1	2	3
7.	1	2	3
8.	1	2	3
9.	1	2	3
10.	1	2	3

Listen and repeat. Circle the one letter _a_ that is pronounced [æ] in each word.

EXAMPLE   b a n ⓐ n a

1. a n i m a l
2. A f r i c a
3. C a l i f o r n i a
4. f a s c i n a t e
5. A l a s k a
6. a t t a c k
7. S a t u r d a y
8. C a n a d a
9. D a l l a s
10. p a c k a g e

Read the story of the _Titanic_. Circle all words that are pronounced with the vowel [æ]. The number in parentheses represents the total number of [æ] words in each sentence.

EXAMPLE   One of the great (tragedies) in the (last) century was the sinking of the (Titanic.) (3)

1. The _Titanic_ was traveling to New York across the Atlantic in 1912. (3)
2. This grand and elaborate ship had over 2,200 passengers. (4)
3. It crashed into an iceberg and sank in about two and a half hours. (3)
4. Telegraph warnings reached the _Titanic_ too late. (2)
5. After the crash, upper and lower class passengers ran about in a panic. (6)
6. Women and children had a chance to cram into small boats at the last minute. (5)
7. The captain and other passengers could not abandon the ship. (3)
8. Actors and actresses reenacted the accident in an Academy Award movie. (5)
9. The story of the _Titanic_ remains a sad and tragic chapter in our past. (5)

EXERCISE A

📖 **Read the following letter aloud. Pay attention to the boldfaced [æ] words.**

> Dear **Dad**,
>
> **At last Carol** and I are in **San Francisco**. It's an **absolutely fabulous** city! **As** we **stand at** the top of **Telegraph** Hill, we **can** see **Alcatraz**. We **plan** to **catch** a cable car and visit **Grant Avenue** in Chinatown. **After that**, we'll **grab** a **taxicab** to the **Japanese** Gardens. Yesterday, we **traveled** to **Napa Valley**. We also **passed** through the **National** Park. **After San** Diego, our **last** stop is **Disneyland** in Los **Angeles**. **California** is a **fantastic** state. We **have** lots of **photographs** and **packages** for the **family**. We'll be **back Saturday afternoon**, **January** 1st.
>
> Love,
Gladys
>
> P.S. We need **cash**. Please send money **as fast as** you **can**!

EXERCISE B

👥 **Find a set of directions for something (for example, using an appliance, assembling an item). Circle all words pronounced with [æ]. Read the directions aloud to a partner. Ask your partner to repeat the directions back to you. Practice the words your listener has difficulty understanding.**

Practice, practice, practice, and you'll have [æ] down pat!

Lesson 6 — [a] as in *arm*, *hot*, and *father*

PRONOUNCING [a]

[a]

Lips: Completely apart in a "yawning" position
Jaw: Lower than for any other vowel
Tongue: Flat, on the floor of the mouth

Possible Pronunciation Problems

Irregular English spelling patterns are the main reason you may have pronunciation problems with the vowel [a]. The letter *o* in English is frequently pronounced [a], like the *a* in *father*.

EXAMPLES If you say [oʊ] instead of [a]: **not** will sound like **note**.

If you say [ʌ] instead of [a]: **not** will sound like **nut**.

If you say [ɔ] instead of [a]: **cot** will sound like **caught**.

Remember to open your mouth wider than for any other vowel when you pronounce [a].

We're p*o*sitive you'll soon be *o*n t*o*p of [a]!

Practice

EXERCISE A 🎧 **Listen and repeat.**

[a] At the Beginning of Words			[a] In the Middle of Words		
on	are	honest	top	shop	block
odd	arch	option	cot	wasp	March
arm	oxen	artist	lock	watch	rocket

The vowel [a] does not occur at the end of words in English.

[a] Spelled

a	*o*
want	fox
wallet	hot
dark	spot
father	opera
pardon	follow

The letter *o* followed by *b, d, g, p, t,* or *ck* is usually pronounced [a].

ro**b**in   ro**d**   lo**g**   sto**p**   lo**t**   po**ck**et

The letter *a* followed by *r* is usually pronounced [a].

f**ar**m   al**ar**m   c**ar**t   st**ar**t   **ar**e

EXERCISE B

🎧 **Listen and repeat the following pairs of words. Be sure to open your mouth wider when producing the words with the [a] vowel.**

[a]	[æ]
cop	cap
hot	hat
pot	pat
odd	add
mop	map
top	tap
log	lag
lock	lack
cot	cat
solid	salad

EXERCISE C

🎧 **Listen and repeat the following phrases and sentences. The boldfaced words all include the vowel [a].**

1. **alarm clock**
2. **stock market**
3. **not far apart**
4. **top** to **bottom**
5. **cops** and **robbers**
6. Did **Father park** the **car**?
7. It was **hard** to **start** the **car**.
8. The **doctor wants** to **operate**.
9. **Honest politicians solve problems**.
10. My **watch stopped** at five **o'clock**.

🎧 **Listen and circle the one word in each group of three that is pronounced with [a].**
(For answers to Check Yourself 1–3, see Appendix II, pages 274–275.)

EXAMPLE
You hear	not	note	nut
You circle	①	2	3

1. 1 2 3
2. 1 2 3
3. 1 2 3
4. 1 2 3
5. 1 2 3
6. 1 2 3
7. 1 2 3
8. 1 2 3
9. 1 2 3
10. 1 2 3

CHECK YOURSELF 2 🎧 **Imagine you are a photographer for a well-known magazine. Your assignment is to photograph animals whose names contain the vowel [a]. Listen and repeat. Circle the animal names that include the vowel [a].**

1. (condor)   (collie)   leopard   (llama)
2. cat   crocodile   elephant   sea otter
3. fox   tiger   hippopotamus   dolphin
4. iguana   kangaroo   lobster   octopus
5. parrot   rhinoceros   opossum   lion

CHECK YOURSELF 3 📖 🧍 **Read the dialogue. Then work with a partner. Circle the words that contain the vowel [a].**

Donna: (Bob), I (want) to talk to you.

Bob: Are you all right, Donna?

Donna: Don't be alarmed. I saw Dr. Johnson at the hospital. You're going to be a father! Our new baby will be born in October.

Bob: I'm in shock. How do you feel?

Donna: I'm feeling on top of the world. I've got a list of names for the baby.

Bob: If it's a girl, let's call her Donna after her mom.

Donna: Donna is fine for a middle name. How about Connie or Barbara for her first name?

Bob: Fine. If it's a boy, we'll name him Don.

Donna: Better yet, if it's a boy, let's call him Bob after his father. If it's a girl, we'll call her Barbara.

Bob: Donna, maybe you want to name her Rhonda after your father's sister. Then, if it's a boy, we can name him Ron.

Donna: We don't want to forget your mother Carla. So, let's call him Carl if it's a boy.

Bob: I think we ought to stop. This could go on and on.

Donna: It's not really a problem. Now we have names for our first four darling babies.

Bob: Donna, you've gone too far. One at a time is enough for this mom and pop. Donna or Don is a good start for now!

Now practice reading the dialogue with a partner. Open your mouth wide when pronouncing [a] words.

More Practice

EXERCISE A

Read aloud the paragraph about the Constitution. Pay attention to the [a] sound in the boldfaced words.

The **Constitution**

The U.S. **Constitution** is the basis of our **democracy**. Much **compromise** was necessary before the **Constitution** was **adopted**. Some **modifications** to the **Constitution** caused **problems** that were **resolved** by forming two houses in **Congress**. The Supreme Court has final **authority** to explain the **Constitution**. It can void laws that conflict with any **part** of the **Constitution**. The U.S. **Constitution** has been **constant** but **responsive** to change. We thank our founding **fathers**, including George **Washington** and **Thomas** Jefferson, for this **remarkable** **document**.

EXERCISE B

Read the limerick aloud. Pay attention to the [a] sound in the boldfaced words.

A **Farmer** Named **Bob**

Tom's father was a **farmer** named **Bob**,
Who **got** very confused **on** the **job**,
    Among his misdeeds,
        Was mixing some seeds—
His **squash** looked like corn **on** the **cob**!

EXERCISE C

Listen to a segment of your favorite radio or TV news program. Listen specifically for words pronounced with [a]. List as many as you can. Write a short summary of the segment, including as many of the words on your list as possible. Bring your summary to class, and read it to a partner.

Complete *all* the activities and you'll be *on target* with [a]!

Contrast and Review of [eɪ], [ɛ], [æ], and [a]

PRONOUNCING OF [eɪ], [ɛ], [æ], AND [a]

JAW LOWERS (MOUTH OPENS)

English key words: **ate   game   they**

[e] + [ɪ] = [eɪ]

[eɪ] is a *long* sound; be sure to prolong it!

English key words: **egg   pet   head**

[ɛ]

[ɛ] is a shorter sound than [eɪ]; your jaw should be dropped more.

English key words: **at   fat   happy**

[æ]

The mouth is open wide for [æ], but not as much as for [a]!

English key words: **arm   hot   father**

[a]

The jaw is completely dropped; the mouth is open wider than for any other sound.

🎧 **Listen and repeat. Feel your mouth open wider as you progress through the pronunciation of [eɪ], [ɛ], [æ], and [a].**

	[eɪ]	[ɛ]	[æ]	[a]
1.	aid	Ed	add	odd
2.	rake	wreck	rack	rock
3.	paid	ped	pad	pod
4.	Nate	net	gnat	not
5.	pained	penned	panned	pond
6.	I had a rake.	I had a wreck.	I had a rack.	I had a rock.
7.	Can you tape it?		Can you tap it?	Can you top it?
8.	Do you know Jane?		Do you know Jan?	Do you know John?
9.	The paste is gone.	The pest is gone.	The past is gone.	
10.	He took the bait.	He took the bet.	He took the bat.	

     [eɪ]   [æ]   [a]
11. I **hate** wearing a **hat** when it's **hot**.

     [eɪ]   [æ]   [a]
12. The house at the **lake lacks** a **lock**.

    [a]   [æ]   [eɪ]
13. **Ron ran** in the **rain**.

     [a]   [ɛ]   [æ]
14. It's **odd** that **Ed** can't **add**.

    [æ]   [eɪ]   [ɛ]
15. **Dan**, the Great **Dane**, sleeps in the **den**.

Lesson 8 — [u] as in *you*, *too*, and *rule* and [ʊ] as in *cook* and *put*

PRONOUNCING [u]

[u]

Lips: Tense and in a "whistling" position
Jaw: Almost completely raised
Tongue: High, near the roof of the mouth

Possible Pronunciation Problems

Pronunciation problems occur because of confusing English spelling patterns and the similarity of [u] and [ʊ] (the sound to be discussed next).

EXAMPLES   When you substitute [ʊ] for [u]:   **pool** becomes **pull**.

suit becomes **soot**.

Your lips should be tense and in a "whistling" position when you say [u]. [u] is a *long* sound; be sure to *prolong* it.

You can *do* it! If *you* remember to protrude your lips when producing [u], *you*'ll never confuse "pull" with "pool"!

Practice

EXERCISE A

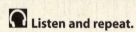 **Listen and repeat.**

[u] In the Middle of Words			[u] At the End of Words		
food	suit	group	do	shoe	threw
pool	truth	ruler	new	flew	through
room	goose	school	you	chew	canoe

The vowel [u] does not occur at the beginning of words in English.
Exception: "ooze."

[u] Spelled

u	oo	o	ew	ue
rule	cool	do	new	due
rude	fool	to	drew	blue
June	too	who	stew	clue
tune	noon	tomb	knew	glued
tuna	stool	lose	news	avenue

note

Less frequent spelling patterns for [u] consist of the letters *ui, ou, oe, ieu,* and *ough.*

fr**ui**t   gr**ou**p   sh**oe**   li**eu**tenant   thr**ough**

hint

The letters *oo* followed by *l, m,* or *n* are usually pronounced [u].

sch**oo**l   b**oo**m   m**oo**n

When the letter *u* follows *t, d, n,* or *s,* some Americans pronounce it [ju].

T**u**esday   d**u**ty   n**u**ew   s**u**it

hint

When speaking English, international students frequently forget to prolong the [u] vowel before consonants. (Consonants are all the sounds that are not vowels.)

EXERCISE B

🎧 **Listen and repeat. The [u] vowel is prolonged before consonants. The dots in the following exercise are there to remind you to lengthen the [u].**

new	new . . . s (news)
due	due . . . s (dues)
sue	sue . . . d (sued)
who	who . . . m (whom)
glue	glue . . . d (glued)

EXERCISE C

🎧 **Listen and repeat the following phrases and sentences. The boldfaced words all contain the vowel [u].**

1. What's **new**?
2. **Who** is it?
3. How are **you**?
4. **loose tooth**
5. in the **mood**
6. **School** will **soon** be **through**.
7. **You** must **chew** your **food**.
8. He **proved** he **knew** the **truth**.
9. The **group flew** to **New** York in **June**.
10. **Who ruined** my **new blue shoes**?

Listen. Circle the number of the word with the vowel [u]. (For answers, see Appendix II, page 275.)

EXAMPLE   *You hear*   comb   cool   call
           You circle   1   ②   3

1. 1   2   3
2. 1   2   3
3. 1   2   3
4. 1   2   3
5. 1   2   3
6. 1   2   3
7. 1   2   3
8. 1   2   3
9. 1   2   3
10. 1   2   3

More Practice

Read aloud the paragraph about New Orleans. Pay attention to the [u] sound in the boldfaced words.

New Orleans

One of the most **beautiful** cities in the **United** States is **New** Orleans. This city on the **bayou** is full of **unique** sights and sounds. **New** Orleans offers good **food** and **music**. Famous chefs create **soups** and **stews** **influenced** by the Creole and Cajun **communities**. Jazz and the **blues** started in **New** Orleans with **musicians** like **Louis** Armstrong. Tourists come to Mardi Gras dressed in **costumes** to look at the **truly super** homes on St. Charles **Avenue**. Whether **you** take a **cruise** down the Mississippi or **choose** fine dining spots, **you** should visit **New** Orleans in the **future**.

What are you in the mood to use? List the names of five things that contain the vowel [u]. Then work with a partner. Ask each other, "What are *you* in the m*oo*d to *u*se?" Respond with the things on your list.

EXAMPLE   **A:** What are y**ou** in the m**oo**d to **u**se?

B: I'm in the m**oo**d to **u**se my n**ew** sh**oe**s.

PRONOUNCING [ʊ]

Lips: Relaxed and slightly parted
Jaw: Slightly lower than for [u]
Tongue: High, but lower than for [u]

Remember NOT to protrude your lips and tense them as you would for [u]. [ʊ] is a short, quick sound; your lips should barely move while saying it.

Practice [ʊ] as you sh*ou*ld, and you'll be underst*oo*d!

Practice

EXERCISE A

 Listen and repeat. Remember to relax your lips and jaw as you produce [ʊ].

[ʊ] In the Middle of Words

cook	shook	foot
full	push	brook
book	could	hood
good	put	sugar
stood	wood	woman
look	took	cushion

The vowel [ʊ] occurs only in the middle of words in English.

[ʊ] Spelled

u	*oo*	*ou*
pull	wool	could
put	wood	would
push	hook	should
bullet	good	
pudding	cookie	

 note

A less frequent spelling pattern for [ʊ] is the letter *o*.

w**o**lf   w**o**man

The letters *oo* followed by *d* or *k* are usually pronounced [ʊ].

    hoo**d**   **g**oo**d**   **w**oo**d**   **b**oo**k**   **l**oo**k**   **c**oo**k**

The letter *u* followed by *sh* is usually pronounced [ʊ].

    bu**sh**   **p**u**sh**   **c**u**sh**ion

EXERCISE B

Listen and repeat. Pay attention to the [ʊ] sound in the boldfaced words.

1. **Look** out!
2. Take a **good look**.
3. It's **good-looking**.
4. He **couldn't** come.
5. **Should** we go?
6. Who **took** my **book**?
7. **Put** the **wood** away.
8. He **took** a **look** at the **crook**.
9. The **woman stood** on one **foot**.
10. **Could** you eat ten **sugar cookies**?

CHECK YOURSELF

Listen carefully to the following sentences. Some words that should be pronounced with [ʊ] will be said incorrectly. Circle C if the pronunciation of the words in the sentence is correct. Circle *I* if the pronunciation of the words in the sentence is incorrect. (For answers, see Appendix II, page 275.)

| **EXAMPLES** | *You hear* | I was fool after eating. | *You circle* | C Ⓘ |
| | *You hear* | The cushion is soft. | *You circle* | Ⓒ I |

1.   C   I
2.   C   I
3.   C   I
4.   C   I
5.   C   I
6.   C   I
7.   C   I
8.   C   I
9.   C   I
10.   C   I

EXERCISE A

📖 **Read aloud the paragraph about Little Red Riding Hood. Pay attention to the boldfaced words containing the vowel [ʊ]. Remember to relax your lips as you say [ʊ].**

Little Red Riding **Hood**

One of our favorite **childhood books** is *Little Red Riding **Hood***. Little Red Riding **Hood** walked through the **woods** to bring a basket of **cooked goods** and **sugar cookies** to her grandmother. Meanwhile, a **wolf** came from behind the **bushes** into Grandmother's house. He **put** the poor **woman** in the closet. He **put** her clothes on, hoping Red Riding **Hood would** think he was Grandma. When Red Riding **Hood stood** at the door, she **looked** at the **wolf**. (Now, we all know that the **wolf couldn't** "**pull** the **wool** over Red Riding **Hood's** eyes." Who **wouldn't** recognize a **wolf** in a **woman's** clothing?) A hunter was walking through the **woods**, and he heard Red Riding **Hood's** screams. He shot a **bullet** and killed the **wolf**. Moral of the story: A **wolf** by any other name or clothing is still a **wolf**!

EXERCISE B

👤 **Read the following sentences aloud. Fill in the blank with a phrase or word that is pronounced with [ʊ]. Think of as many responses as you can for each blank. Share your sentences with a partner.**

EXAMPLE   He is a **good** *cook* _____.

1. I **took** a **look** at _____.
2. I wish I **could** _____.
3. The **woman put** _____.
4. She **should** _____.
5. The **butcher couldn't** _____.

LESSON REVIEW: [u] AND [ʊ]

EXERCISE

🎧 **Listen and repeat. Remember to feel tension and protrude your lips when you repeat words that include the vowel [u] and to relax your muscles when you pronounce words that include the vowel [ʊ].**

[u]	[ʊ]
1. fool	full
2. suit	soot
3. Luke	look
4. pool	pull

	[u]	[ʊ]
5.	stewed	stood

6. I hate the black **suit**. I hate the black **soot**.
7. She went to **Luke**. She went to **look**.
8. I have no **pool**. I have no **pull**.
9. He's not a **fool**! He's not **full**!
10. The beef **stewed** for an hour. The beef **stood** for an hour.

        [ʊ]   [ʊ]   [u]
11. Take a **good look** at **Luke**.

    [ʊ]   [u]
12. **Pull** him from the **pool**.

        [ʊ]   [u]
13. He has **soot** on his **suit**.

     [u]   [ʊ]
14. The **fool** was **full** of fun.

     [ʊ]   [u]
15. She **stood** and **stewed** about the problem.

CHECK YOURSELF 1   📖 **Read the sentences aloud. Write the phonetic symbol [u] or [ʊ] above each boldfaced word. (For answers to Check Yourself 1–3, see Appendix II, page 276.)**

         [ʊ]   [u]
EXAMPLE   **Pull** the raft from the **pool**.

    [ ]   [ ]   [ ]
1. **Too** many **cooks** spoil the **soup**!

          [ ]   [ ] [ ]
2. There **should** be a **full moon**.

      [ ]   [ ] [ ]
3. Mr. **Brooks** is **good looking**.

    [ ]   [ ]   [ ]
4. **June** is a **good** month to **move**.

      [ ]   [ ]   [ ]
5. The **butcher cooked** a **goose**.

       [ ]   [ ]   [ ]
6. The **news bulletin** was **misunderstood**.

       [ ] [ ]   [ ] [ ]
7. Did **you choose** a pair of **new shoes**?

    [ ]   [ ] [ ] [ ]
8. **Lucy** had a **loose tooth pulled**.

    [ ]   [ ]   [ ] [ ]
9. **Students should** read **good books**.

      [ ]   [ ]   [ ]   [ ]
10. The **room** is **full** of **blue balloons**.

🎧 **Listen and circle the number of the word that is different.**

EXAMPLE	*You hear*		fool	fool	full
	You circle		1	2	③

1. 1   2   3
2. 1   2   3
3. 1   2   3
4. 1   2   3
5. 1   2   3
6. 1   2   3
7. 1   2   3
8. 1   2   3
9. 1   2   3
10. 1   2   3

📖 **Read the paragraph about Houdini. Then read the paragraph again. Circle the words pronounced with [u] and underline the words pronounced with [ʊ].**

Houdini

Harry (Houdini) was a magician known (throughout) world. He <u>could</u> remove himself from chains and ropes and could walk through walls! Houdini was born in Budapest, Hungary. He moved to New York when he was twelve and soon took up magic. Rumors spread that Houdini had supernatural powers. However, he was truthful and stated that his tricks could be understood by all humans! Houdini is an idol for all would-be magicians.

📖 **After checking your answers, practice reading the paragraph aloud again. Remember—your lips must be in a tense "whistling" position for [u] and in a relaxed position when pronouncing [ʊ].**

EXERCISE A

📖 Read two headline news stories from the front page of a newspaper. Circle all [u] and [ʊ] words. Read aloud the sentences containing the circled words. Carefully pronounce the [u] and [ʊ] vowel sounds.

EXERCISE B

Read the dialogue aloud with a partner. Pay careful attention to the [ʊ] and [u] words in boldfaced type.

         [ʊ]   [u]   [ʊ]   [u]   [u]
Lou: **Good afternoon. Brooks** Travel **Group. Lou** speaking.

          [u]   [u]   [ʊ]   [u]   [ʊ]
Lucy: Hi, **Lou**. This is **Lucy Fuller**. I'm **due** for a trip and **would** like a

    [u]   [u]   [u]
few days away from my **two** children and my husband **Drew**!

           [ʊ]   [u]   [u]
I'd like to **book** a **cruise** for **June**.

     [u] [ʊ]   [u]   [u]   [u]
Lou: **You should** try the **newest** ship, the "**Super Cruiser**." It sails down

     [u]   [u]   [u]   [u]   [u]
the **Blue Danube. You** fly to the ship from **New** York on **Tuesday**,

  [u]   [ʊ]   [u]   [u]   [u] [u]
June 1st. I just **took** a **cruise** on it, **too**. It was **truly super**!

        [u]   [u]   [u]   [u]   [u]
Lucy: Is it **true** the **rooms** on **cruises** are **usually** small and **gloomy**?

                [u]   [ʊ]   [u]
Lou: No. The cabins are **roomy** and **full** of light. They all have **beautiful**

    [u]
views.

           [u]
Lucy: How's the **food**?

        [ʊ]   [u]   [u]   [u]
Lou: The **cooks** prepare **unique menus**. There's so much to **choose** from.

          [u]   [u]   [u]   [u]
That's why I **usually lose** a **few** pounds before the **cruise**.

             [u] [u] [u]   [u]
Lucy: Besides eating, what **do you do** on a **cruise**?

    [u]   [ʊ] [u]   [u]   [u]   [u]
Lou: **You** will have a **full routine**. There is a **huge pool**, and the **crew**

    [ʊ]   [u] [u] [ʊ]   [u]
will take **good** care of **you. You could** relax on deck with a **cool**

      [ʊ] [ʊ]   [u]   [u]
drink, read a **good book**, watch a **movie**, or even take a **snooze**.

Lucy: I don't want to be **rude** [u], but how much is the **cruise** [u]?

Lou: Here's the **good** [ʊ] **news** [u]. For **June** [u], the fares are **reduced** [u]. **Two** [u] can **cruise** [u] for the price of one.

Lucy: Are **you** [u] **pulling** [ʊ] my leg? This is **too** [u] **good** [ʊ] **to** [u] be **true** [u]. Well, I'm no **fool** [u]. **Who** [u] says a **woman** [ʊ] **should** [ʊ] leave her **good-looking** [ʊ] [ʊ] husband alone? **Put** [ʊ] us down for **two** [u]. **Drew** [u] and I will **cruise** [u] the beautiful [u] **Blue** [u] **Danube** [u] in **June** [u]!

Practice [u] and [ʊ] as yo**u sho**u**ld and y**o**u will be understo**o**d!**

[ʌ] as in *up*, *but*, and *come*

PRONOUNCING [ʌ]

Lips: Relaxed and slightly parted
Jaw: Relaxed and slightly lowered
Tongue: Relaxed and midlevel in the mouth

Possible Pronunciation Problems

The vowel [ʌ] may not exist in your language and may be difficult for you to hear and pronounce. It is easy to become confused by irregular English spelling patterns and to substitute sounds that are more familiar to you.

EXAMPLES   If you say [a] instead of [ʌ]:   **color** will sound like **collar**.

If you say [oʊ] instead of [ʌ]:   **come** will sound like **comb**.

If you say [ɔ] instead of [ʌ]:   **done** will sound like **dawn**.

Remember, [ʌ] is a short, quick sound. You shouldn't feel any tension, and your lips should barely move during its production.

Just relax as you say [ʌ] and you won't run into trouble!

Practice

EXERCISE A   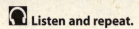 **Listen and repeat.**

[ʌ] At the Beginning of Words			[ʌ] In the Middle of Words		
us	ugly	onion	hug	much	rough
up	other	under	won	must	month
of	uncle	upper	nut	come	trouble
oven			does		

The vowel [ʌ] does not occur at the end of words in English.

[ʌ] Spelled _____

u	*o*
but	love
cut	done
sun	some
lucky	mother
funny	Monday

EXERCISE B

🎧 **Listen and repeat. The boldfaced words in the following phrases and sentences should all be pronounced with the vowel [ʌ].**

1. **Come** in.
2. What **does** it mean?
3. **bubble gum**
4. **once** a **month**
5. **Once** is **enough**.
6. **cover up**
7. My **uncle** is my **mother's brother**.
8. My **cousin** is my **uncle's son**.
9. The **gloves** are **such** an **ugly color**.
10. **Come** and have **some fun** in the **sun**.

CHECK YOURSELF 1

🎧 **Listen. Circle the word that you hear. (For answers to Check Yourself 1–3, see Appendix II, pages 276–277.)**

EXAMPLES	[ʌ]	[a]
	(luck)	lock
	hut	(hot)
1.	cut	cot
2.	stuck	stock
3.	come	calm
4.	wonder	wander
5.	color	collar
6.	nut	not
7.	bum	bomb
8.	pup	pop

9. fund   fond
10. shut   shot

📖 **Check your answers. Then read each pair of words aloud. Remember, when you pronounce the words with [ʌ], your lips should be completely relaxed and should barely move.**

CHECK YOURSELF 2 🎧 **Listen. Circle the one word in each group that is not pronounced with [ʌ].**

EXAMPLE	once	lovely	(alone)	funny
1.	something	wonder	ugly	open
2.	trouble	come	locker	once
3.	color	cups	dozen	collar
4.	peanut	muddy	modern	bunny
5.	stood	stuff	stump	stuck
6.	lucky	brother	just	lock
7.	Monday	month	Tuesday	Sunday
8.	comb	coming	cutting	country
9.	cover	over	oven	other
10.	rust	must	rot	nothing

CHECK YOURSELF 3 🎧 👥 **Listen to the dialogue. Then work with a partner. Circle the words pronounced with the vowel [ʌ]. Practice reading the dialogue together.**

Gus: Hi, (Justine!) How's my (fun-loving) (cousin?)

Justine: Very worried. I just had a run of tough luck.

Gus: Why, what's up?

Justine: My bus got stuck in the mud, and I lost some money. I should carry something for luck!

Gus: Yes. Here's some other advice. Never walk under ladders. And run from black cats. They're nothing but trouble!

Justine: Oh, Gus. You must be a nut! Do you really believe such mumbo jumbo?

Gus: Don't make fun, Justine. Customs come from many countries. You must know some others!

Justine: Well, the number 13 is unlucky. And a blister on the tongue means someone is lying!

Gus: Right! But you can have good luck, too. Discover a four-leaf clover or find bubbles in your coffee cup and you'll get a sum of money.

Justine: OK, Gus. Maybe I'll have some luck this month. Knock on wood!

EXERCISE A

📖 **Read the recipe aloud. Remember that all the boldfaced words should be pronounced with [ʌ].**

Recipe for **Fudge** Brownies

Everyone loves mother's fudge brownies. **Just** follow these easy-to-**understand instructions**, and the brownies will **come** out **wonderfully**!

You'll need:

One cup flour

One cup sugar

Two **country** fresh eggs

One-half **cup butter**

One cup nuts

Half-**dozen** tablespoons cocoa

One package chocolate **fudge** frosting mix

One package tiny marshmallows

Melt **butter** over low heat in **double**-boiler, **uncovered**. Beat eggs and sugar **until color** is clear; add **butter** and cocoa. Stir in flour **just until** smooth. Mix in **nuts**. Pour into **ungreased** eight-inch-square pan. Turn **oven up** to three **hundred** degrees and bake **one**-half hour or **until done**. **Cover** with marshmallows. Leave in **oven until** marshmallows are **runny**. **Once** it is cool to the **touch**, top with **fudge** icing. **Cut up** into squares. **Yum-yum**!

EXERCISE B

👥 **Read the limerick aloud to a partner. Be sure to pronounce the boldfaced words with [ʌ] correctly.**

A Man **from Kentucky**

A man **from Kentucky** named **Bud**,
Had a **lucky young** racehorse named **Jud**,
   When he bet on his horse,
   Bud won money, of course,
But one day **Jud** got **stuck** in the **mud**!

Now work together to write a limerick with words that include the vowel [ʌ].

Just relax as you say [ʌ], and you won't *run* into *trouble* with [ʌ]. **And may** good *luck* be yours!

10 [OU] as in *oh*, *no*, and *boat*

PRONOUNCING [OU]

Lips: Tense and very rounded

Jaw: Rises with the tongue and closes slightly

Tongue: Glides from midlevel to near the roof of the mouth

[oʊ] is a diphthong. A diphthong is a compound vowel sound made by blending two vowels together very quickly. The diphthong [oʊ] begins with [o] and ends with [ʊ].

Possible Pronunciation Problems

Once again, your pronunciation problems with this sound occur because of confusing English spelling patterns and similarities with other vowel sounds.

EXAMPLES

If you say [ʌ] instead of [oʊ]: **coat** will sound like **cut**.

If you say [ɔ] instead of [oʊ]: **bold** will sound like **bald**.

If you say [a] instead of [oʊ]: **note** will sound like **not**.

When producing the diphthong [oʊ], round your lips into the shape of the letter *o*. [oʊ] is a long sound; be sure to prolong it.

Listen and practice and kn*ow* your [oʊ] will be *O*K!

Practice

EXERCISE A

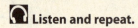 **Listen and repeat.**

[oʊ] At the Beginning of Words			[oʊ] In the Middle of Words			[oʊ] At the End of Words		
oat	odor	oval	boat	roam	spoke	go	sew	snow
own	only	open	both	loan	soul	no	ago	hello
oak	over	ocean	coast	known	don't	so	show	though
old			nose			toe		

[ou] Spelled

o	oa	ow	oe	ou
no	soap	know	toe	dough
rope	goat	owe	hoe	though
vote	loan	grow	goes	shoulder
home	foam	throw		
fold	load	bowl		

hint

When *o* is in a syllable ending in silent *e*, the letter *o* is pronounced [ou] (the same as the name of the alphabet letter *o*).

ph**o**ne   n**o**te   h**o**me   r**o**pe

The letters *oa* are usually pronounced [ou].

c**oa**l   b**oa**t   r**oa**sting   t**oa**ster

The letter *o* followed by *ld* is usually pronounced [ou].

c**o**ld   **o**ld   s**o**ldier   t**o**ld

hint

When speaking English, many international students frequently forget to prolong the diphthong [ou] before consonants.

EXERCISE B

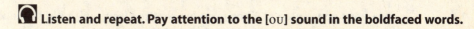

Listen and repeat. Remember that the diphthong [ou] is a prolonged sound. The dots in the following exercise are there to remind you to lengthen it.

toe	toe . . . s (toes)
sew	sew . . . s (sews)
grow	grow . . . s (grows)
know	know . . . n (known)
blow	blow . . . n (blown)

EXERCISE C

Listen and repeat. Pay attention to the [ou] sound in the boldfaced words.

1. Leave me **alone**!
2. I **suppose so**.
3. **only joking**
4. **Hold** the **phone**.
5. **open** and **close**
6. at a **moment's notice**
7. **Tony Jones broke** his **toe**.
8. **Don't go** down the **old road**.
9. Repeat the [ou] words **slowly over** and **over**!
10. **No** one **knows** how **old Flo** is.

CHECK YOURSELF 1 🔊 **Listen and circle the word that you hear. (For answers to Check Yourself 1–3, see Appendix II, pages 277–278.)**

	[oʊ]	[ʌ]
EXAMPLES	(comb)	come
	boat	(but)
1.	phone	fun
2.	bone	bun
3.	roam/Rome	rum
4.	boast	bust/bused
5.	tone	ton
6.	coat	cut
7.	wrote	rut
8.	hole/whole	hull
9.	rogue	rug
10.	most	must/mussed

📖 **Check your answers. Then read each pair of words aloud. Be sure to prolong the diphthong [oʊ].**

CHECK YOURSELF 2 📖 **Read the names of the following household items. Circle the items pronounced with the diphthong [oʊ].**

1.	(toaster)	frying pan	bookcase	freezer
2.	clock	telephone	faucet	radio
3.	stove	sofa	lawn mower	table
4.	doorknob	window	television	coatrack
5.	can opener	mixing bowl	clothes dryer	iron

👥 **Check your answers. Then imagine that the items with names containing the [oʊ] sound are broken. Work with a partner. Tell each other, "The _____ is broken." Be sure to prolong the sound of [oʊ].**

EXAMPLE   "The **toaster** is **broken**."

CHECK YOURSELF 3 📖 👥 **Read the dialogue. Then work with a partner. Circle all the words containing the diphthong [oʊ].**

Joe: (Rose,) let's (go) on a trip. We need to be (alone.)

Rose: OK, Joe. Where should we go?

Joe: I know! We'll go to Ohio.

Rose: Great! We'll visit my Uncle Roland.

Joe: No, it's too cold in Ohio. We'll go to Arizona.

Rose: Fine. We'll stay with your Aunt Mona!

Joe: No, it's too hot in Arizona. Let's go to Rome.

Rose: Oh, good! You'll meet my Cousin Tony.

Joe: No, no, no!! We won't go to Rome. Let's go to Nome, Alaska. We don't know anyone there!!

Rose: You won't believe it, but I have an old friend . . .

Joe: Hold it, Rose, we won't go anywhere! I suppose we'll just stay home.

Check your answers to make sure you circled all the words containing the diphthong [oʊ]. Practice reading the dialogue aloud with your partner.

More Practice

EXERCISE A

What don't you know? List five things. Be sure your responses each contain words with the diphthong [oʊ]. Then work with a partner. Ask each other "What don't you know?" Answer with the things on your list.

EXAMPLE   **A:** What d**o**n't you kn**ow**?

  B: I d**o**n't kn**ow** (if **Jo**e will **go** al**o**ne/h**ow** I'll get h**o**me/when **To**ny wr**o**te the n**o**te . . .)

EXERCISE B

Read the limericks aloud. Pay attention to the pronunciation of the boldfaced words with the [oʊ] sound.

A Young Lady Named **Joan**

Moe loved a young lady named **Joan**.
But she spent all her time on the **phone**.
    Though Moe did **propose**,
    It was voicemail **Joan chose**.
So they each lived their lives out, **alone**.

A **Fellow** Named **Joe**

There once was a **fellow** named **Joe**.
Who wore **yellow** wherever he'd **go**.
    His **clothes** were **so** bright
    You'd **know** him on sight.
He **glowed** from his head to his **toe**.

Practice [oʊ] *over* and *over* and your [oʊ] will be *OK*!

PRONOUNCING [ɔ]

Lips: In a tense oval shape and slightly protruded

Jaw: Open more than for [oʊ]

Tongue: Low, near the floor of the mouth

Possible Pronunciation Problems

The vowel [ɔ] is another troublemaker. Confusing English spelling patterns can cause you to substitute more familiar vowels.

EXAMPLES   If you say [a] instead of [ɔ]:   **caller** will sound like **collar**.

If you say [oʊ] instead of [ɔ]:   **bought** will sound like **boat**.

If you say [ʌ] instead of [ɔ]:   **bought** will sound like **but**.

Listen carefully and your pronunciation of [ɔ] will improve.

Remember to protrude your lips and drop your *jaw* as you say [ɔ].

Practice

EXERCISE A   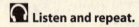 **Listen and repeat.**

[ɔ] At the Beginning of Words

all	awful	always
off	often	August
also	ought	audience

[ɔ] In the Middle of Words

boss	wrong	taught
fall	broad	across
song	bought	naughty

[ɔ] At the End of Words

awe	flaw	thaw
raw	draw	straw
law	claw	jaw

[ɔ] Spelled

o	a	aw	au
dog	fall	jaw	auto
toss	call	lawn	fault
lost	mall	dawn	cause
long	salt	drawn	taught
offer	stall	awful	auction

note

Less frequent spelling patterns for [ɔ] consist of the letters *oa* and *ou*.

br**oa**d   c**ou**gh   th**ou**ght

hint

The letter *o* followed by *ff*, *ng*, and *ss* is usually pronounced [ɔ].

offer   **o**ff   l**o**ng   str**o**ng   l**o**ss   t**o**ssing

The letters *aw* are usually pronounced [ɔ].

l**aw**n   dr**aw**   **aw**ful

The letter *a* followed by *ll*, *lk*, *lt*, and *ld* is usually pronounced [ɔ].

b**a**ll   t**a**lk   s**a**lt   b**a**ld

EXERCISE B

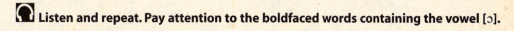 **Listen and repeat the pairs of words. When you pronounce the [ɔ] words, remember to protrude your lips.**

I		II		III	
[ɔ]	[ʌ]	[ɔ]	[ou]	[ɔ]	[a]
1. dog	dug	saw	so	for	far
2. dawn	done	law	low	stalk	stock
3. long	lung	tall	toll	taught	tot
4. cough	cuff	bald	bold	caught	cot
5. bought	but	bought	boat	caller	collar

EXERCISE C

Listen and repeat. Pay attention to the boldfaced words containing the vowel [ɔ].

1. **call** it **off**
2. **call** it quits
3. **call** the **shots**
4. **all talk**
5. **walk all** over
6. It's **all wrong**.
7. Is **Paul's** hair **long** or short?
8. How much does **coffee cost**?
9. What is the **reward** for the **lost dog**?
10. Did you make a **long**-distance **call** to **Boston**, **Albany**, or **Baltimore**?

🔊 **Listen. You will hear two sentences. Circle the letter of the sentence that contains a word with the vowel [ɔ]. (For answers to Check Yourself 1–3, see Appendix II, page 278.)**

EXAMPLE   *You hear*   (a) It's in the hall.   (b) It's in the hole.

    You circle   (a)   (b)

    1.   (a)   (b)

    2.   (a)   (b)

    3.   (a)   (b)

    4.   (a)   (b)

    5.   (a)   (b)

🔊 **Listen to the following sentences. Some words that should be pronounced with [ɔ] will be pronounced incorrectly. Circle C for correct or I for incorrect.**

EXAMPLES   *You hear*   She played with the small child.   *You circle*   (C)   I

    You hear   Please sew the piece of wood.   *You circle*   C   (I)

    1.   C   I

    2.   C   I

    3.   C   I

    4.   C   I

    5.   C   I

    6.   C   I

    7.   C   I

    8.   C   I

    9.   C   I

   10.   C   I

📖 **Read the dialogue. Circle the words pronounced with the vowel [ɔ].**

Audrey: Hi, Paula. Did you hear the awful news? Maude called off her wedding to Claude!

Paula: Why, Audrey? I thought they were getting married in August.

Audrey: Maude kept stalling and decided Claude was the wrong man.

Paula: Poor Claude. He must be a lost soul.

Audrey: Oh, no. He's abroad in Austria having a ball!

Paula: I almost forgot. What about the long tablecloth we bought them?

Audrey: I already brought it back. The cost of the cloth will cover the cost of our lunch today.

Paula: Audrey, you're always so thoughtful!

⚱ **Check to make sure you circled the words with the vowel [ɔ]. Practice reading the dialogue aloud with a partner.**

More Practice

EXERCISE A

📖 **Read aloud the following story of the Gettysburg Address. Pay attention to the boldfaced words containing the vowel [ɔ]. Remember to drop your jaw when you say [ɔ].**

hint When followed by *r*, the sound of the vowel [ɔ] changes slightly.

The **Story** of the Gettysburg Address

"**Four score** and seven years ago, our fathers **brought forth** upon this continent a new nation, conceived in liberty and dedicated to the proposition that **all** men are created equal."

Four months after the Gettysburg Civil **War** battle was **fought**, President Abraham Lincoln delivered these **immortal** words in the Gettysburg Address. He **talked** to an **audience** of **more** than **fourteen** thousand to dedicate this battlefield to those **unfortunate** soldiers who had **lost** their lives **for** the **cause**. He stood **tall** and gave a **short** but **strong oration**. Many **stories** about the Address are **false**. Lincoln did not write it on a train right **before** he arrived. He worked on it in his **office**, as **authors often** do. He **also** made at least **four** revisions. **Nor** was there a **lukewarm** response to the speech. From the start, people were **awed** by his words, and **according** to newspaper **reports**, his speech was **lauded**. **Almost all** of us **recall** being **taught** these famous words in school. His **thoughts** seem as **authentic** today as they were **long** ago.

EXERCISE B

⚱ **Find an advertisement for a department store. List the names of ten items in the ad. Bring the ad and your list to class. Exchange lists with a partner, but keep your ad. Ask the prices of items on each other's lists, using the phrase "How much do/does the _____(s) cost?" Use your ads to answer.**

EXAMPLE **A:** How much does <u>the toaster</u> *cost*?

B: It *costs* <u>$19.99</u>.

Remember you *ou*ght to protrude your lips and dr*o*p your j*aw* whenever you try to produce the sound [ɔ]! Practice *o*ften!

PRONOUNCING [ʌ], [oʊ], [ɔ], AND [a]

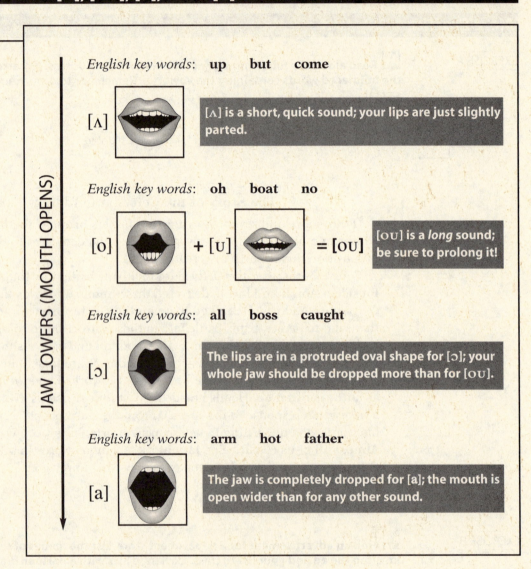

JAW LOWERS (MOUTH OPENS)

English key words: **up** **but** **come**

[ʌ] — [ʌ] is a short, quick sound; your lips are just slightly parted.

English key words: **oh** **boat** **no**

[o] + [ʊ] = [oʊ] — [oʊ] is a *long* sound; be sure to prolong it!

English key words: **all** **boss** **caught**

[ɔ] — The lips are in a protruded oval shape for [ɔ]; your whole jaw should be dropped more than for [oʊ].

English key words: **arm** **hot** **father**

[a] — The jaw is completely dropped for [a]; the mouth is open wider than for any other sound.

🎧 **Listen and repeat. Feel your mouth open wider as you progress through the pronunciation of [ʌ], [ou], [ɔ], and [a] words.**

[ʌ]	[ou]	[ɔ]	[a]
1. cut	coat	caught	cot
2. nut	note	naught	not
3. mud	mode	Maude	mod
4. fund	phoned	fawned	fond
5. Chuck	choke	chalk	chock
6. The dog **bucks**.		The dog **balks**.	The dog **barks**.
7. Here's a **nut**.	Here's a **note**.		Here's a **knot**.
8. It's in the **hull**.	It's in the **hole**.	It's in the **hall**.	
9. Don't **suck** it.	Don't **soak** it.		Don't **sock** it.
10.	Was it **sewed**?	Was it **sawed**?	Was it **sod**?

EXERCISE B

📖 **Read each sentence aloud. Pay attention to the [ʌ], [ou], [ɔ], and [a] sounds in the boldfaced words.**

   [a]   [ʌ]   [ɔ]
1. **Don** was **done** at **dawn**.

    [ɔ]   [ou]   [ɔ]   [ʌ]
2. **Maude mowed** the **lawn** in the **mud**.

    [ʌ] [ɔ]   [ou]
3. **Bud bought** a **boat**.

    [ɔ]   [ou]   [a]
4. She **caught** her **coat** on the **cot**.

    [ɔ]   [a]   [ʌ]
5. The **caller's collar** is a nice **color**.

Lesson 13   [ə] as in *a*, *upon*, and *soda*

The schwa vowel [ə] is a very short, quick sound. Your lips should be completely relaxed and barely move during its production.

[ə] is the sound that results when ANY vowel in English is unstressed in a word. The vowels in all unstressed syllables almost always sound like [ə]. Any letter or combination of letters can represent the schwa [ə].

Possible Pronunciation Problems

In most languages, vowels are pronounced clearly and distinctly. The schwa [ə] does not exist. In English, unstressed vowels should receive much less force than other vowels in the word. In order to speak fluent English, you must unstress or reduce any vowels that are NOT in accented syllables of words. Vowel reduction to [ə] is not sloppy speech. It is an important feature of spoken English.

Practice

EXERCISE A   🎧 **Listen and repeat. Notice how the syllable with the [ə] vowel receives less stress than the other syllables in the word.**

[ə] At the Beginning of Words		[ə] In the Middle of Words		[ə] At the End of Words	
ago	upon	agony	relative	soda	famous
away	contain	holiday	seventy	sofa	lemon
along	asleep	company	telephone	zebra	cousin
amaze	suppose	buffalo	photograph	reason	circus

[ə] Spelled

a	*e*	*i*	*o*	*u*
arrive	oven	liquid	occur	upon
ashamed	open	humid	obtain	suppose
asleep	cement	capital	lemon	circus
away	jacket	typical	lesson	column
signal	belief	cousin	contain	support

note

Other spellings of [ə] include *eo, ou, iou, io,* and *ai.*

    pigeon   famous   delicious   nation   certain

The schwa [ə] can occur more than once and can be represented by different letters in the same word.

president   elephant   accident

EXERCISE B

🎧 **Listen and repeat. Be sure to pronounce the syllable with [ə] with less force than other syllables.**

1. How are you today?
2. See you tonight.
3. See you tomorrow.
4. Don't complain.
5. I suppose so.
6. I suppose it's possible.
7. Consider my complaint.
8. Complete today's lesson.
9. Don't complain about the problem.
10. My cousin will arrive at seven.

CHECK YOURSELF 1

🎧 **Listen and circle the schwa vowel [ə] in each word. (For answers to Check Yourself 1–3, see Appendix II, page 279.)**

EXAMPLE   t e l ⓔ g r a p h

1. a l p h a b e t   6. p r e v e n t
2. u t i l i z e   7. i m i t a t e
3. d e p e n d i n g   8. b r e a k f a s t
4. p h o t o g r a p h   9. c o n t r o l
5. p a p a   10. a l a r m

CHECK YOURSELF 2

📖 **Read aloud each group of four words. Circle the one word in each group that does NOT contain [ə].**

EXAMPLE   (slipper)   soda   finally   agree

1. about   oven   create   olive
2. minute   second   seven   leaving
3. after   attend   allow   annoy
4. something   support   supply   suppose
5. combine   complete   camper   compare

6.	Canada	Russia	Norway	Colombia
7.	lavender	maroon	yellow	orange
8.	strawberry	banana	vanilla	chocolate
9.	lettuce	tomato	carrot	cucumber
10.	giraffe	zebra	monkey	camel

CHECK YOURSELF 3 📖 **Read the words aloud. Each word contains TWO unstressed syllables. Circle the schwa [ə] vowels in BOTH unstressed syllables of each word.**

EXAMPLES   m a g i c a l

e l e p h a n t

1. f a v o r i t e

2. p r i n c i p a l

3. a s s i s t a n c e

4. m e d i c a l

5. a t t e n d a n c e

6. e v i d e n c e

7. o f f e n d e d

8. d i p l o m a

9. a p a r t m e n t

10. C a n a d a

More Practice

EXERCISE A   📖 **Read aloud the verses from the poem "Annabel Lee," by Edgar Allen Poe. Remember, the underlined schwa [ə] vowels receive less stress than other vowels.**

from "Annabel Lee"
Edgar Allen Poe

It was many and many a year ago in a kingdom by the sea
That a maiden there lived whom you may know
By the name of Annabel Lee,
And this maiden she lived with no other thought
Than to love and be loved by me.

I was a child and she was a child, in this kingdom by the sea
But we loved with a love that was more than love
I and my Annabel Lee,
With a love that the winged seraphs of heaven coveted her and me.

And this was the reason that long ago, in this kingdom by the sea,
A wind blew out of a cloud, chilling my beautiful Annabel Lee,
So that her highborn kinsman came and bore her away from me,
To shut her up in a sepulcre in this kingdom by the sea.

And neither the angels in heaven above
Nor the demons down under the sea,
Can ever dissever my soul from the soul
Of the beautiful Annabel Lee.

EXERCISE B

Names of ten of the presidents of the United States are listed on the left. On the right are listed the names of ten states in the United States. Look up the birth states of each of the presidents in an encyclopedia or on the Internet. Match the president on the left with the correct state on the right. Then work with a partner. Ask each other where each president was born. Pay attention to the underlined schwa [ə] sound.

EXAMPLE   **A:** Where was Thomas Jefferson born?

B: Thomas Jefferson was born in Virginia.

President	State
_b_ 1. Thomas Jefferson	a. Kentucky
___ 2. Lyndon Johnson	b. Virginia
___ 3. Bill Clinton	c. California
___ 4. Harry Truman	d. Illinois
___ 5. Gerald Ford	e. Massachusetts
___ 6. Richard Nixon	f. Texas
___ 7. Ronald Reagan	g. Nebraska
___ 8. Andrew Jackson	h. Arkansas
___ 9. Abraham Lincoln	i. South Carolina
___ 10. John Kennedy	j. Missouri

Spend a few minutes every day practicing the schwa, and progress is possible!

Answers to More Practice Exercise B

1. b, 2. f, 3. h, 4. j, 5. g, 6. c,
7. d, 8. i, 9. a, 10. e

[ɝ] as in *turn*, *first*, and *serve* and [ɚ] as in *father* and *actor*

PRONOUNCING [ɝ]

[ɝ]

Lips: Protruded and slightly parted
Jaw: Slightly lowered
Tongue: Midlevel in the mouth

[ɝ] is a sound that occurs only in stressed syllables of words.

Possible Pronunciation Problems

The vowel [ɝ] does not exist in most languages. Just remember that [ɝ] always receives strong emphasis and is found only in stressed syllables. It is produced with slightly protruded lips and tense tongue muscles.

Be s*ur*e to practice and you'll be c*er*tain to l*ear*n [ɝ]!

Practice

EXERCISE A

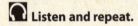 **Listen and repeat.**

[ɝ] At the Beginning of Words

urge	early
herb	urban
earn	earnest
earth	irk

[ɝ] In the Middle of Words

turn	curve
word	learn
verb	circus
third	Thursday

[ɝ] At the End of Words

fur	prefer
sir	stir
her	purr
occur	defer

[ɝ] Spelled

ir	*ur*	*er*
bird	hurt	fern
girl	curl	term
firm	curb	stern
third	purple	German
circle	turkey	servant

note

Less frequent spelling patterns for [ɝ] consist of the letters *ear*, *our*, and *or*.

h**ear**d   j**our**ney   w**or**k

EXERCISE B   🎧 **Listen and repeat. The boldfaced words in the following phrases and sentences all include the vowel [ɝ].**

1. **turn** it off
2. **heard** the **words**
3. slow as a **turtle**
4. **first** things **first**
5. a **turn** for the **worse**
6. left **work early**
7. The **early bird** catches the **worm**.
8. The **girl** saw the **circus first**.
9. The **servant served dessert**.
10. **Irma** had **her thirty-third birthday**.

CHECK YOURSELF   ⚱ **The boldfaced words in the following sentences contain the vowel [ɝ]. Work with a partner. Read the following sentences aloud, filling in each blank with a word from the box. (For answers, see Appendix II, page 279.)**

purse	perfume	curly	church	bird
work	desserts	turkey	verbs	skirt

1. The **girl** wore a **purple** _____.
2. The **Germans** bake good _____.
3. At Thanksgiving we **serve** _____.
4. Some people **worship** in a _____.
5. I **heard** the **chirping** of the _____.
6. Another **word** for handbag is _____.
7. A **permanent** makes your hair _____.
8. I **prefer** the scent of that _____.
9. You should **learn** your nouns and _____.
10. A **person** collects unemployment when he is out of _____.

EXERCISE

📖 **Read aloud the paragraph about turkeys. Pay attention to your pronunciation of the boldfaced words with the [ɝ] sound.**

The **Turkey**

Everyone **learns** about the **early** settlers who **journeyed** to America. These Pilgrims celebrated their **first** Thanksgiving feast with the famous **turkey**. One Native American name for **turkey** is **"firkee,"** and this may have been how the **bird** got its name. **Turkey** is always **served** for Thanksgiving dinner on the fourth **Thursday** in each November, but it is **certain** to please on other occasions. Age will **determine** the taste of a **turkey**. An older male or younger **"girl" turkey** is **preferred**. **Turkeys** are **nourishing** and can be **turned** into **versatile** meals. There is some **work** involved in cooking a **turkey**, but it is **worth** the trouble. The **world concurs** that Americans prepare the most **superb turkeys**.

PRONOUNCING [ɚ]

It is difficult to hear the difference between [ɚ] and [ɝ] when these sounds are produced in isolation. However, [ɚ] is produced with much less force and occurs only in unstressed syllables.

Possible Pronunciation Problems

[ɚ] does not exist in most languages. The position of the lips and jaw is the same as for [ɝ], but the tongue muscles are completely relaxed. [ɚ] never receives strong emphasis and is found only in unstressed syllables.

Practice

EXERCISE A

🎧 **Listen and repeat. Be sure to emphasize [ɚ] less than the other vowels in words.**

[ɚ] In the Middle of Words		[ɚ] At the End of Words	
liberty	butterfly	baker	sooner
perhaps	flowerpot	butter	teacher
surprise	understood	mirror	deliver
		mother	weather

The vowel [ɚ] does not occur at the beginning of words.

[ɚ] Spelled

ar	er	or	ure
sugar	after	color	nature
dollar	paper	actor	picture
collar	father	flavor	feature
regular	farmer	doctor	failure
grammar	silver	razor	measure

The major spellings of [ɚ] are *ar*, *er*, and *or* when the sound occurs in the middle or at the ends of words.

sug**ar**   ad**ver**tise   summ**er**   col**or**ful   doct**or**

EXERCISE B

🎧 **Listen and repeat the following phrases and sentences. Pay attention to the boldfaced words that include the [ɚ] sound. Remember that syllables with the sound [ɚ] are unstressed and should be pronounced with much less force than other syllables in the same word.**

1. **sooner** or **later**
2. **Measure** the **sugar**.
3. **better** late than **never**
4. **Water** the **flowers**.
5. **Consider** the **offer**.
6. The **actor** was **better** than **ever**.
7. Was the **afternoon paper delivered**?
8. The **razor** is **sharper** than the **scissors**.
9. **Summer** is **warmer** than **winter**.
10. A **wonderful picture** is showing at the **theater**.

CHECK YOURSELF

📖 **Read the words aloud. Circle the words that are pronounced with [ɚ]. (For answers, see Appendix II, page 280.)**

EXAMPLE   (acre)   shirt   (afternoon)

1. return   supper   purple
2. enter   curtain   dirty
3. third   backward   inform
4. nurse   soldier   pleasure
5. silver   weather   Saturday

EXERCISE 📖 **Read aloud the paragraph about Mother Goose. Remember NOT to stress the [ɚ] sound.**

Mother Goose

Mother Goose was supposed to be an **older** lady who told **popular** rhymes to **younger** children. **Printers** and **publishers** put **together** these **familiar** rhymes. Some were **finger** plays such as **"Tinker, tailor, soldier, sailor**, rich man, poor man, **beggar** man, thief!" Many **remember** such favorites as "Little Jack **Horner** sat in a **corner** eating his Christmas pie." The king of England's **steward** was called Jack **Horner**. He was a **messenger** who may have **delivered** a Christmas pie with hidden **papers** baked inside. **Whether** or not we believe these **colorful** tales, we know that **nursery** rhymes are **wonderful!**

LESSON REVIEW: [ɝ] AND [ɚ]

Practice

EXERCISE 🎧 **Listen and repeat. The words in the three columns contain both the [ɝ] and [ɚ] sounds. The first syllable of each word should be pronounced with much more stress than the second syllable.**

murder	firmer	Herbert
curler	server	furniture
surfer	burner	merger

CHECK YOURSELF 1 📖 **Read aloud the following phrases and sentences. Identify the [ɝ] and [ɚ] sounds. Write the sounds above the syllables. Remember the [ɝ] sound is stressed and the [ɚ] sound is unstressed. (For answers to Check Yourself 1 and 2, see Appendix II, page 280.)**

      [ ][ ]
1. silver urn
      [ ]   [ ]
2. dangerous curve
    [ ]   [ ]
3. sermon in church
      [ ] [ ]
4. regular exercise
      [ ]   [ ]
5. grammar teacher
       [ ]   [ ] [ ]   [ ]
6. The grammar teacher worked on verbs.

$\qquad$ [ ]　　[ ]　　　[ ]
7. One good turn deserves another.
$\qquad$ [ ]　　　　[ ]　　　　[ ]
8. Birds of a feather flock together.
$\qquad$ [ ]　　[ ]
9. Actions speak louder than words.
$\qquad$ [ ] [ ]　　[ ] [ ] [ ]
10. Actors perform better after rehearsing.

CHECK YOURSELF 2 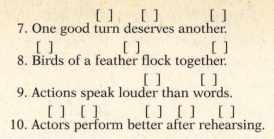 **Read the following paragraph about pearls carefully. Underline words pronounced with [ɝ], and circle words pronounced with [ɚ].**

Pearls

The <u>pearl</u> is one of the <u>world</u>'s most (treasured) gems. <u>Pearls</u> are formed inside the shells of oysters. The largest pearl fisheries are in Asia. Cultured pearls were developed by the Chinese in the twentieth century. They are larger than nature's pearls. A perfect pearl that is round and has great luster is worth a lot of money. Perhaps "diamonds are a girl's best friend," but pearls will always win a woman's favor!

Check your answers to see if you underlined all the words pronounced with [ɝ] and circled words pronounced with [ɚ]. Practice reading the paragraph again.

More Practice

EXERCISE A **Work with a partner. Complete the dialogue together by choosing one word in each set of parentheses. Practice reading the dialogue aloud together. Pay attention to the words with the [ɝ] and [ɚ] sounds.**

Bert: Hello, Mrs. Kirk. I'm here to buy a birthday present for my (sister/brother/daughter). (Her/his) name is (Irma/Curtis). I think (he/she) would like a new (sweater/skirt/shirt).

Mrs. Kirk: We have a wonderful selection. Tell me, Bert, what is (her/his) favorite color?

Bert: (Irma/Curtis) loves (purple/turquoise/amber). I like that (sweater/skirt/shirt) over there.

Mrs. Kirk: Do you know (her/his) size?

Bert: Well, (Irma/Curtis) is (taller/shorter) than you and a little (heavier/thinner).

Mrs. Kirk: I just remembered that I have (Irma's/Curtis's) measurements on file. I will order the (sweater/skirt/shirt) today, and you should have it by Thursday.

Bert: Perfect. (Her/His) birthday is on Saturday, September 1st. By the way, I like that (purse/pearl necklace/perfume). I'll give my younger daughter a gift as well.

Mrs. Kirk: (Irma/Curtis) certainly has a generous (brother/father).

Bert: Well, one good turn deserves another. My birthday is coming up on (October/November/December) 3rd. You could do me a favor. Tell (her/him) you heard I like those (silver/copper) cufflinks!

EXERCISE B

Make a list of all the occupations you can think of that are pronounced with [ɝ] or [ɚ] (doctor, dancer, clerk). Then work with a partner. Practice pronouncing the occupations in the context of sentences.

EXAMPLES Mr. Rogers is a wonderful dancer.

I saw my doctor yesterday.

Lea*r*n to say [ɝ] and [ɚ], and your pronunciation of many wo*r*ds will sound bette*r* than eve*r*!

PRONOUNCING [aʊ]

Lips: Glide from an open position

Jaw: Rises with the tongue and closes

Tongue: Glides from low to high near the roof of the mouth

[aʊ] is a diphthong. A diphthong is a compound vowel sound made by blending two vowels together very quickly. [aʊ] begins with [a] and ends with [ʊ].

Possible Pronunciation Problems

[aʊ] should be easy for you to pronounce if you remember it is a diphthong, which is a combination of two vowel sounds. [aʊ] is a combination of the sounds [a] and [ʊ]. Be sure your lips glide from a wide, open position to a closed one, or you might simply be pronouncing the vowel [a].

EXAMPLES   If you say [a] instead of [aʊ]:   **pound** will sound like **pond**.

down will sound like **Don**.

[aʊ] is always represented by the letter *o* followed by *u*, *w*, or *ugh*.

You won't have many d*ou*bts ab*ou*t which words include the s*ou*nd [aʊ]!

Practice

EXERCISE A   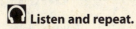 **Listen and repeat.**

[aʊ] At the Beginning of Words

owl	ounce	ourselves
out	outlet	outside
hour	outfit	outline

[aʊ] In the Middle of Words

loud	mouse	mountain
down	vowel	pronounce
crowd	flower	scout

[aʊ] At the End of Words

cow	allow
how	plough
now	

[aʊ] Spelled

ou	*ow*
foul	town
sour	crown
cloud	power
thousand	eyebrow
announce	clown

EXERCISE B

🎧 **Listen and repeat. When producing words with the diphthong [aʊ], be sure to glide your articulators from [a] to [ʊ].**

[aʊ]	[a]
bound	bond
pound	pond
shout	shot
proud	prod
doubt	dot

EXERCISE C

🎧 **Listen and repeat the following phrases and sentences. The boldfaced words should be pronounced with the diphthong [aʊ].**

1. **How** are you?
2. **How about** it?
3. **round** and **round**
4. I **doubt** it!
5. **hour** after **hour**
6. **around** the **house**
7. **Pronounce** the **vowel sounds**.
8. Don't **shout out loud** in the **house**.
9. The ball **bounced out** of **bounds**.
10. **Howard** is **proud** of his **town**.

CHECK YOURSELF 1

Circle the word in each group of four that does NOT contain the diphthong [aʊ]. (For answers to Check Yourself 1 and 2, see Appendix II, pages 280–281.)

EXAMPLE	bounce	round	found	would
1.	brown	down	flow	frown
2.	foul	group	shout	loud
3.	know	how	now	cow
4.	sour	hour	tour	our
5.	could	count	crown	crowd
6.	thought	plough	drought	thousand

7.	ounce	out	own	ouch
8.	flounder	flood	flour	pounce
9.	allow	about	power	arose
10.	noun	consonant	vowel	sound

CHECK YOURSELF 2 📖 **Read the following dialogue. Circle the words that contain the diphthong [aʊ].**

Mr. Brown: You look (out) of sorts. (How) come?

Mrs. Brown: I'm tired out. Didn't you hear the loud noise outside all night?

Mr. Brown: I didn't hear a sound. I was out like a light!

Mrs. Brown: Our neighbors had a big crowd; they were shouting and howling!

Mr. Brown: Why didn't you tell them to stop clowning around?

Mrs. Brown: I didn't want to sound like a grouch.

Mr. Brown: Next time I'll go out. I'm not afraid to open my mouth.

Mrs. Brown: I knew I could count on you. Here comes our noisy neighbor,

                   Mr. Crowley, right now.

Mr. Brown: Sorry, dear, I have to go downtown, NOW!

Mrs. Brown: Come back, you coward!

⬇ **Check to make sure you circled all the words pronounced with the diphthong [aʊ]. Then read the dialogue with a partner.**

More Practice

EXERCISE A 📖 **Read the poem aloud. Be sure to pronounce the boldfaced words containing the diphthong [aʊ] correctly.**

The Hungry **Owl**
Anonymous

The **owl** looked **down** with his great **round** eyes
At the lowering **cloud** and the darkening skies.
"A good night for **scouting**," says he,
"A **mouse** or two may be **found** on the **ground**
Or a fat little bird in a tree."
So **down** he flew from the old church **tower**,
The **mouse** and birdie **crouch** and **cower**,
Back he flies in an **hour**,
"A very good supper," says he.

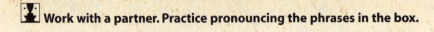 **Work with a partner. Practice pronouncing the phrases in the box.**

down and **out**	three's a **crowd**
loud mouth	**count** on you
beats **around** the bush	a **wallflower**
throw in the **towel**	paint the **town** red

Now take turns making statements and responses, completing each response with a phrase from the box. Pay attention to your pronunciation of the boldfaced words containing the diphthong [aʊ].

1. Statement: **Howard** is always **shouting** and attracting attention.

    Response: **Sounds** like he's a _____.

2. Statement: Mr. **Crowley** has lost all his money.

    Response: **Sounds** like he's _____.

3. Statement: Tim wouldn't leave my **spouse** and me alone last night.

    Response: **Sounds** like _____.

4. Statement: We may not be able to attend your **house** party.

    Response: **Sounds** like we won't _____.

5. Statement: Betty stayed in the corner for **hours** at the party.

    Response: **Sounds** like she's _____.

6. Statement: The **accountant** talks on and on and never gets to the

    point.

    Response: **Sounds** like she _____.

7. Statement: My **housekeeper** wants to quit.

    Response: **Sounds** like he is ready to _____.

8. Statement: **Paulo** is going **out** to party and dance all night.

    Response: **Sounds** like he wants to _____.

Practice [aʊ] out loud, and you will have few doubts about the sound [aʊ]!

Lesson 16 [aɪ] as in *I, my,* and *pie*

Lips: Glide from an open to a slightly parted position

Jaw: Rises with the tongue and closes

Tongue: Glides from low to high near the roof of the mouth

[aɪ] is a diphthong. A diphthong is a compound vowel sound made by blending two vowels together very quickly. The diphthong [aɪ] begins with [a] and ends with [ɪ].

Possible Pronunciation Problems

The diphthong [aɪ] should be quite easy for you to pronounce. Just watch out for irregular spelling patterns. Remember that [aɪ] is frequently represented by the letters *i* or *y*.

EXAMPLES   **i**ce   m**y**

Keep tr*y*ing. Your [aɪ] will be qu*i*te f*i*ne.

EXERCISE A   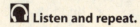 **Listen and repeat.**

[aɪ] At the Beginning of Words

eye/I	item	idea
ice	aisle	icon
I'm	island	ivory
I've		

[aɪ] In the Middle of Words

bite/byte	fight	kind
five	rhyme	time/thyme
mind	while	height
sign		

[aɪ] At the End of Words

by/buy	lie/lye	sigh
cry	rye	apply
die/dye	try	deny
tie		

[aɪ] Spelled

i	*y*	*ie*	*igh*
I	my	die	high
ice	fly	pie	sight
fire	why	tie	night
bite	type	cries	delight
nice	style	fried	frighten

The letter *i* followed by *gh*, *ld*, or *nd* is usually pronounced [aɪ].

sight   wild   find

When *i* is in a syllable ending in silent *e*, the letter *i* is pronounced [aɪ] (the same as the alphabet letter *i*).

bite   fine   refinement   confine

EXERCISE B

Listen and repeat. Pay attention to the boldfaced words containing the diphthong [aɪ].

1. **Hi**!
2. **Nice** to meet you.
3. **I'm fine**.
4. What **time** is it?
5. **Nice try**!
6. **Rise** and **shine**!
7. The store is open from **nine** to **five**.
8. **I'll buy** the **item** if the **price** is **right**.
9. **I'm trying** to **type** it by **tonight**.
10. **My driver's license expires** in July.

CHECK YOURSELF 1

Read the words aloud. Circle the word in each group that does NOT contain the diphthong [aɪ]. (For answers to Check Yourself 1 and 2, see Appendix II, page 281.)

EXAMPLE	pie	line	(rich)	rice
1.	price	crime	pity	pile
2.	mind	kind	spinning	finding
3.	sign	high	fright	freight
4.	list	cite	aisle	cried
5.	gyp	bye	cry	reply
6.	niece	nice	knife	night
7.	style	failed	filed	fire
8.	pretty	try	resign	good-bye
9.	ice	eye	aim	aisle
10.	flight	fine	duty	dying

📖 **Read the dialogue. Practice it with a partner. Circle all the words that contain the diphthong [aɪ].**

Mike: (Hi,) (Myra,) It's (nice) to see you.

Myra: Likewise, Mike. How are you?

Mike: I'm tired. I just came in on a night flight from Ireland.

Myra: What time did your flight arrive?

Mike: I arrived at five forty-five in the morning.

Myra: I'm surprised the airlines have a late-night flight.

Mike: If you don't mind, Myra, I think I'll go home and rest for a while. I'm really wiped out!

Myra: Why, Mike, I have a whole night lined up—dining out and going night-clubbing!

Mike: Myra, are you out of your mind?

Myra: I'm only joking. You're going right home. Sleep tight!

More Practice

📖 **Read the paragraph aloud. Pay attention to the boldfaced words containing the diphthong [aɪ].**

Lying!

    Psychologists say that **lying** well is a special talent that is not easily **acquired**. Good **liars** can be **quite likeable**, have a charming **style**, and can look you **right** in the **eye**. **Lie**-detector tests are used about 1 million **times** a year by **private** companies, police departments, and even the **CIA**. Some people insist that **lie**-detector tests are **reliable**. However, many experts **find** that **lie**-detectors can be fooled by **biting** one's tongue. From the beginning of **time**, people have **tried** to detect **lies**. In ancient India, suspected **liars** were sent **by** themselves into a hut without any **light**. They were instructed to pull the tail of a donkey in the hut. They were told the donkey would **cry** out if the person pulling its tail was **lying**. They had no **idea** that the donkey's tail was covered in soot. The real **liars** were **identified** because they had no soot on their hands when they came out of the hut!

Read "Going to St. Ives" aloud. Pay attention to your pronunciation of the boldfaced words with the diphthong [aɪ]. Then answer the question in the last line.

Going to St. Ives

As **I** was going to St. **Ives**
I met a man with **nine wives**.
Each **wife** had **nine** sacks
Each sack had **nine** cats
Each cat had **nine** kits
Kits, cats, sacks, **wives**.
How many were going to St. **Ives**?

List five things that you like. The names of the things should contain the diphthong [aɪ]. Then work with a partner. Ask each other, "What do you like?" Answer with the things on your list.

EXAMPLE **A:** What do you like?

B: I like (to spend time by myself/to ride my bike at night/. . .)

Keep trying and in time your [aɪ] will be quite fine!

PRONOUNCING [ɔɪ]

Lips: Glide from a tense oval shape to a relaxed, slightly parted position

Jaw: Rises with the tongue and closes

Tongue: Glides from a low position to a high position near the roof of the mouth

[ɔɪ] is a diphthong. A diphthong is a compound vowel sound made by blending two vowels together very quickly. The diphthong [ɔɪ] begins with [ɔ] and ends with [ɪ].

Possible Pronunciation Problems

You shouldn't have many problems with the diphthong [ɔɪ]. English words with this diphthong are spelled *oy* or *oi*. There are virtually no exceptions to this rule!

You'll enj*oy* pronouncing [ɔɪ]!

Practice

EXERCISE A   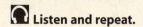 **Listen and repeat.**

[ɔɪ] At the Beginning of Words		[ɔɪ] In the Middle of Words			[ɔɪ] At the End of Words		
oil	oyster	join	foil	noise	toy	enjoy	destroy
oink	ointment	boil	coin	poison	boy	annoy	
oily		broil	avoid	choice	ploy	decoy	

EXERCISE B   📖 **Read the phrases aloud. Pay attention to the boldfaced words containing the diphthong [ɔɪ].**

1. girls and **boys**
2. flip a **coin**
3. Don't **annoy** me!
4. **Enjoy** yourself.
5. Lower your **voice**.

Read the following words. Circle the word in each group that is NOT pronounced with [ɔɪ]. (For answers to Check Yourself 1 and 2, see Appendix II, pages 281–282.)

EXAMPLE	joy	join	enjoy	(jaunt)
1.	voice	avoid	void	vows
2.	noise	nose	hoist	annoy
3.	towel	toy	toil	spoil
4.	Detroit	Illinois	St. Croix	New York
5.	oil	oily	foil	owl
6.	boil	broil	bow	boy
7.	poison	pounce	point	appoint
8.	poise	Joyce	Joan	soil
9.	coil	coal	coy	coin
10.	lobster	sirloin	oyster	moist

Read the dialogue. Circle the words that are pronounced with the diphthong [ɔɪ].

Mrs. Royce: Hi, Mr. (Lloyd.) Can I help you?

Mr. Lloyd: Yes, Mrs. (Royce,) I'd like a (toy) for my son, (Floyd.)

Mrs. Royce: We have quite a choice of toys. What about a fire truck?

Mr. Lloyd: That's too noisy. Besides, my boy would destroy it!

Mrs. Royce: Here's an oil paint set.

Mr. Lloyd: That's messy. His mother will be annoyed if he soils anything.

Mrs. Royce: Let me point out this electric train.

Mr. Lloyd: Wow! I never had a toy like that as a boy!

Mrs. Royce: Your boy will enjoy it. Mr. Lloyd? Please turn off the set. Mr. Lloyd!

Mr. Lloyd: Did you say something, Mrs. Royce? I'm playing with Floyd's new toy!

Mrs. Royce: I guess you've made your choice! I hope you let your boy use it once in a while!

Check to make sure you circled all the [ɔɪ] words. Then practice the dialogue with a partner.

More Practice

EXERCISE A

📖 **Read the limerick aloud. Pay attention to your pronunciation of the boldfaced words with the [ɔɪ] sound.**

> ### The **Boy** from **Troy**
>
> **Roy** was a **boy** from **Troy**.
> Who ate **oysters** with absolute **joy**.
> He **boiled** them, he **broiled** them
> He baked them, he **oiled** them,
> And sometimes he dipped them in **soy**.

EXERCISE B

🏆 **Ask and answer the questions with a partner.**

1. **A:** Would you rather have **broiled** or **boiled** lobster?

   B: I'd rather have _____.

2. **A:** Would you prefer to cook fish in **oil** or wrap it in **foil** and steam it?

   B: _____.

3. **A:** Do you ever buy **choice sirloin** or pork **loin**?

   B: _____.

4. **A:** Do you think **noisy** children are **annoying** or **enjoyable**?

   B: I think **noisy** children are _____.

5. **A:** Which would you **enjoy** more—a trip to **Detroit** or a trip to **Troy**?

   B: I'd **enjoy** a trip to _____.

You'll soon enj*oy* pronouncing [ɔɪ]!

Part 2 Stress, Rhythm, and Intonation

Lesson 18 — Introducing Stress, Rhythm, and Intonation

Thus far, you have been studying the individual sounds of English. The sounds can be significantly affected by vocal features known as stress, rhythm, and intonation. These vocal features help to convey meaning and must be used correctly if you are to be completely understood.

Stress is the first vocal feature we will deal with. Speakers must stress certain syllables in words; otherwise the words would be misunderstood or sound strange. For example, improperly placed stress when pronouncing ***in**valid* (a chronically ill or disabled person) may make it sound like *in**valid*** (null; legally ineffective). Stress can also change the meaning of a sentence. "**I** saw a movie" is different from "I saw a **movie**." "**He** won't go" implies a meaning different from "He won't **go**." In English, proper use of stress enables you to clearly understand the difference between such words as the noun ***pres**ent* (a gift) and the verb *pre**sent*** (to introduce; to offer).

Rhythm is the second feature we will present. Rhythm is created by the strong stresses or beats in a sentence. In many languages, the rhythm is syllable-timed. This means that all vowels in all syllables are pronounced almost equally. Syllables are rarely lost or reduced as they are in English. For example, a three-word phrase in your language is not likely to become two words. In English, "ham and eggs" is squeezed into two words, "ham'n eggs."

This reduction results because English has a stress-timed rhythm. This means that its rhythm is determined by the number of stresses, not by the number of syllables. English speakers slow down and emphasize heavily stressed words or syllables. They speed up and reduce unstressed ones. For example, the five-word phrase "I will see you tomorrow" may become "I'll seeya t'morrow."

Intonation is the final vocal feature you will learn about. Intonation patterns involve pitch and are responsible for the melody of the language. Speakers frequently depend more on intonation patterns to convey their meaning than on the pronunciation of the individual vowels and consonants. For example, in English, the same words can be used to make a statement or ask a question. If your vocal intonation rises, you are asking a question: "He speaks English?" The sentence "That's Bill's car" becomes the question "That's Bill's car?" when you raise the pitch of your voice at the end.

So now you can appreciate the common expression, "It's not **what** you say, it's **how** you say it!"

Although your English grammar might be perfect and you might be able to pronounce individual sounds correctly, you will still have a noticeable foreign accent until you master the stress, rhythm, and intonation patterns of English.

Stress Within the Word

Definition

Stress refers to the amount of volume that a speaker gives to a particular sound, syllable, or word while saying it. Stressed sounds and syllables are **louder** and **longer** than unstressed ones. The words *accent*, *stress*, and *emphasis* are frequently used interchangeably.

Stress in English

A major characteristic of the English language is the use of strong and weak stress. Every word of more than one syllable has a syllable that is emphasized more than the others. Accented syllables receive more force and are **louder** than unaccented ones. Correct use of stress is essential for achieving proper pronunciation of words.

Possible Pronunciation Problems

Many languages have specific rules for accenting words. When there is an exception to the rule, an accent mark is generally written above the stressed syllable. There are NO consistent rules in English. Consequently, you may have difficulty when attempting to accent syllables correctly.

1. If you place the stress on the **wrong** syllable:

EXAMPLES   **désert** (dry barren region) will sound like **dessért** (sweet foods)
                       ínvalid (bedridden/ill person) will sound like **inválid** (void, null)

2. If you stress every vowel in a word equally and forget to reduce vowels in unaccented syllables:

EXAMPLES   **tomórrow**   will sound like **tómórrów**
                       becáuse   will sound like **bécáuse**

As you practice imitating your teacher or the instructor on the CD, your ability to use proper stress patterns when speaking English will improve. BE POSITIVE AND KEEP PRACTICING!

Words Stressed on the First Syllable

1. The majority of two-syllable words are accented on the FIRST syllable.

EXAMPLES   Túesday   áwful   éver   bróther   óven   wíndow

2. Compound nouns are usually accented on the FIRST syllable.

EXAMPLES   bédroom   stóplight   schóolhouse   bóokstore

3. Numbers that are multiples of ten are accented on the FIRST syllable.

EXAMPLES   twénty   thírty   fórty   fífty   síxty   séventy

Words Stressed on the Second Syllable

1. Reflexive pronouns are usually accented on the SECOND syllable.

EXAMPLES   mysélf   yoursélf   himsélf   hersélf   oursélves

2. Compound verbs are usually accented on the SECOND or LAST syllable.

EXAMPLES   outdóne   outsmárt   outdó   outrún   overlóok

Practice

EXERCISE A

Listen and repeat. Be sure to stress the FIRST syllable of the words on the left and the SECOND syllable of the words on the right.

Stress on FIRST Syllable	Stress on SECOND Syllable
ápple	aróund
táble	allów
móther	invíte
téacher	compléte
wínter	suppórt
páper	belíeve
báseball	mysélf
bréakfast	outrún
síxty	behínd
éighty	

EXERCISE B

The following three-syllable words have a variety of stress patterns. Listen and repeat. Remember to EMPHASIZE the stressed syllable.

Primary Stress on FIRST Syllable	Primary Stress on SECOND Syllable	Primary Stress on THIRD Syllable
áccident	accéptance	afternóon
stráwberry	vanílla	absolúte
séventy	exámine	seventéen
yésterday	tomórrow	recomménd
président	policeman	guarantée
sálary	emplóyer	employée
pérsonal	repáirman	personnél
tránslating	transláition	gasolíne
élephant	gorílla	kangaróo
Fébruary	Decémber	overlóok

Stress in Noun/Verb Homographs

There are many two-syllable nouns and verbs that are the same in the written form. We can distinguish between these word pairs in their spoken form through the use of stress. In these pairs, the noun will always be stressed on the first syllable and the verb on the second syllable.

EXERCISE C 🔊 **Listen and repeat the noun/verb pairs. Remember to stress the *noun* on the FIRST syllable and *verb* on the SECOND.**

Nouns		Verbs	
cónflict	(controversy)	conflíct	(to clash)
cónduct	(one's behavior)	condúct	(to lead or guide)
cóntent	(subject matter)	contént	(to satisfy)
désert	(barren region)	desért	(to abandon)
dígest	(synopsis)	digést	(to absorb)
cóntest	(competition)	contést	(to dispute or challenge)
pérmit	(written warrant)	permít	(to allow or consent)
éxploit	(notable act, adventure)	exploít	(to take advantage of)
óbject	(material thing)	objéct	(to oppose or disagree)
íncrease	(enlargement)	incréase	(to make larger)

EXERCISE D 🔊 **Listen and repeat the sentences. Carefully pronounce the stress pattern differences between the boldfaced words in each sentence.**

1. Please **recórd** the **récord**.
2. Please don't **desért** me in the **désert**.
3. We **projéct** that the **próject** will be good.
4. The sheik was **fífty** with **fifteén** wives!
5. His hairline began **recéding récently**.
6. The teacher was **contént** with the **cóntent** of the report.
7. He **objécts** to the ugly **óbjects**.
8. I **mistrúst Míster** Smith.
9. She will **presént** you with a **présent**.
10. He will **contést** the results of the **cóntest**.

The Prefix *re-*

1. When the prefix *re-* means "again," it receives strong stress.

EXAMPLES   rédo   réname   ré-dress   ré-sort   rémake

2. When the syllable *re* begins a word, and it doesn't mean "again," it is unstressed.

EXAMPLES   remárk   redeém   remínd   rewárd   requíre

Listen and repeat the pairs of words and the sentences. Remember to stress *re-* only when it means "again."

1. ré-mark (to mark something again)   remárk (to comment)

2. ré-press (to press or iron something again)   repress (to inhibit)

3. ré-lay (to lay something down again)   reláy (to pass on a message)

4. ré-dress (to dress again)   redress (to correct a wrong)

5. ré-sort (to arrange or organize again)   resórt (to take action in order to succeed)

6. Rédo this model, but redúce the size.

7. Remínd me to ré-sort the index cards.

8. Will he refúse to ré-press the shirts?

9. The teacher will require you to réwrite the letter.

10. His mom remárked that she ré-marked the clothes.

CHECK YOURSELF 1

Read the sentences aloud. Fill in the blank with compound nouns formed from the two boldfaced words. Be sure to stress the first syllable of each compound noun. (For answers to Check Yourself 1–4, see Appendix II, pages 282–284.)

EXAMPLE   A **rack** that holds **coats** is a _____coatrack_____.

1. **Juice** made from **oranges** is called _____.

2. A **box** used for storing **bread** is called a _____.

3. A **store** that sells **books** is called a _____.

4. A **ball** you kick with your **foot** is called a _____.

5. A **hat** you wear in the **rain** is called a _____.

6. A **store** that sells **toys** is called a _____.

7. A **man** that delivers the **mail** is called a _____.

8. A **sign** that signals you to **stop** is called a _____.

9. When you have an **ache** in your **head**, you have a _____.

10. A **store** that sells **drugs** is called a _____.

🎧 **Listen and repeat the words. Circle the ONE word in each group that has a stress pattern different from the others.**

EXAMPLE	connect	control	contain	(constant)
1.	agent	annoy	allow	agree
2.	upon	until	undo	under
3.	protect	program	pronoun	protein
4.	token	toaster	today	total
5.	supper	sunken	suffer	support
6.	explain	extra	excite	exam
7.	deepen	deny	devote	degree
8.	repair	reason	recent	reader
9.	invite	invent	inform	instant
10.	open	oppose	over	only

🎧 **Listen and repeat the sentences. Circle the number of the stressed syllable in each italicized word.**

                            ① 2

EXAMPLE   The *convict* escaped from jail.

                       1 2

1. Keep a *record* of your expenses.

                            1 2

2. The police don't *suspect* anyone.

                          1 2

3. The student will *present* a speech.

               1 2

4. The *present* was not wrapped.

               1 2 3

5. The *invalid* was in the hospital.

                        1 2

6. Please print your *address* clearly.

                     1 2

7. I will send a *survey* to all students.

                 1 2

8. Be sure to *record* your speech.

                     1 2 3

9. The letter is in the *envelope*.

                 1 2 3

10. I want to *envelop* the baby in my arms.

Read the poem aloud line by line. Observe how the noun in each line is emphasized. Circle the number of the stressed syllable in each two-syllable word.

    ① 2

Money

  ① 2 ① 2

Richard Armour

  1 2

Workers earn it,

  1 2

Spendthrifts burn it,

  1 2

Bankers lend it,

  1 2

Women spend it,

  1 2

Forgers fake it,

  1 2

Taxes take it,

  1 2

Dying leave it,

   1 2

Heirs receive it,

   1 2

Thrifty save it,

  1 2

Misers crave it,

  1 2

Robbers seize it,

   1 2

Rich increase it,

  1 2

Gamblers lose it . . .

I could use it!

Check your answers. Then read the poem aloud again using proper stress patterns.

EXERCISE   🏆 **Work with a partner. Take turns explaining the type of work that each person in the list does. Then use the word in a sentence. Be sure to stress the correct syllable in each compound noun.**

EXAMPLES   A **mail**man puts the mail in our **mail**box.

                    Mailman is another name for **post**man or **mail** carrier.

1. mailman
2. fisherman
3. milkman
4. fireman
5. policeman
6. garbage man
7. paperboy
8. seamstress
9. lifeguard
10. babysitter
11. disc jockey
12. repairman
13. lineman
14. quarterback
15. ice skater
16. movie star
17. cameraman
18. bartender
19. dog trainer
20. saleswoman
21. salesman
22. busboy

Lesson 20 | Stress Within the Sentence

Sentence Stress in English

You have already learned that word stress is a major feature of English. Stress patterns go beyond the word level. Just as it sounds awkward to stress the syllables in a word incorrectly or to stress them all equally, it sounds unnatural to stress all the words in a sentence equally or improperly. Effective use of strong and weak emphasis in phrases and sentences will help you achieve your goal of sounding like a native English speaker.

Possible Pronunciation Problems

English sentence-level stress patterns may not be used the same way as in your language. In English, specific words within a sentence are emphasized or spoken louder to make them stand out. ("It's not **his** house; it's **her** house.") Your language may use its grammar instead of word stress to convey the same meaning. Consequently, you may be confused about when to use strong stress (and when not to use it!) in English sentences. Using the stress patterns of your native language when speaking English will contribute to your foreign accent.

1. If you place the stress on the wrong word, you will:

   a. completely change the meaning of your statement.

   EXAMPLE   "He lives in the green **house**" (the house painted green) will sound like "He lives in the **green**house" (where plants are grown).

   b. distort your intended meaning of the sentence.

   EXAMPLE   "**Steve's** my cousin" (not Sam) will sound like "Steve's my **cousin**" (not my brother).

2. If you give too much or equal stress to unimportant or "function words":

   EXAMPLES   "I'm in the **house**" will sound like "I'm **in the** house."
   "He's at the **store**" will sound like "**He's at the store**."

After reading the explanations and listening to the CD a few times, you will begin to understand the use of English sentence stress patterns. YOU SHOULD BE VERY PROUD OF YOURSELF. YOU'VE ALREADY COME A LONG WAY!

Words Generally Stressed in Sentences: Content Words

Content words are the important words in a sentence that convey meaning. We normally STRESS content words when speaking. Content words include all the major parts of speech such as nouns, verbs, adjectives, adverbs, and question words.

Words Generally Unstressed in Sentences: Function Words

Function words are the unimportant words in a sentence. They don't carry as much meaning as content words. We normally do NOT stress function words when speaking. Function words include the following parts of speech:

		Examples
1.	Articles	*the, a*
2.	Prepositions	*for, of, in, to*
3.	Pronouns	*I, her, him, he, she, you*
4.	Conjunctions	*but, as, and*
5.	Helping verbs	*is, was, are, were, has, can*

Practice

EXERCISE A   **Listen and repeat the common expressions. Be sure to stress the content words, NOT the function words.**

1. **sooner** or **later**
2. in a **moment**
3. an **apple** a **day**
4. to **tell** the **truth**
5. as **soft** as a **kitten**
6. **Silence** is **golden**.
7. **Honesty** is the **best policy**.
8. **Truth** is **stranger** than **fiction**.
9. A **penny saved** is a **penny earned**.
10. To **err** is **human**; to **forgive** is **divine**.

Stressing Words to Clarify or Change Meaning

Sometimes a speaker wants his or her sentence to convey a special meaning that it wouldn't have in the written form. This can be done by stressing a specific word in order to call attention to it. The word that receives the stress depends on the personal motive of the speaker.

EXAMPLES   I **bought** ten ties. (I wasn't *given* the ties; I *bought* them.)

I bought ten **ties**. (I didn't buy *shirts*; I bought *ties*.)

EXERCISE B   **Listen and repeat the questions and responses. The boldfaced words should receive more emphasis than the other words.**

1. **Who** likes candy?   **Sam** likes candy.
2. **What** does Sam like?   Sam likes **candy**.
3. Is that **his** car?   No, that's **her** car.
4. Will she **stay**?   No, she'll **leave**.

5. **Where** are you going?   I'm going **home**.
6. **Who's** going home?   **I'm** going home.
7. **When** are you going home?   I'm going home **now**.
8. Did Mary **buy** a book?   No, Mary **borrowed** a book.
9. Did **Mary** buy a book?   No, **Sue** bought a book.
10. Did Mary buy a **book**?   No, she bought a **pen**.

Stress in Adjective/Noun Combinations

When you speak, it's important to use words that describe what you are talking about. Words that describe nouns (people, places, or things) are called adjectives. When you use adjective/noun combinations, the noun normally receives greater stress.

EXAMPLES   big **dog**   good **book**   pretty **dress**   nice **boy**

By accidentally stressing the adjective, you might mistakenly say a compound noun with a completely different meaning. Your listeners will be confused!

EXAMPLES   cheap **skates** (inexpensive skates) will sound like **cheap**skates (stingy people)

yellow **jacket** (a yellow coat) will sound like **yellow**jacket (a stinging insect)

EXERCISE C   🎧 **Listen and repeat the sentences. Be sure to stress only the boldfaced words or syllables.**

Sentences with Adjective/ Noun Combinations	Sentences with Compound Nouns
I like all *blue* **birds**.	I like **blue**jays and **blue**birds.
We live in the *white* **house**.	The president lives in the **White** House.
I don't like *dark* **rooms**.	Photographers work in **dark**rooms.
He sawed a *black* **board**.	The teacher writes on the **black**board.
I don't like the *green* **house**.	Plants grow in the **green**house.

EXERCISE D   🎧 **Listen to the dialogue. Pay careful attention to the sentence stress patterns used.**

John: **Anna**, who was on the **phone**?

Anna: My old friend **Mary**.

John: Mary **Jones**?

Anna: **No**. Mary **Hall**.

John: I don't know Mary **Hall**. Where is she **from**?

Anna: She's from **Washington**.

John: Washington the **state** or Washington the **city**?

Anna: Washington, **D.C.**, our nation's **capital**.

John: Is that where she **lives**?

Anna: Yes, she still lives in the white **house**.

John: The **White** House? With the **president**?

Anna: No, **silly**. The white **house** on **First** Street.

John: What did she **want**?

Anna: She wants to **come** here.

John: Come **here**? **When**?

Anna: In a **week**. She's bringing her black **bird**, her **collie**, her **snakes**, her . . .

John: **Stop**! She's bringing a **zoo** to **our** house?

Anna: **No**, John. She's opening a **pet** store here in **town**.

Now practice the dialogue with a partner. Be sure to STRESS the boldfaced words.

CHECK YOURSELF 1   Read the sentences aloud. Circle all content words and underline all function words. (For answers to Check Yourself 1–3, see Appendix II, page 284.)

EXAMPLE   The dogs are barking.

1. Mary is a good friend.
2. Steve is tall and handsome.
3. It's early in the morning.
4. The baby caught a cold.
5. I ate a piece of pie.
6. The store opens at nine.
7. My shoes hurt my feet.
8. Please look for the book.
9. He's leaving in a week.
10. We walked in the snow.

Check your answers. Then read the sentences aloud again. Be sure to *stress* all *content words* and *unstress* all *function words*.

CHECK YOURSELF 2   Read the sentences aloud. In each sentence, the function words have been omitted. Fill in the blanks with appropriate function words.

EXAMPLE   I went ___to___ ___the___ store.

1. Mary wants _____ cup _____ coffee.
2. _____ show started _____ eight.
3. _____ movie _____ very funny.
4. Sue ate _____ slice _____ cake.
5. We met _____ couple _____ friends _____ mine.

Check your answers. Then practice reading the sentences aloud again. Remember, do not stress the function words!

📖 **Read the sentences aloud. One word in each sentence will be stressed more than the others. Circle the word that you must stress to clarify the intended meaning of the sentence.**

EXAMPLES   Mary (Hall) will visit John and Anna. (Not Mary Jones.)

Mary is from (Washington.) (She isn't from New York.)

1. Mary is Anna's friend. (She isn't her cousin.)

2. John is married to Anna. (They aren't engaged anymore.)

3. She's from Washington, D.C. (She's not from Washington state.)

4. She lives in the white house. (She doesn't live in the White House.)

5. Her house is on First Street. (It isn't on First Avenue.)

6. Anna and John got married three years ago. (They didn't get married five years ago.)

7. They own a small home. (They don't rent.)

8. Mary wants to come in a week. (She doesn't want to wait a month.)

9. She'll bring her collie and snakes. (She's not bringing her poodle.)

10. Mary is opening a pet store. (She isn't opening a toy store.)

More Practice

EXERCISE   📖 **Read the paragraph aloud. Remember, the boldfaced words should receive more emphasis than the other words in the sentence.**

Everybody, Somebody, Anybody, and Nobody!

Once upon a **time**, there were **four** people. They were named **Everybody**, **Somebody**, **Anybody**, and **Nobody**. An **important** job had to be done. **Everybody** was sure that **Somebody** would do it. **Anybody** could have done it, but **Nobody** did it. **Somebody** got angry about that, because it was **Everybody's** job. **Everybody** thought **Anybody** could do it and that **Somebody** would do it. It ended **up**, **however**, that **Everybody** blamed **Somebody** when **Nobody** did what **Anybody** could have done!

We hope this chapter on stress didn't cause you any stress! You did a beautiful job! It's time to take a break and *RELAX* for a while. When you're well rested, move on to the next lesson. *You'll soon get the* RHYTHM!

Rhythm in English

The rhythm of conversational English is more rapid than that of formal speech. Every spoken sentence contains syllables or words that receive primary stress. Certain words within the sentence must be emphasized, while others are spoken more rapidly. To keep the sentence flowing smoothly, words are linked together into phrases and separated by pauses to convey meaning clearly. Effective use of rhythm will help you to achieve more natural-sounding speech.

Possible Pronunciation Problems

In many languages, all vowels in all syllables are pronounced almost equally. Syllables are rarely lost or reduced as they are in English. It is likely that you are using your language's conversational rhythm patterns when speaking English. This habit will contribute to a noticeable foreign accent.

1. If you stress each word equally or too precisely:

EXAMPLE   "He will **leave** at **three**" will sound like "**He will leave at three**."

2. If you avoid the use of contractions or reduced forms:

EXAMPLES   "I **can't** go" will sound like "I **can not** go."
"He likes **ham'n eggs**" will sound like "He likes **ham and eggs**."

3. If you insert pauses incorrectly between the words of the sentence, you will distort the meaning of your sentence and create a choppy rhythm.

EXAMPLE   "I don't know Joan" will sound like "I don't know, Joan."

We know this can be slightly confusing at first. Please do not be concerned! THE EXERCISES IN THIS CHAPTER WILL GET YOU RIGHT INTO THE RHYTHM!

Contractions

Contractions are two words that are combined together to form one. Contractions are used frequently in spoken English and are grammatically correct. If you use the full form of the contraction in conversation, your speech will sound stilted and unnatural.

Contraction	Full Form
I'll	I will
you're	you are
he's	he is
we've	we have
isn't	is not

EXERCISE A

📖 **Read the pairs of sentences aloud. The first sentence is written in full form; the second contains a contraction. Listen to how smooth and natural the second sentence sounds compared with the choppy rhythm of the first sentence.**

1. I am late again.   I'm late again.
2. Mary does not know.   Mary doesn't know.
3. You are next in line.   You're next in line.
4. We have already met.   We've already met.
5. That is right!   That's right!
6. They will not sing.   They won't sing.
7. Steve has not eaten.   Steve hasn't eaten.
8. He is very nice.   He's very nice.
9. Please do not yell.   Please don't yell.
10. We will be there.   We'll be there.

Blending and Word Reductions

In conversational English, the words in phrases and short sentences are often blended together as if they were one word.

EXAMPLES   "How are you?" is often pronounced "Howaryou?"

"Do it now!" is often pronounced "Doitnow!"

When words are blended together in this manner, sounds are frequently reduced or omitted completely. (The blending of words and the reductions and omissions of sounds occur ONLY in conversational speech. They are NEVER written this way.)

EXAMPLES   "I miss Sam" sounds like "I misam."

"Don't take it" sounds like "Don'take it."

This style of speaking (the use of *contractions*, *blending*, and *word reductions*) is used by American English speakers in normal conversation and is perfectly acceptable spoken language. Try to use these forms as often as possible when speaking English. YOU'LL SOON GET THE RHYTHM!

EXERCISE B

🎧 **Listen and repeat the phrases. Be sure to blend the words together smoothly and to use reduced forms.**

1. cream'n sugar   (cream and sugar)
2. bread'n butter   (bread and butter)
3. ham'n cheese   (ham and cheese)
4. pieceapie   (piece of pie)
5. I gota school.   (I go to school.)
6. He had a cupacoffee.   (He had a cup of coffee.)
7. I wanna takeabreak.   (I want to take a break.)

8. Seeyalater.   (See you later.)
9. Leavmealone.   (Leave me alone.)
10. Whatimeisit?   (What time is it?)

Linking

Linking sounds while speaking is necessary to speak English smoothly and to sound like a native speaker of English. Linking is the connecting of the last sound in one word to the first sound of the next word. The amount of linking in a person's speech varies from speaker to speaker. However, there are two situations in which most native speakers of English use linking regularly.

When a word begins with a vowel sound, it is often pronounced as if it began with the final consonant sound of the previous word.

EXAMPLES "Don't ask" sounds like "Don 'task."

"We've eaten" sounds like "We 'veaten."

When the same consonant sound that ends one word also begins the next word, that sound should not be pronounced twice. It should be pronounced one time but with a slightly lengthened articulation.

EXAMPLES warm milk = war milk

cold day   = col day

EXERCISE C   🎧 **Listen and repeat the phrases. Be sure to pronounce the words beginning with vowel sounds as if they begin with the last consonant sound of the previous word.**

1. take over   (ta kover)
2. look up   (loo kup)
3. It's open.   (It sopen.)
4. Make a wish.   (Ma ka wish.)
5. Kiss aunt Alice.   (Ki saun talice.)
6. Leave him alone.   (Leave hi malone.)
7. Let's eat now.   (Let seat now.)
8. Call another friend.   (Ca lanother friend.)
9. Jump up and down.   (Jum pu pan down.)
10. Buy a red envelope.   (Buy a re denvelope.)

EXERCISE D   🎧 **Listen and repeat the phrases. Be sure to pronounce the identical consonant letters in the adjacent words as ONE sound.**

1. Get two tickets.   (Ge two tickets.)
2. Stop pushing me.   (Sto pushing me.)
3. It's less serious.   (It's le serious.)
4. My mom made lemon pie. (My mo made lemon pie.)
5. Will Linda be there?   (Wi Linda be there?)

Double Consonants

Many words in English are spelled with the same two consecutive consonant letters (e.g., "little" or "coffee"). Pronouncing the same sound twice will disrupt your rhythm of spoken English and contribute to your accent.

EXAMPLES   **pretty** will sound like **pret-ty**

happen will sound like **hap-pen**

EXERCISE E   📖 **Read the words aloud. Be sure to pronounce the identical consonant letters in each word as ONE sound.**

1. trigger	9. parrot
2. coffee	10. paddle
3. fussy	11. little
4. silly	12. passing
5. cotton	13. butter
6. happy	14. pillow
7. penny	15. traffic
8. offer	

Phrasing and Pausing

Phrase: A phrase is a thought group or a group of words that convey meaning.

Pause: A pause is a brief moment during which the speaker is silent.

Sentences should be divided into phrases or thought groups through the use of pauses. The speaker can use a pause to convey or emphasize meaning or simply to take a breath!

EXERCISE F   🎧 **Listen and repeat the sentences. Be sure to PAUSE between phrases (marked by the slanted lines) and to blend the words in each phrase.**

1. The phone book // is on the shelf.
2. Steve said // "Sue is gone."
3. "Please help me // Sally."
4. Mr. White // our neighbor // is very nice.
5. I don't agree // and I won't change my mind.
6. Please finish your homework // before you go out.
7. Dr. Stevens // our new dentist // cancelled my appointment.
8. Do you prefer to eat // steak with French fries // or steak with rice?
9. I like to go for long walks // when the weather is sunny and cool.
10. My dog barks at people // when they knock on the door.

📖 **Read the pairs of sentences aloud. Be sure to pause between phrases. Listen to how the meanings of the sentences change when you vary your phrasing and pausing.**

1. I know Ana.   (You're talking to someone else *about* Ana.)
   I know // Ana.   (You're talking directly *to* your friend Ana.)

2. Please call me Mary.   (You're telling someone that *your* name is Mary.)
   Please call me // Mary.   (You're asking *your friend* Mary to telephone you.)

3. Who will help Steve?   (You're making an inquiry *about* Steve.)
   Who will help // Steve?   (You're *directly* asking Steve a question.)

4. Tammy said // "The teacher is smart."   (Tammy says her teacher is smart.)
   "Tammy" // said the teacher // "is smart."   (The teacher says Tammy is smart.)

5. Ricky thought his friend was lazy.   (Ricky is thinking his friend is lazy.)
   "Ricky" // thought his friend // "was lazy."   (The friend is thinking Ricky is lazy.)

Sound Changes

The rapid speech of native American English speakers might be difficult for you to understand at times. Sounds in words may run together, disappear, or actually change.

EXAMPLES   "When did you see her?" might sound like "Whenja see-er?"

"I'll meet you" might sound like "I'll meetcha."

It's true that such expressions are not "the King's English." In fact, the king would probably turn over in his grave if he were to hear them! Nevertheless, American English speakers use such rhythm patterns in informal, rapid speech. It is important for you to be able to understand these expressions when you hear them.

🎧 **Listen to the commonly used expressions presented using the rapid, informal rhythm.**

1. Whatsidoin?   (What is he doing?)
2. Whenjarive?   (When did you arrive?)
3. Saniceday!   (It's a nice day!)
4. Nicetameetcha.   (Nice to meet you.)
5. Whervyabeen?   (Where have you been?)

📖 **Read the sentences aloud. Fill in the blanks with the contraction. Check your answers. (For answers to Check Yourself 1–3, see Appendix II, pages 285–286.)**

EXAMPLES   _____He's_____ my favorite teacher. (He is)

                 _____We're_____ good friends. (We are)

1. _____ a good student. (I am)

2. Lynn _____ play tennis. (does not)

3. _____ seen that movie. (We have)

4. _____ quite right. (You are)

5. His brother _____ come. (cannot)

📖 **Read the sentences aloud, pausing where indicated. Underline the sentence in each pair that is correctly marked for pauses.**

EXAMPLE   <u>I finished my homework // and watched TV.</u>

            I finished my // homework and watched TV.

1. Meet me at the bus stop // after you're done.
   Meet me at the bus // stop after you're done.

2. Bill Brown the mayor will // speak tonight.
   Bill Brown // the mayor // will speak tonight.

3. Please clean your room // before leaving.
   Please clean your // room before leaving.

4. The truth is I don't // like it.
   The truth is // I don't like it.

5. Cervantes // the famous author // wrote Don Quixote.
   Cervantes the famous author wrote // Don Quixote.

6. He was there // for the first time.
   He was there for // the first time.

7. Where there's a will // there's a way.
   Where there's a // will there's a // way.

8. Do unto others as // you would have them do // unto you.
   Do unto others // as you would have them // do unto you.

9. Patrick Henry said // "Give me liberty // or give me death."
   Patrick Henry // said "Give me // liberty or give me death."

10. When in Rome do // as the Romans do.
    When in Rome // do as the Romans do.

Check your answers. Then read aloud again the correctly marked sentences. Be sure to PAUSE where marked by the slanted lines and blend the words in each phrase.

Read the dialogue aloud with a partner. Circle all contractions and linked words. Then on the lines below, list these shortened forms and write their full form equivalent.

Frances Black: Hello, this is the Black residence. This is Frances Black speaking.

Ellie White: Howarya Frannie? It's Ellie. Doyawanna come over for a cupacoffee?

Frances Black: Eleanor, I am very sorry I can not visit you. I am going to lunch at the club.

Ellie White: That's OK. I'm gonna eat at Burger Palace. Why don't we go tathamovies tonight?

Frances Black: We will not be able to join you. We have tickets for the opera.

Ellie White: My husband Sam won't like that. He's more of a wrestling fan. We'll meetcha some other night.

Frances Black: Eleanor, I really have to go now. It has been most pleasant speaking with you.

Ellie White: I hafta go now, too. It's been great talking to you. (*hangs up the phone*) Frannie's a nice girl, but she hasta learnta relax!

Reduced Forms	Full Form
Howarya?	How are you?
It's	It is

Check your answers. Then change roles and read the dialogue again with a partner. Be sure to blend the words together smoothly and use the appropriate shortened forms.

More Practice

EXERCISE A

Record yourself while speaking to a friend by telephone. Listen to your responses carefully. Write down any sentences in which you could have used a contraction instead of the full form. Practice saying the sentences again using the contractions.

Read the poems aloud several times. Thought groups or phrases have been marked for you to follow. Be sure to blend the words within each phrase together smoothly without chopping them up with unnecessary pauses. Also, concentrate on linking the final consonant of one word to the initial vowel sound of the next word within each phrase.

Gifts
James Thomson

Give a man // a horse he can ride, //
Give a man // a boat he can sail; //
And his rank and wealth, // his strength and health //
On sea // nor shore // shall fail. //

Give a man // a pipe he can smoke, //
Give a man // a book he can read; //
And his home is bright // with a calm delight, //
Though the room be poor // indeed. //

Give a man // a girl he can love, //
As I, // O my love, // love thee; //
And his hand is great // with the pulse of Fate, //
At home, // on land, // on sea.

Paul Revere's Ride *(Excerpt)*
Henry Wadsworth Longfellow

Paul Revere is famous for his part in the American Revolution. He rode through the streets at midnight, warning "The British are coming!" to everyone who would listen.

Listen, // my children, // and you shall hear //
Of the midnight ride // of Paul Revere, //
On the eighteenth of April, // in Seventy-Five: //
Hardly a man // is now alive //
Who remembers // that famous day // and year. //

He said to his friend, // "If the British march //
By land or sea // from the town tonight, //
Hang a lantern aloft // in the belfry arch //
Of the North Church tower // as a signal light, //
One // if by land, // and two // if by sea; //
And I // on the opposite shore will be, //
Ready to ride // and spread the alarm //
Through every Middlesex village // and farm,
For the country-folk // to be up // and to arm." //

So through the night // rode Paul Revere; //
And so through the night // went his cry of alarm //
To every Middlesex village // and farm, //
A cry of defiance // and not of fear, //
A voice in the darkness, // a knock at the door, //
And a word // that shall echo // forevermore! //
For, // borne on the night-wind // of the Past, //
Through all our history, // to the last, //
In the hour of darkness // and peril // and need, //
The people will waken // and listen to hear //
The hurrying hoof-beats // of that steed, //
And the midnight message // of Paul Revere. //

Lesson 22 Intonation

Definition

Intonation refers to the use of melody and the rise and fall of the voice when speaking. Each language uses rising and falling pitches differently and has its own distinctive melody and intonation patterns. In fact, babies usually recognize and use the intonation of their native language before they learn actual speech sounds and words.

Intonation in English

Intonation can convey grammatical meaning as well as the speaker's attitude. It will "tell" whether a person is making a statement or asking a question; it will also indicate if the person is confident, doubtful, shy, annoyed, or impatient. Correct use of intonation is necessary to convey your message correctly and to make you sound like a native English speaker.

Possible Pronunciation Problems

English has several basic intonation contours. However, there are many more possible variations that change with a speaker's intended meaning, attitude, and emotional state of mind. Without realizing it, you can confuse your listeners by using incorrect English intonation patterns.

1. If your voice rises when it should fall, you will:
   a. change a declarative sentence into a question.

   EXAMPLE   "That's Bill's car" will sound like "That's Bill's car?"

   b. sound doubtful or annoyed.

2. If your voice stays level when it should either rise or fall, you will:
   a. sound bored or uninterested.
   b. confuse your listeners into thinking you didn't finish your sentence or question.

   EXAMPLE   "I went home" will sound like "I went home . . . and . . . "

Listen to the CD several times before trying to imitate the instructor. With practice, you will soon notice a great improvement. KEEP UP THE GOOD WORK!

Phrases Ending with a Falling Pitch

1. Declarative sentences

EXAMPLES   Linda is my sister. ↘   He is not going. ↘

2. Questions that require more than a *yes/no* response (such question words include *who, what, when, why, where, which, how*)

EXAMPLES   Where is my book? ↘   (On the table. ↘)

When did he leave? ↘   (At three o'clock. ↘)

Phrases Ending with a Rising Pitch

1. Questions that ask for a *yes/no* response (such question words include *can, do, will, would, may,* and *is*)

EXAMPLES   Will you stay? ↗   (No, I can't. ↘)

Do you like school? ↗   (Yes, I do. ↘)

2. Statements that express doubt or uncertainty

EXAMPLES   I'm not positive. ↗

I think he's coming. ↗

Practice

EXERCISE A

 Listen and repeat the statements. Make your voice *fall* at the end of each of the sentences. Remember, questions that cannot be answered with *yes* or *no* take the same *downward* intonation as declarative sentences.

1. I have four brothers. ↘

2. He is not my friend. ↘

3. We like ice cream. ↘

4. Tim bought a new car. ↘

5. She likes to play tennis. ↘

6. What is your name? ↘

7. How is your family? ↘

8. Who will drive you home? ↘

9. Why did he leave? ↘

10. Which book is yours? ↘

EXERCISE B

🎧 **Listen and repeat the *yes/no* questions and sample responses. Be sure your voice *rises* ↗ at the end of each question and *falls* ↘ at the end of each response.**

Yes/No Questions ↗	Responses ↘
1. Can you see?	Yes, I can.
2. Does he play golf?	Yes, he does.
3. May I borrow it?	Yes, you may.
4. Will she help?	No, she won't.
5. Did he arrive?	Yes, he's here now.
6. Is Susan your sister?	No, she's my friend.
7. Have they eaten?	Yes, they ate at two.
8. May I help you?	Yes, please do.
9. Are we leaving?	No, we're staying.
10. Can my friends stay?	Yes, they can.

Sounding Confident Instead of Uncertain

As was already discussed, a *falling* pitch should be used at the end of declarative sentences. It will help you sound confident and sure of yourself. On the other hand, using an *upward* pitch at the end of the same sentences indicates that the speaker is doubtful or uncertain about what he or she is saying.

EXAMPLE They have twenty children. ↘ (stated as a fact)

They have twenty children. ↗ (stated with doubt or disbelief)

EXERCISE C

🎧 **Listen and repeat the statements. Use a *falling* pitch to end the sentences on the left and an *upward* pitch to end the sentences on the right. (Notice how the *falling* pitch in the first reading helps you to sound sure of yourself, while the *rising* pitch in the second reading makes you sound doubtful or uncertain.)**

Stated with Certainty ↘	Stated with Doubt ↗
1. He ate twenty-five hot dogs.	He ate twenty-five hot dogs.
2. The boss gave him a raise.	The boss gave him a raise.
3. You ran 55 miles.	You ran 55 miles.
4. Mike was elected president.	Mike was elected president.
5. It's already three o'clock.	It's already three o'clock.

Intonation in Sentences with Two or More Phrases

Intonation also tells the listener whether a speaker has completed the statement or question or whether he or she has more to say. Many sentences are spoken with two or more phrases joined together with such connecting words as *and, if, so,* or *but.*

EXAMPLES He can sing, **but** he can't dance.

We were hungry, thirsty, **and** tired.

If your voice drops after the first phrase, your listener will think you are finished with the sentence. To make it clear that you have more to say, you must keep your voice *level* → before the connecting word. There are three main types of sentences:

1. Declarative sentences with two or more phrases

Keep your voice *level* → before the connecting word and *lower* it at the end. ↘

EXAMPLES   I must buy coffee →, tea →, and milk. ↘
    She speaks French → but not Spanish. ↘

2. Questions presenting two or more choices

This intonation pattern is the same as for declarative sentences with two or more phrases. Keep your voice *level* → before the connecting word and *lower* it when you finish your question. ↘

EXAMPLES   Would you like cake → or pie? ↘
    Is he leaving tomorrow → or Sunday? ↘

3. *Yes/No* questions with two or more phrases

Keep your voice *level* → before the connecting word, and use a *rising pitch* ↗ at the end of your question.

EXAMPLES   Will you come → if I drive you? ↗
    Did he like the new belt → and gloves I bought? ↗

EXERCISE D

🎧 **Listen and repeat the statements and questions. (The arrows are there to remind you to use the proper intonation patterns.)**

1. May I leave now →, or should I wait ↘?
2. Did you buy a new hat → or pants ↘?
3. He missed his bus → but arrived on time ↘.
4. Call me later →, if it's not too late ↘.
5. Will you visit us → if you're in town ↗?
6. I'll leave early →, so I won't miss the plane ↘.
7. Do you like grapes →, pears →, and plums ↗?
8. He's good at math → but not spelling ↘.
9. You may stay up late → if you finish your homework ↘.
10. He went sailing →, swimming →, and fishing ↘.

🎧 **Listen and repeat the statements and questions. Indicate whether they have a falling or rising intonation by marking an *X* in the appropriate column. (For answers to Check Yourself 1–3, see Appendix II, pages 286–287.)**

		Falling	Rising
EXAMPLES	I feel fine.	X	
	Can you sing?		X
1.	When's your birthday?	___	___
2.	Did you see my friend?	___	___
3.	How are you?	___	___
4.	I'm fine, thank you.	___	___
5.	Why were you absent?	___	___
6.	Can you have dinner?	___	___
7.	How do you know?	___	___
8.	I don't like beets.	___	___
9.	Where is my pencil?	___	___
10.	Will you drive me home?	___	___

📖 **Read the multiple-phrase sentences aloud. Draw the correct intonation arrows in the blanks (↘ = *voice falls*; → = *voice stays level*; ↗ = *voice rises*).**

EXAMPLE   Do you want coffee __→__, tea __→__, or milk __↘__?

1. We enjoy swimming _____, hiking _____, and tennis _____.

2. Is a barbecue all right _____ if it doesn't rain _____?

3. If it rains tomorrow _____, the game is off _____.

4. Is he sick _____? I hope not _____.

5. Please bring me the hammer _____, nails _____, and scissors _____.

6. Do you like grapes _____, pears _____, and plums _____?

7. May I leave now _____, or should I wait _____?

8. He's good at math _____ but not spelling _____.

9. Call me later _____ if it's not too late _____.

10. Will you visit us _____ if you're in town _____?

📖 **Read the joke. In the blank spaces, draw the correct intonation arrows (↘ = *voice falls*; → = *voice stays level*; ↗ = *voice rises*). To help you, sentence stress patterns and some intonation arrows are already provided.**

Sam Can't Tell a Joke!

Sam __→__, a convicted **felon** _____, was sentenced to life in **prison** __↘__. When he arrived at the **prison** _____, the other inmates were sitting around calling out **numbers** _____. He heard **Bill** call _____, "One thousand **twenty**" _____. Then **Joe** bellowed _____, "Two hundred **forty**" _____. "Does anyone know three thousand **two**" __↗__? asked **Mark** happily _____. Each time a number was **called** _____, the men **roared** with laughter _____. **Sam** asked _____, "**What's** so funny _____? **What** is everyone laughing at" _____?

Bill explained _____. "**Well** _____, we know **thousands** of jokes _____. It would take **too** long to **tell** each one _____. So we've **numbered** all of them _____. When we want to tell a **joke** _____, we simply call out its **number**" _____. Sam asked hopefully _____, "Will you guys teach **me** all the jokes _____ **and** their numbers" _____?

Bill taught Sam **all** of the jokes **and** their numbers _____. One **day** _____, while the inmates were telling **jokes** _____, **Sam** called _____, "**Five hundred**" _____. **No** one laughed _____. He **shouted** _____, "**Five hundred**" _____. Still **no** one laughed _____. "I don't **get** it _____. **Why** isn't anyone laughing _____? Isn't number **five hundred** one of our **funniest** jokes" _____? "**Yes**" _____, replied **Bill** _____, "but you didn't **tell** it right" _____!

More Practice

📖 **Read the dialogue aloud with a partner. Use the correct sentence stress and intonation patterns as indicated by the boldfaced words and intonation arrows (↘ = *voice falls*; → = *voice stays level*; ↗ = *voice rises*).**

Husband: **Hi, honey** ↘. What did you do **today** ↘?

Wife: I went **shopping** ↘.

Husband: You went **shopping** ↗? **Again** ↗?

Wife: **Yes** ↘. The store had a **big** sale ↘. **Everything** was **half**-price ↘.

Husband: What did you buy **now** ↘?

Wife: I bought this **blouse** for thirty dollars ↘. Isn't it **stunning** ↗?

Husband: **Yes** →, it's stunning ↘. **I'm** the one that's stunned ↘.

Wife: Do you like the **green** hat → or the **red** one ↘?

Husband: I like the **cheaper** one ↘.

Wife: I also bought a **belt** →, **scarf** →, **dress** →, and **shoes** ↘.

Husband: **Stop** it ↘! I'm afraid to hear **any more** ↘. Do we have **any** money left ↗?

Wife: **Yes**, dear →, we have **lots** of money left ↘. I **saved** two hundred dollars on my new clothes →, so I bought **you** a set of **golf** clubs ↘.

Husband: **Really** ↗? I always said you were a **great** shopper ↘!

Part 3 | Consonants

Lesson 23 — Pronouncing the Consonants of American English

You have probably discovered that English spelling patterns are inconsistent and are not always a reliable guide to pronunciation. For example, in the following words, the letters *ch* represent *three* different sounds.

ma**ch**ine   **ch**ain   me**ch**anic

Pretty confusing, right? That's why the International Phonetic Alphabet (IPA) is helpful. The IPA, which is used all over the world, consists of a set of symbols in which ONE symbol always represents ONE sound.

As with the vowels in Part 1, each consonant will be introduced and explained one at a time. To help you learn the exact pronunciation of the phonetic symbols and key words, a Key to Pronouncing the Consonants of American English is presented on page 117. Refer to it, and listen to the pronunciation of the sounds, as needed.

Definitions

As you progress through the consonant lessons, you will frequently see the terms *gum ridge*, *soft palate*, *aspiration*, *voiced consonant*, *voiceless consonant*, and *articulators*. We will now define these terms for you.

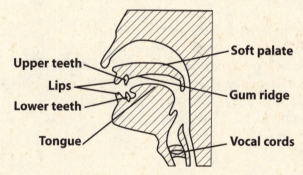

Articulators: The articulators are the different parts of the mouth area that we use when speaking, such as the lips, tongue, soft palate, teeth, and jaw.

Gum ridge: The gum ridge is the hard part of the roof of your mouth just behind your upper front teeth.

Soft palate: The soft palate is the soft, movable, rear portion of the roof of your mouth.

Aspiration: Aspiration means the action of pronouncing a sound with a puff of released breath. The English consonants [p], [t], [k], and [h] are "aspirate" sounds. They should be produced with a strong puff of air.

Voiced consonant: A voiced consonant is a sound produced when the vocal cords are vibrating. Place your hand on your throat over your vocal cords while making a humming sound. You can feel your vocal cords vibrate as you say "mmmmmmmmmm."

Voiceless Consonant: A voiceless consonant is a sound made with no vibration of the vocal cords. Put your hand over your vocal cords and make the hissing sound "sssssssss." You will not feel any vibration this time!

The various consonant sounds are created by:

1. The position of your articulators. For example, the tip of your tongue must touch the upper gum ridge to say sounds like [t], [d], [n], or [l], but must protrude between your teeth to say [θ] as in *think* or [ð] as in *them*.

2. The way the breath stream comes from your mouth or nose. For example, the breath stream, or airstream, is continuous for the consonants [s] or [f], but is completely stopped and then exploded for [p] or [t]. The airstream flows through the *nose* for [m], [n], and [ŋ] and through the *mouth* for all other consonants.

3. The vibration of your vocal cords. For example, your vocal cords do not vibrate for the sounds [s], [f], or [t], but you must add "voicing" for the sounds [z], [v], or [d].

The chart on the right categorizes the voiced and voiceless consonants. Don't try to memorize the chart! Just put your hand over your vocal cords as you practice saying the sounds. You will be able to hear and *feel* the difference between voiced and voiceless consonants.

Voiced	Voiceless
[b]	[p]
[d]	[t]
[g]	[k]
[v]	[f]
[z]	[s]
[ð]	[θ]
[dʒ]	[tʃ]
[ʒ]	[ʃ]
[m], [n], [ŋ]	[h]
[j], [w], [l], [r]	

Key to Pronouncing the Consonants of American English

INTERNATIONAL PHONETIC ALPHABET SYMBOL	ENGLISH KEY WORDS
[s]	**s**it, ba**s**ket, ki**ss**
[z]	**z**oo, bu**s**y, bu**zz**
[t]	**t**op, re**t**urn, ca**t**
[d]	**d**ay, la**dd**er, be**d**
[θ]	**th**ink, ba**th**tub, mou**th**
[ð]	**th**e, fa**th**er, smoo**th**
[ʃ]	**sh**oe, na**ti**on, wi**sh**
[tʃ]	**ch**air, wi**tch**
[ʒ]	rou**g**e, vi**si**on, mea**s**ure
[dʒ]	**j**aw, ma**g**ic, a**ge**
[j]	**y**ou, **y**es
[p]	**p**ay, a**pp**le, sto**p**
[b]	**b**oy, ra**bb**it, tu**b**
[f]	**f**un, o**ff**ice, i**f**
[v]	**v**ery, o**v**er, sa**v**e
[k]	**c**ake, **c**ar, boo**k**
[g]	**g**o, be**g**in, e**gg**
[w]	**w**e, a**w**ay
[l]	**l**amp, pi**ll**ow, be**ll**
[r]	**r**ed, ma**rr**y, ca**r**
[h]	**h**at, be**h**ind
[m]	**m**e, swi**m**
[n]	**n**o, ru**n**
[ŋ]	si**ng**, playi**ng**

[s] as in *sit*, *basket*, and *kiss* and [z] as in *zoo*, *busy*, and *buzz*

PRONOUNCING [s]

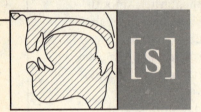

[s]

Tongue tip: Near but not touching gum ridge behind upper front teeth

Airstream: Continuous without interruption

Vocal cords: Not vibrating

Possible Pronunciation Problems

The sound [s] is a common sound. Some speakers may incorrectly say [ɛ] before [s] in English. Others may say [ʃ] instead of [s] before [i] and [ɪ].

EXAMPLES If you produce [ɛ] before [s]: **state** will sound like **estate**.

If you say [ʃ] instead of [s]: **sip** will sound like **ship**.

As you say [s], keep the airstream steady, like the hissing sound of a snake (sssssssss)!

So *s*tudy and practi*c*e; you'll *s*oon have *s*ucce*ss* with [s]!

Practice

EXERCISE A   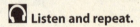 **Listen and repeat.**

[s] At the Beginning of Words

sky	skip	snake
sad	spell	skate
spin	study	school
slow		

[s] In the Middle of Words

lesson	custom	castle
racing	basket	history
listen	answer	fast
pencil		

[s] At the End of Words

bus	face	course
yes	makes	class
box	house	plus
miss		

[s] Spelled

s	*c*	*x* ([ks])	*ss*
spy	cell	six	kiss
ski	ice	fix	less
smoke	lace	fox	dresser
steal	cent	tax	message
desk	center	oxen	

Less frequent spelling patterns for [s] consist of the letters *z* and *sc*.

wal**z**   pret**z**el   **sc**ent   **sc**ene

The letter *c* followed by *e, i,* or *y* is usually pronounced [s].

cent   pla**c**e   so**c**iety   fan**c**y

The letter *s* in plural nouns is pronounced [s] when it follows most voiceless consonants.

book**s**   coat**s**   cuff**s**   map**s**

EXERCISE B

🎧 **Listen and repeat. Pay attention to the consonant [s] in the boldfaced words.**

1. **stop sign**
2. **small mistake**
3. **start** and **stop**
4. **Nice** to **see** you.
5. **Stand straight.**
6. **Sit still!**
7. **Speak** for **yourself.**
8. The **swimmer** was **slow** and **steady.**
9. The **grocery store started selling seafood.**
10. **Stan stopped smoking cigars.**
11. We had **steak** and **spinach** for **supper.**
12. **Students study** in **school.**
13. I **rest** on **Saturday** and **Sunday.**
14. The **sportsman likes** to **ski** and **skate.**
15. **Stacy speaks Spanish.**

CHECK YOURSELF

🎧 **Listen and circle the letter *s* in each word that is pronounced [s]. (Only ONE *s* in each word is actually pronounced [s].) (For answers, see Appendix II, page 287.)**

EXAMPLE   ⓢ u r p r i s e

1. s u p p o s e
2. S u s a n
3. d i s a s t e r
4. e a s i e s t
5. p o s t e r s
6. s a l e s m a n
7. s e a s o n
8. r e s i s t
9. p r e s e n t s
10. b u s i n e s s

Check your answers. Then practice pronouncing the words.

EXERCISE

📖 **Read aloud the essay about Thomas Edison. Pay attention to the boldfaced words containing the [s] sound.**

Silence Is Literally Golden!

Thomas Edison was a great American inventor. **This** is a true **story** about how **silence** really paid off for him. He invented a new ticker; the **Western** Union Company wanted to **purchase** it. **Edison** didn't know how much to **ask**. He **requested several** days to think about the **selling price**.

Thomas and **Mrs. Edison discussed Western** Union's offer. **Mrs. Edison suggested** that he **ask** twenty thousand dollars ($20,000). He was **stunned** by this **staggering price** but **accepted** his **wife's advice**.

When the **Western** Union **officer asked** Mr. **Edison**, "What **price** have you **decided** to **ask**?" Mr. **Edison started** to **state** $20,000, but the amount got **stuck** on his tongue. He **stood** there **speechless**. The **Western** Union negotiator became impatient with Mr. **Edison's silence** and **asked**, "Will you **accept** one hundred thousand dollars ($100,000)?" **So**, as you can **see**, **silence** can be golden!

PRONOUNCING [z]

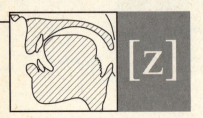

Tongue tip: In the same position as for [s]

Airstream: Continuous without interruption

Vocal cords: Vibrating

Possible Pronunciation Problems

The sound [z] is not a common sound. Many students pronounce the letter *z* in English as an [s] or [d]. Also, irregular English spelling patterns contribute to problems with this consonant.

EXAMPLES   If you say [s] instead of [z]:   **zoo** will sound like **Sue**.

                                                             eyes will sound like **ice**.

               If you say [dʒ] instead of [z]:   **zest** will sound like **jest**.

Remember, [z] is a voiced sound; your vocal cords MUST vibrate or you will say [s] by mistake.

Think of the buzzing sound of a bee (bzzzzzzzzz) and you'll say your Zs with ease!

Practice

EXERCISE A

🎧 **Listen and repeat. Put your hand on your throat so that you can feel your vocal cords vibrate as you pronounce the consonant [z].**

[z] At the Beginning of Words

zoo	zinc	zebra
zeal	zero	zipper
zest	zone	

[z] In the Middle of Words

lazy	crazy	dizzy
busy	razor	cousin
easy	dozen	puzzle

[z] At the End of Words

as	was	raise
is	buzz	amaze
his	daze	breeze

[z] Spelled

z	s
zip	has
size	eyes
seize	rose
lizard	these
sneeze	bruise

---

note

The letter *x* is a less common spelling pattern for [z].

xylophone   **X**erox

---

hint

The letter *s* is usually pronounced [z] when between vowels and in a stressed syllable.

de**s**erve   becau**s**e   re**s**ign

The letter *s* in plural nouns is pronounced [z] when it follows a vowel or most voiced consonants.

shoe**s**   leg**s**   leave**s**   bed**s**   car**s**

The vowel BEFORE [z] at the end of a word is always prolonged more than before [s]. (Vowels are also prolonged before [b], [d], [v], and [g] at the end of a word.) Prolonging the vowel before [z] helps to distinguish it from [s].

ey**es**   bre**ez**e   ri**s**e   bu**zz**

Listen and repeat. Remember to add voicing when pronouncing the consonant [z] in the boldfaced words.

1. **Easy does** it.
2. **zero degrees**
3. a cool **breeze**
4. a **dozen eggs**
5. **busy as** a bee
6. **Close** your **eyes.**
7. The **puzzle is easy.**
8. **Does Zachary raise flowers**?
9. There are **zebras** and **lions** at the **zoo.**
10. **His cousin comes** from New **Zealand.**
11. The **museum is closed** on **Tuesday.**
12. My **husband** gave me a **dozen roses.**
13. I'm **crazy** about **raisins** and **apples.**
14. **Zelda** took a **cruise** to **Brazil.**
15. The **jazz music is pleasant.**

Listen and circle the word in each group that is NOT pronounced with [z]. (For answers, see Appendix II, pages 287–288.)

EXAMPLE	is	was	his	(this)
1.	eyes	nose	wrist	ears
2.	walls	waltz	wells	ways
3.	carrots	apples	peas	raisins
4.	pleasing	pleasant	pleasure	please
5.	deserve	daisy	serve	design
6.	cease	seize	size	sings
7.	Tuesday	Thursday	Wednesday	Saturday
8.	east	ease	easy	tease
9.	rose	rice	raise	rise
10.	fox	xylophone	clothes	zero

EXERCISE

🔺 **Zelda and Zachary need help completing their crossword puzzle. Read the dialogue with a partner, filling in the missing words containing [z]. Also pay attention to your pronunciation of the boldfaced words containing [z].**

Zelda: **Zachary**, this crossword **puzzle is** driving me **crazy**. What's a seven-letter word that **means** "**surprising** or unbelievable"?

Zachary: **Zelda**, I'll give you a hint. It **rhymes** with *hazing*.

Zelda: Oh, "<u>a __ __ z __ __ __</u>." Thanks. How about a four-letter word **representing** a form of American **Music**? Never mind, I've got it: "<u>__ __ z z</u>." That **was easy**.

Zachary: **These** are **flowers**, but they're not **zinnias** or **daisies**.

Zelda: "<u>__ __ s e s</u>." Let's try another one. What **is** a trip on a boat called? It **rhymes** with **lose**. Oh, wait; I know. It's "<u>__ __ __ __ s __</u>."

Zachary: I got this one. The name of a mineral that **begins** with z: "<u>z __ __ __</u>."

Zelda: This **quiz is** getting **easier**. An animal with stripes that **is** seen at the **zoo**.

Zachary: "<u>Z __ __ __ __</u>." Here **is** the last one. A **musical** instrument that **begins** with *x*. **Please** help me.

Zelda: I **always** want to **please** my **husband**. So **here's** the word: "<u>x __ __ __ __ __ __ __</u>."

LESSON REVIEW: [s] and [z]

EXERCISE A

🎧 **Listen and repeat each pair of words or sentences. Remember, [z] is a voiced sound; your vocal cords should vibrate. And be sure to prolong any vowel BEFORE the sound [z].**

	[s]	[z]
1.	**S**ue	**z**oo
2.	face	phase
3.	race	raise
4.	bus	buzz
5.	ice	eyes
6.	We saw the **place**.	We saw the **plays**.
7.	They made **peace**.	They made **peas**.
8.	The **price** was $100.	The **prize** was $100.
9.	Did you see the **racer**?	Did you see the **razor**?
10.	He lost the **race**.	He lost the **raise**.

🎧 **Listen and repeat.**

      [s]   [z]
1. **Sue** went to the **zoo**.

      [s]   [z]
2. Put **ice** on your **eyes**.

      [s]   [z]
3. My **niece** hurt her **knees**.

      [z]   [s]
4. The **president** set a **precedent**.

      [z]   [s]
5. The baby will **lose** his **loose** tooth.

[s] vs. [z] in Noun/Verb Homographs

Several nouns and verbs are the same in the written form. However, we can distinguish between these word pairs in their spoken form. The letter *s* in the noun form is usually pronounced [s]; in the verb form, it is usually pronounced [z].

🎧 **Listen and repeat. Be sure to add "voice" to the letter *s* when saying the verbs.**

Nouns s = [s]	Verbs s = [z]
excuse (a reason)	excuse (to forgive)
house (residence)	house (to shelter)
use (purpose)	use (utilize)
abuse (mistreatment)	abuse (injure)

🎧 **Listen and repeat. Pay attention to the boldfaced words. Be sure to distinguish between the voiceless [s] in the nouns and the voiced [z] in the verbs.**

      [z]   [z]
1. **Please excuse** me.

      [z]   [s]
2. He **has** a good **excuse**.

      [z]
3. May I **use** your car?

           [z] [s]
4. The object **has** no **use**.

      [z]   [z]
5. The **museum** will **house** the painting.

           [s]
6. We bought a new **house**.

      [s]
7. Child **abuse** is a terrible thing.

      [z]   [z]
8. **Please** don't **abuse** me.

🎧 **Listen. Two of the words in each group will be the same; one will be different. Circle the number of the word that is different. (For answers to Check Yourself 1–4, see Appendix II, pages 288–289.)**

EXAMPLE   *You hear*   prize   price   price

              You circle   ①   2   3

     1.   1   2   3

     2.   1   2   3

     3.   1   2   3

     4.   1   2   3

     5.   1   2   3

     6.   1   2   3

     7.   1   2   3

     8.   1   2   3

     9.   1   2   3

   10.   1   2   3

📖 **Read the sentences aloud. In the brackets above each boldfaced word, write [s] or [z].**

               [s]   [s]   [z]

EXAMPLE   **S**ilence i**s** golden.

        [ ]   [ ]   [ ]

     1. **It's** raining **cats** and **dogs**.

        [ ] [ ]   [ ]   [ ]

     2. Come **as soon as possible**.

        [ ]   [ ]

     3. **Strike** while the iron **is** hot.

          [ ]   [ ]

     4. Kill two **birds** with one **stone**.

        [ ]   [ ]

     5. **Misery loves** company.

🎧 **Listen and circle the word used to complete each sentence.**

                                        [s]   [z]

EXAMPLE   The sweater was (fussy / (fuzzy)).

                                   [s]   [z]

1. We finally won the (race / raise).

                           [s]   [z]

2. I know that (face / phase).

                                 [s]   [z]

3. He gave me a good (price / prize).

                             [s]   [z]

4. Look at her small (niece / knees).

                           [s]   [z]

5. We must accept the (loss / laws).

                         [s]   [z]

6. The sheep have (fleece / fleas).

                       [s]   [z]

7. Did you hear the (bus / buzz)?

                           [s]   [z]

8. His dog has a large (muscle / muzzle).

                     [s]   [z]

9. How much is the (sink / zinc)?

                     [s]   [z]

10. I can identify the (spice / spies).

🎧 📖 **Listen. Circle the words pronounced with [s] and underline the words pronounced with [z]. Then practice reading the limericks aloud.**

A Man Named (Stu)

A man from (Texas) named Stu
Was crazy about Silly Sue.
    He proposed twenty times,
    Using song, dance, and rhymes
Until Sue said to Stu, "I do!"

A Girl Named Maxine

There was a slim girl called Maxine
Who loved cooking Spanish cuisine.
    She spent days eating rice,
    Lots of chicken and spice.
Now Maxine is no longer lean!

EXERCISE

📖 **Read the paragraph about Julius Caesar aloud. Be sure to pronounce all the boldfaced [s] and [z] words correctly.**

Julius Caesar

     [s] [s] [z]   [z]   [s]   [s]   [z]   [s]
Julius Caesar is one of the **most famous leaders** in **history**. He

     [s]   [z]   [z][s] [z] [z][s]
became **master** of Italy **because** of **his skills as soldier** and

[s]   [s]   [z][z]   [z]   [z]   [z]
statesman. His zeal and **wisdom** brought **positive changes**.

       [z]   [z]   [s]   [s]
He **reorganized** the government and **raised** the **status** of the poor. But

  [z][s]   [z]   [z]   [s]   [s]
he **was stabbed** to death by **his enemies Brutus** and **Cassius**.

[s]   [s]   [z]   [s][s] [z]   [s]
Shakespeare said in **his** play about **Julius Caesar**, "Men at **some** time

    [s] [z]   [s]   [s] [z]   [s] [z]
are **masters** of their **fates**: The fault, dear **Brutus**, **is** not in our **stars**,

        [s] [z]   [z]
but in **ourselves**, that we are **underlings**."

Lesson 25 [t] as in *top*, *return*, and *cat*

PRONOUNCING [t]

Tongue tip: Firmly pressed against gum ridge behind upper front teeth

Airstream: Stopped and then exploded

Vocal cords: Not vibrating

Possible Pronunciation Problems

The consonant [t] is a common sound and, for many learners, it does not cause much difficulty. When pronouncing [t], your tongue tip should touch the upper gum ridge, NOT the back of your upper front teeth. [t] must be said with strong aspiration and a puff of air or it might sound like [d]. Some speakers tend to say [ts] instead of [t] before [u] or [tʃ] in place of [t] before [i] and [ɪ].

EXAMPLES   If you say [d] instead of [t]:   **two** will sound like **do**.

If you say [ts] instead of [t]:   **tune** will sound like **tsune**.

If you say [tʃ] instead of [t]:   **tease** will sound like **cheese**.

Practice saying [t] while loosely holding a tissue in front of your mouth. If you aspirate [t] correctly and say it with a puff of air, your tissue will flutter.

So—be sure to practice all the time; you'll make a terrific [t].

Practice

EXERCISE A   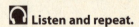 **Listen and repeat.**

[t] At the Beginning of Words			[t] In the Middle of Words			[t] At the End of Words		
to	talk	time	until	attend	between	it	went	state
ten	tell	table	after	return	contain	but	late	fruit
try	tree	terrible	empty	winter	printing	ate	light	apart
top			wanted			boat		

The letter *t* is usually pronounced [t].

The letters *ed* in past tense verbs are pronounced [t] when they follow a voiceless consonant.

stopp**ed**   look**ed**   kiss**ed**   wash**ed**

When [t] is between two vowels and follows a stressed syllable (as in *water*, *butter*, and *city*), it is NOT aspirated.

When [t] follows *s* (as in *stop*, *stay*, *stick*), it is NOT aspirated with a puff of air.

Some speakers of various Asian languages tend to add the sound [o] to words ending in [t] in English (the word *cat* becomes *cato*, the word *sit* becomes *sito*). Be sure you avoid this extra vowel when practicing words with final [t].

EXERCISE B

Listen and repeat. The letter *t* in the following words occurs between vowels, so it is NOT aspirated.

city	water
pretty	writing
better	sitting
notice	pattern
butter	cutting

EXERCISE C

Listen and repeat. Pay attention to the [t] sound in the boldfaced words and phrases. Be sure to aspirate [t] at the beginning of words.

1. **Tell** the **teacher**.
2. **tea** and **toast**
3. **to** be or **not to** be
4. **Take** your **time**.
5. **Today** is **Tuesday**, **October tenth**.
6. **Turn** off the **light**.
7. **Tim bought two tickets to** the **tennis tournament**.
8. **Pat wrote** a poem.
9. The **boat won't return until eight**.
10. Should we leave a **fifteen percent tip**?

📖 **Read the words aloud. Circle the ONE letter *t* in each word that is pronounced [t]. (For answers to Check Yourself 1 and 2, see Appendix II, page 289.)**

EXAMPLE t h o u g h(t)

1. t r a c t i o n
2. t h a t
3. p a t i e n t
4. t e x t u r e
5. t e m p e r a t u r e
6. t o o t h
7. p r e s e n t a t i o n
8. a r i t h m e t i c
9. t o g e t h e r
10. s u b t r a c t i o n

📖 **Complete each sentence with a word from the box. Then practice saying the sentences aloud. Pay attention to the boldfaced words containing the consonant [t].**

too	write	not	two	aunt
knot	right	ant	knight	night
toe	tow	thyme	time	tail
tale				

1. **Tess** had _____ much to **eat**.
2. I **must return** _____ books.
3. **Two** wrongs **don't** make a _____.
4. Please _____ me a **note**.
5. **Tim's** _____ is **twenty-two**.
6. **Tie** a **tight** _____.
7. When you go **to** bed, please leave the _____ **light** on.
8. **Tony** broke his **little** _____.
9. **What** _____ is the **party**?
10. **That tiger** has a **tiny** _____.

More Practice

🔉 **Read the dialogue aloud with a partner. Pay attention to the boldfaced words containing the consonant [t].**

Tom: **Tina**, who were you **talking to** on the **telephone**?

Tina: **Terry White**. She **wanted to** know **what time** the **party** is **tonight**.

Tom: **Terry** is always **late**. She **missed** our **tennis** game **last Tuesday**.

Tina: **Two** days ago, she **didn't** come **to breakfast until two**. **Terry** is always in a **tizzy**.

Tom: **Terry missed** her **flight to Texas last** week.

Tina: She's never on **time** for any **appointment**.

Tom: This is **terrible**! **What time** did you **tell** her **to** come **tonight**?

Tina: **Don't** worry. I had a **terrific** idea. I **told Terry to** come **at** six **fifteen**. The **party** really is **set** for **eight**!

Tom: **To tell** the **truth**, I wish you **told** her **it** was **at two fifteen**. I **just don't trust** her!

EXERCISE B

 Read the anecdote aloud. Pay attention to the consonant [t] in the boldfaced words.

A **hotel guest went into** the bar one **night to** have a few drinks. He had **caught** a bad cold and **kept** sneezing. The **bartender**, who had known the **guest** for the **past ten** days, **told** him, "You look **tired** and sound **terrible**."

"Yes, I have a **terrific** cold," the **hotel guest stated**. The **bartender turned to** him and said, "**It's too** bad **that** you **don't** have pneumonia. The **doctors** know **what to** do for **that**!"

EXERCISE C

 Practice reading the questions and answers aloud with a partner. Fill in the blanks with words containing the consonant [t]. Pay attention to the boldfaced words containing [t].

1. **A: What time** does the **party start**?

   B: The **party starts at** _____.

2. **A: What time** is your **appointment** with the **dentist**?

   B: My **appointment** is **at** _____ on _____ **afternoon**.

3. **A: What** is your **telephone** number?

   B: My **telephone** number is _____.

4. **A:** Do you **turn left** or **right** on **Tenth Street**?

   B: Turn _____ on **Tenth Street**.

5. **A:** Where are you **taking** a **trip** this **winter**?

   B: I'm **taking** a **trip to** _____

Every *t*ime you *t*alk, *t*ry to achieve perfec*t* pronunciation of [*t*]!

Lesson 26 [d] as in *day*, *ladder*, and *bed*

PRONOUNCING [d]

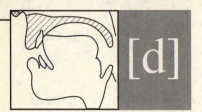

Tongue tip: Firmly pressed against gum ridge behind upper front teeth

Airstream: Stopped and then exploded

Vocal cords: Vibrating

Possible Pronunciation Problems

1. The sound [d] should be produced with the tongue tip touching the upper gum ridge. It should NOT touch the back of your upper front teeth or be placed between your teeth.

EXAMPLES   If you say [ð] instead of [d]:   **ladder** will sound like **lather**.

breeding will sound like **breathing**.

2. When [d] is the last sound in a word, many speakers forget to make their vocal cords vibrate. This will make [d] sound like a [t] and confuse your listeners.

EXAMPLES   If you say [t] instead of [d]:   **card** will sound like **cart**.

bed will sound like **bet**.

Press your tongue tip against the gum ridge behind your upper front teeth and add voicing when you pronounce [d].

Don't forget to practice [d] every *d*ay!

Practice

EXERCISE A   **Listen and repeat. Be sure your tongue tip touches the upper gum ridge.**

[d] At the Beginning of Words			[d] In the Middle of Words			[d] At the End of Words		
do	door	dozen	body	older	pudding	bad	food	bread
dog	dime	doctor	soda	order	Sunday	did	card	build
day	down	different	under	window	medicine	end	cold	would/wood
desk			today			said		

🔊 **Listen. Repeat the pairs of words. Be sure to press your tongue against the upper gum ridge and to make your vocal cords vibrate for [d]. Remember to prolong any vowel BEFORE the consonant [d].**

[d]	[t]
bed	bet
mad	mat
need	neat
hard	heart
bride	bright
hide	height
wade	wait

🔊 **Listen and repeat. Pay attention to the consonant [d] in the boldfaced words.**

1. a **good idea**
2. one **hundred dollars**
3. **end** of the **road**
4. a **bad cold**
5. What's **today's date**?
6. How **do** you **do**?
7. What **did** you **order** for **dinner**?
8. **Wendy** is a **wonderful dancer**.
9. We **landed** in **London** at **dawn**.
10. **Send dad** a **birthday card**.

🔊 **Listen carefully. Some words that should be pronounced with the consonant [d] will be said incorrectly. Circle C for Correct or I for Incorrect. (For answers to Check Yourself 1 and 2, see Appendix II, page 290.)**

EXAMPLES   *You hear*   I'm reading a **good** book.   *You circle*   Ⓒ   I

You hear   **Sat** is the opposite of happy.   *You circle*   C   Ⓘ

1. C   I
2. C   I
3. C   I
4. C   I
5. C   I

📖 **Read this wedding invitation. Circle the words that contain the consonant** [d].

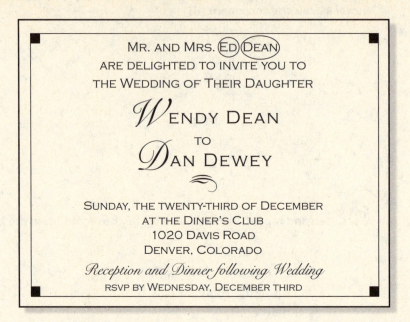

MR. AND MRS. ⟨ED⟩ ⟨DEAN⟩
ARE DELIGHTED TO INVITE YOU TO
THE WEDDING OF THEIR DAUGHTER

Wendy DEAN

TO

Dan DEWEY

SUNDAY, THE TWENTY-THIRD OF DECEMBER
AT THE DINER'S CLUB
1020 DAVIS ROAD
DENVER, COLORADO
Reception and Dinner following Wedding
RSVP BY WEDNESDAY, DECEMBER THIRD

Now read the invitation aloud. Pay attention to the words containing the consonant [d].

More Practice

EXERCISE A

📖 **Read the essay aloud. Pay attention to the boldfaced words containing the consonant** [d].

Daydreaming

Almost all people **daydream during** a normal **day**. They **tend** to **daydream** the most **during** quiet times. Most people have **said** that they enjoy their **daydreams**. Some have very **ordinary daydreams**, while others have unrealistic ones, such as inheriting a million **dollars**. Men **daydream** as much as women **do**, but the subject of their **dreams** is **different**. Men **daydream** about being **daring** heroes or **good** athletes. Women **delight** in **daydreaming** about fashion and beauty. As **individuals** grow **older**, they **tend** to **daydream** less, although it is still **evident** in their **old** age. **Children daydream**, too. Psychologists believe **daydreaming** is an important part of **children's development** because it helps them to **develop** their imaginations. **Daydreaming** has **advantages** and **disadvantages**. It can keep people **entertained under dull conditions**. The **downside** is that, when **daydreaming**, they **need** to **divert** their attention from their **surroundings**. When it is important for people to pay attention to something like **driving**, **daydreaming** can be a risky or **dangerous diversion**.

Work with a partner. Write a short conversation beginning with one of the following questions:

- What **day** is **today**?
- Can you **drive** me to the **doctor** on **Monday**?
- **Do** you think we **should do** something for **Don's birthday**?

Practice your conversation together. Pay attention to all the words containing the consonant [d].

*D*on't forget to practice [d] every *d*ay!

PRONOUNCING [θ]

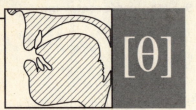

[θ]

Tongue tip: Between the teeth
Airstream: Continuous without interruption
Vocal cords: Not vibrating

Possible Pronunciation Problems

The sound [θ] does not exist in most languages. Because it may be difficult for you to recognize, you probably substitute more familiar sounds.

EXAMPLES   If you say [s] instead of [θ]:   **thank** will sound like **sank**.
If you say [ʃ] instead of [θ]:   **thin** will sound like **shin**.
If you say [f] instead of [θ]:   **Ruth** will sound like **roof**.
If you say [t] instead of [θ]:   **path** will sound like **pat**.

When you pronounce [θ], concentrate on placing your tongue between your teeth. Look in a mirror, and keep the airstream continuous.

Keep *th*inking about [θ]!

Practice

EXERCISE A   🎧 **Listen and repeat. Remember to place your tongue between your teeth when you say [θ].**

[θ] At the Beginning of Words		
thaw	theme	theory
thin	thick	thirsty
thank	thorn	thought
thief		

[θ] In the Middle of Words		
wealthy	healthy	anything
nothing	toothpaste	birthday
method	something	northwest
author		

[θ] At the End of Words		
bath	teeth	truth
both	mouth	south
cloth	month	oath
path		

note   The consonant [θ] is always spelled *th*.

🎧 **Listen and repeat. Remember to place your tongue BETWEEN your teeth for [θ] and BEHIND your teeth for [t] and [s].**

[θ]	[t]	[s]
thank	tank	sank
thin	tin	sin
thought	taught	sought
bath	bat	bass
thick	tick	sick
Beth	bet	Bess
path	pat	pass

🎧 **Listen and repeat. Pay attention to the consonant [θ] in the boldfaced words.**

1. **Thank** you.
2. I **think** so.
3. **something** else
4. Open your **mouth**.
5. **healthy** and **wealthy**
6. a penny for your **thoughts**
7. **Thanksgiving** Day falls on **Thursday**.
8. Do birds fly **north** or **south** in the winter?
9. **Thank** you for your **thoughtful birthday** card.
10. The baby got his **third tooth** this **month**.
11. **Thelma** had her **thirty-third birthday**.
12. Brush your **teeth** with a **toothbrush** and **toothpaste**.
13. Good friends stick **with** you **through thick** and **thin**!
14. **Beth** walked back and **forth** on the **path**.
15. The **oath** is, "Tell the **truth**, the whole **truth**, and **nothing** but the **truth**."

🎧 **Listen. Ten of the following words contain the consonant [θ]. Circle the words containing the consonant [θ]. (For answers to Check Yourself 1 and 2, see Appendix II, page 290.)**

Thomas	clothes	(teeth)	feather
(Ruth)	further	(moth)	father
although	thick	other	faith
throw	clothing	breathe	breath
rather	method	cloth	thorough

Read aloud the paragraph about Jim Thorpe. Circle the words that should be pronounced with the consonant [θ].

Jim (Thorpe)

Do you know (anything) about Jim Thorpe? He was a Native American athlete. He excelled in everything at the Olympics. Thousands were angry when Thorpe's medals were taken away because he was called a professional athlete. In 1973, long after his death, Thorpe's medals were restored. Throughout the world, Jim Thorpe is thought to be one of the greatest male athletes.

Check your answers, and practice reading the paragraph aloud again.

More Practice

EXERCISE A
Work with a partner. Practice these tongue twisters. Which of you will be first to read them quickly with no mistakes? Pay attention to the boldfaced words containing the consonant [θ]. Remember to place your tongue between your teeth when you say [θ].

1. **Theopholus Thistle,** the successful **thistle** sifter, in sifting a sieveful of unsifted **thistles, thrust three thousand thistles through** the **thick** of his **thumb.**

2. **Thirty thousand thoughtless** boys **thought** they'd make a lot of noise. So with **thirty thousand thumbs**, they banged on **thirty thousand** drums!

EXERCISE B
No one ever gets tired of hearing "Thank you!" Work with a partner. Write a dialogue in which one person thanks another person for something. Remember to pay attention to the consonant [θ] in *thank you* and in other words.

Keep *th*inking about [θ]!

Lesson 28 [ð] as in *the*, *father*, and *smooth*

PRONOUNCING [ð]

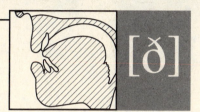

Tongue tip: Between the teeth
Airstream: Continuous without interruption
Vocal cords: Vibrating

Possible Pronunciation Problems

The sound [ð] is another unfamiliar sound. It may be difficult for you to recognize and produce. You probably substitute the more familiar sound [d] or possibly [z] or [dʒ].

EXAMPLES
If you say [d] instead of [ð]:   **they** will sound like **day**.
If you say [z] instead of [ð]:   **bathe** will sound like **bays**.
If you say [dʒ] instead of [ð]:   **than** will sound like **Jan**.

When pronouncing [ð], remember to place your tongue between your teeth and to keep the airstream from your mouth continuous.

Look in the mirror as you pronounce [ð]. Make sure you can see the tip of your tongue, and there won't be a problem with **th**ese, **th**em, and **th**ose.

Practice

EXERCISE A   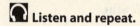 **Listen and repeat.**

[ð] At the Beginning of Words

the	that	there
this	they	these
then	those	though
them		

[ð] In the Middle of Words

other	gather	leather
mother	either	together
father	neither	whether
brother		

[ð] At the End of Words

bathe	breathe
clothe	soothe
smooth	

> The letters *th* followed by *e* are usually pronounced [ð].
>
> **the**   **th**em   o**the**r   ba**the**

EXERCISE B   🎧 **Listen and repeat.**

	[ð]	[d]			[ð]	[z]
1.	they	day		6.	then	Zen
2.	breathe	breed		7.	breathe	breeze
3.	there	dare		8.	soothe	sues
4.	though	dough		9.	writhe	rise
5.	bathe	bade		10.	bathe	bays

EXERCISE C   🎧 **Listen and repeat. Pay attention to the boldfaced words containing the consonant [ð].**

1. **That**'s right.
2. **father** and **mother**
3. **either** one of **them**
4. **This** is it!
5. under **the weather**
6. Don't **bother** me!
7. **This** is my **other brother**.
8. I'd **rather** get **together another** day.
9. **That leather** belt feels **smooth**.
10. I like **this** one better **than the other** one.
11. **Mother** must **bathe the** baby.
12. Will **Grandmother** and **Grandfather** be **there**?
13. Birds of a **feather** flock **together**.
14. **This clothing** is as light as a **feather**.
15. **The rhythm** of **the** music is **soothing**.

CHECK YOURSELF 1   📖 **Circle the word in parentheses that correctly completes each sentence. Then read each sentence aloud. Be sure to place the tip of your tongue between your teeth as you say [θ]. (For answers to Check Yourself 1–3, see Appendix II, pages 291–292.)**

EXAMPLE   I like **this** book better (then /(than))/ **that** book.

1. (This /(These)) shoes are **weatherproof**.
2. I **loathe this** wet (weather / whether).
3. (This / These) board is **smoother than the other** one.
4. **The** family will be (there / their) for **the** wedding.

5. **Mother** told (they / them) not to be late.

6. (They / Them) are **worthy** of **the** award.

7. (Those / That) **brothers** are **rather** tall.

8. I don't know (weather / whether) to buy **this** one or **that** one.

9. (That / Those) **lather** is **soothing**.

10. (Their / There) **father** likes **the weather** in **southern** Florida.

CHECK YOURSELF 2　　🎧 **Listen and circle the word in each group that is NOT pronounced with [ð].**

EXAMPLE　　brother　　mother　　(broth)　　father

1. cloth	clothing	clothes	clothe
2. though	although	thought	those
3. then	them	themselves	den
4. feather	father	faith	further
5. bathing	bath	bathe	breathe
6. thank	than	that	then
7. soothe	sues	soothing	smooth
8. dare	there	their	theirs

CHECK YOURSELF 3　　👥 **Read the dialogue with a partner and circle the words containing the consonant [ð].**

Daughter: (Mother), I like (these) old pictures. Who's (this)?

Mother:　　That's your great-grandmother.

Daughter: The feathered hat is funny! Who's that man?

Mother:　　That's your grandfather. He was from the Netherlands.

Daughter: I know these people! Aren't they Uncle Tom and Uncle Bob?

Mother:　　That's right. Those are my brothers. They always bothered me!

Daughter: This must be either Father or his brother.

Mother:　　Neither! That's your father's uncle.

Daughter: Why are there other people in this photo?

Mother:　　This was a family gathering. We got together all the time.

Daughter: Mother, who's this "smooth-looking" man?

Mother:　　Shhhhhhhhh! I'd rather not say. Your father will hear!

Daughter: Is that your old boyfriend?

Mother:　　Well, even mothers had fun in those days!

Read the dialogue again and check to make sure you circled the words containing the consonant [ð]. Then change roles and read the dialogue aloud again with a partner.

More Practice

📖 Read the weather report aloud. Pay attention to the boldfaced words containing the consonant [ð].

> **This** is **Heather Worthington**, here to give you **another weather** report. **The weather** is **rather** rainy in **northern** areas. Don't **bother** with umbrellas or heavy **clothing** in **the southern** region. **There** will be warm **weather**, **although there** is a slight chance of **either** rain or storms. Seas are **smooth**, so you might take **those bathing** suits out. **Neither** tornado nor hurricane warnings are in effect **this** week, so everyone can **breathe** easy. **That**'s all for tonight.

📖 Select a brief newspaper or magazine article. Circle all words pronounced with the consonant [ð]. Look in a mirror as you read it aloud. Be sure to see and feel the tip of your tongue between your teeth as you say [ð].

[ð] is ano*th*er sound *th*at you can master, if you remember *th*at *th*e tip of your tongue goes between your teeth!

EXERCISE

🎧 **Listen and repeat the words and sentences.**

	[s]	[z]	[t]	[d]	[θ]	[ð]
1.	pass		pat		path	
2.	sink	zinc			think	
3.			set	said	Seth	
4.	Stan			Dan		than
5.		Zen		den		then

    [d]   [ð] [s]
6. **Dan** is older **than Stan**.

           [s] [t]   [θ]
7. Did you **pass Pat** on the **path**?

    [θ]   [z]   [s]
8. I **think** there is **zinc** in the **sink**.

    [θ] [d]   [t]
9. **Seth said** to **set** the table.

  [s]   [d]   [z]   [t]
10. **Sue** is **due** at the **zoo** at **two**.

Lesson 30 [ʃ] as in *shoe*, *nation*, and *wish* and [tʃ] as in *chair*, *teacher*, and *witch*

PRONOUNCING [ʃ]

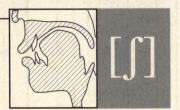

Tongue tip: Near but not touching upper gum ridge

Middle of tongue: Near but not touching hard palate

Airstream: Continuous without interruption

Vocal cords: Not vibrating

Possible Pronunciation Problems

The consonant [ʃ] may not be familiar to you. You may accidentally substitute the more familiar [s] or [tʃ] sound (the sound to be covered next).

EXAMPLES   If you say [s] instead of [ʃ]:   **she** will sound like **see**.

If you say [tʃ] instead of [ʃ]:   **shoe** will sound like **chew**.

The sound [ʃ] will be easy to pronounce if you keep the airstream steady and smooth. Be careful not to let your tongue touch your teeth or upper gum ridge or you will say [tʃ] by mistake.

[ʃ] is a steady, quiet sound. *Shhhhhhh.*

Practice

EXERCISE A   🎧 **Listen and repeat. Remember, your tongue should not touch the roof of your mouth.**

[ʃ] At the Beginning of Words

shy	shoe	sugar
shop	short	shape
ship	share	shower
shine		

[ʃ] In the Middle of Words

ocean	nation	official
washer	patient	machine
tissue	mission	brushing
insure		

[ʃ] At the End of Words

dish	rush	foolish
wish	finish	Spanish
cash	punish	English
wash		

[ʃ] Spelled

sh	*ti*	*ci*	*ss*	*ch*
shelf	option	social	issue	chef
shirt	section	special	assure	chute
brush	fiction	musician	depression	machine
crash	mention	physician	profession	Chicago
shadow	election	conscious	expression	chauffeur

EXERCISE B   🎧 **Listen and repeat. Be sure to pucker your lips for [ʃ] and "smile" for [s].**

[ʃ]	[s]
ship	sip
sheet	seat
shelf	self
sheen	seen
mash	mass

EXERCISE C   🎧 **Listen and repeat. Pay attention to the boldfaced words and phrases containing the [ʃ] sound.**

1. **Sh**ake hands.
2. wa**sh**ing ma**ch**ine
3. I'm **s**ure!
4. **sh**ort on ca**sh**
5. **Sh**ut the door!
6. Poli**sh** your **sh**oes.
7. There are many fi**sh** in the o**ce**an.
8. **Sh**irley **sh**opped for **sh**oes.
9. The **sh**irt **sh**ould be wa**sh**ed.
10. The mu**sh**rooms and **sh**rimp are deli**ci**ous.
11. We had a **sh**ort vaca**ti**on in Wa**sh**ington.
12. **Sh**ine the fla**sh**light in this direc**ti**on.
13. **Sh**e **sh**owed us the **ch**ic new fa**sh**ions.
14. **Ch**arlotte speaks Engli**sh** and Spani**sh**.
15. I wi**sh** you would fini**sh** wa**sh**ing the di**sh**es.

🎧 **Listen and circle the word in each group that is NOT pronounced with the consonant [ʃ]. (For answers, see Appendix II, page 292.)**

EXAMPLE	(pleasure)	sure	surely	sugar
1.	crush	cash	catch	crash
2.	chef	chief	chute	chiffon
3.	machine	parachute	mustache	kitchen
4.	China	Russia	Chicago	Michigan
5.	facial	conscience	science	conscious
6.	pressure	pressed	assure	permission
7.	division	subtraction	addition	multiplication
8.	position	action	patio	motion
9.	Charlotte	Cheryl	Sharon	Charles
10.	tension	resign	pension	mention

More Practice

EXERCISE A

📖 **Read the paragraph aloud. Pay attention to the consonant [ʃ] in the boldfaced words.**

Fashion is a **passion** for every **generation**. **Should** skirts be **short** or **should** we switch to long? That is always the question. **Should** men wear **shirts** with button-down collars? **Should** they change to wider ties? What **shade** is in style, charcoal gray or **chartreuse** green? **Should** **shoes** and handbag match? Today's purchase may be **ancient** history tomorrow! Despite future trends and despite our **shapes**, we must look **chic** for that luncheon or **social** event. **Shopping** is **sure** to be fun!

EXERCISE B

👥 **Work with a partner. Take turns reading the hints and identifying the correct occupation from the box. Pay attention to the consonant [ʃ] in the boldfaced words.**

EXAMPLE   A: A person with this **occupation should** be good at investments.

B: _a financial advisor_____

financial advisor	**musician**	**social** worker	**sheriff**
physician	**chef**	**fashion** designer	**chauffeur**

1. **A:** A person with this **occupation should** be a good driver.

   B: _____

2. **A:** A person with this **occupation should** be a lover of food.

   B: _____

3. **A:** A person with this **occupation should** have a sense of style.

   B: _____

4. **A:** A person with this **occupation should** have **compassion**.

   B: _____

5. **A:** A person with this **occupation should** know about the body and healing.

   B: _____

6. **A:** A person with this **occupation should** fight against crime.

   B: _____

7. **A:** A person with this **occupation should** play an instrument.

   B: _____

PRONOUNCING [tʃ]

Tongue tip: Firmly pressed against gum ridge behind upper front teeth

Airstream: Stopped (as for [t]) and then released (as for [ʃ])

Vocal cords: Not vibrating

Possible Pronunciation Problems

The sounds [tʃ] and [ʃ] are easily confused with one another.

EXAMPLES If you say [ʃ] instead of [tʃ]: **chair** will sound like **share**.

which will sound like **wish**.

Just remember to start [tʃ] with your tongue in the same place as for the sound [t]. Be sure to press your tongue tip against the gum ridge behind your upper front teeth, or you will say [ʃ] by mistake.

[tʃ] is an explosive sound like a sneeze! Think of Ah-CHOO and you'll meet the challenge of pronouncing [tʃ].

Practice

EXERCISE A 🎧 **Listen and repeat the following words. Be sure to begin [tʃ] just like the sound [t].**

[tʃ] At the Beginning of Words

chew	chest	chicken
chair	choose	Charles
child	cherry	cheerful
chalk		

[tʃ] In the Middle of Words

nature	butcher	question
teacher	richer	future
picture	orchard	catcher
hatchet		

[tʃ] At the End of Words

itch	reach	watch
each	touch	speech
match	sandwich	
much	peach	

[tʃ] Spelled

ch	*tu*	*tch*
chop	mature	patch
rich	culture	catch
cheap	posture	butcher
cheese	fortune	kitchen
March	picture	pitcher

note Less frequent spelling patterns for [tʃ] consist of the letters *t* and *ti*.

righ**te**ous diges**ti**on ques**ti**on

EXERCISE B 🎧 **Listen and repeat.**

[tʃ]	[t]	[ʃ]
cheer	tear	sheer
chip	tip	ship
chin	tin	shin
match	mat	mash
watch	what	wash

EXERCISE C 🎧 **Listen and repeat. Pay attention to the [tʃ] sound in the boldfaced words.**

1. **Watch** out!
2. **inch** by **inch**
3. I'm **catching** a cold.
4. **cheese sandwich**
5. Don't **touch** that!
6. **chocolate chip** cookies
7. Does the **butcher charge much** for **chickens**?
8. **Which furniture** did you **choose**?
9. **Natural cheddar cheese** is not **cheap**.
10. Please **watch** the **children** in the **lunchroom**.

11. I **purchased** a **picture** of **China**.
12. The **coach chose Charles** for the team.
13. The **bachelor** plays **checkers** and **chess**.
14. Don't count your **chickens** before they're **hatched**!

CHECK YOURSELF Listen to the sentences. Some words that should be pronounced with [t∫] will be said INCORRECTLY. Circle *C* for Correct or *I* for Incorrect to indicate whether the [t∫] word in each sentence is pronounced properly. (For answers, see Appendix II, page 292.)

EXAMPLES   *You hear*   Sit in the **share**.   *You circle*   C   Ⓘ

            You hear   I had to **change** the tire. *You circle*   Ⓒ   I

1. C   I
2. C   I
3. C   I
4. C   I
5. C   I
6. C   I
7. C   I
8. C   I
9. C   I
10. C   I

More Practice

EXERCISE A

Read aloud the paragraph about Chubby Checker. Be sure to pronounce all the boldfaced [t∫] words correctly.

Chubby Checker

Children and teenagers in the 1960s were **charmed** by the performer known as **Chubby Checker**. **Chubby** became "King of the Twist" and **changed** the **future** of music forever. While he was working in a **chicken** store, **Chubby's** boss recognized **natural** talent and had him sing to the customers. His "**catchy**" name, **Chubby Checker**, was **chosen** over his **actual** name, Ernest Evans. He **actually** recorded the "Twist" while still in high school and was **fortunate** to hit the **charts** immediately. His career was **launched**. His records **reached** people around the world. **Chubby** was **featured** on TV and **watched** by millions in movies and shows. Although **Chubby** is no longer the top-**notch** king of rock, he is still everyone's **champion**.

Rachel and Chuck made a list of all the chores to do around the house. Work with a partner. Pretend you are Rachel and Chuck. Decide which eight chores are the most important and which of you will do each of the eight. Pay attention to the boldfaced words containing the consonant [tʃ].

1. **Change** the sheets.
2. Repair the steps on the **porch**.
3. **Purchase chicken** and **chops** at the **butcher**.
4. **Exchange** the **chair** at the **furniture** store.
5. Prepare the **children's lunch**.
6. Make a **batch** of **chocolate chip** cookies.
7. Make a **pitcher** of lemonade.
8. **Charge** the battery of the lawn mower.
9. Hang the new **picture** over the **couch**.
10. Write the monthly **checks** and pay the **charge** accounts.
11. Bring in **Charles's watch** to be repaired.
12. Put the **china** dishes in the **chest**.
13. **Patch** the leaking roof.
14. **Chop** vegetables for dinner.
15. **Check** the oil in the car.

LESSON REVIEW: [ʃ] AND [tʃ]

Listen and repeat. Remember: Your tongue tip must touch the upper gum ridge for [tʃ] but NOT for [ʃ].

[ʃ]	[tʃ]
1. **sh**oe	**ch**ew
2. **sh**are	**ch**air
3. **sh**ip	**ch**ip
4. wa**sh**	wa**tch**
5. ca**sh**	ca**tch**
6. I have a **crush**.	I have a **crutch**.
7. Please **wash** the dog.	Please **watch** the dog.
8. He can't **mash** it.	He can't **match** it.
9. Give me my **share**.	Give me my **chair**.
10. Get rid of the **sheet**.	Get rid of the **cheat**.

🎧 **Listen and repeat.**

     [tʃ]   [ʃ]
1. Let's **choose** new **shoes**.

    [ʃ]   [tʃ]
2. **She's** eating the **cheese**.

   [ʃ]   [tʃ]
3. **Sherry** likes **cherry** pie.

          [ʃ]   [tʃ]
4. The hull of the **ship** has a **chip**.

        [ʃ]   [tʃ]
5. He paid **cash** for the **catch** of the day.

🎧 **Listen. Two of the words in each series will be the same; one will be different. Circle the number of the word that is different. (For answers to Check Yourself 1–4, see Appendix II, pages 292–293.)**

EXAMPLE   *You hear*   watch   watch   wash

                You circle   1   2   ③

  1. 1   2   3
  2. 1   2   3
  3. 1   2   3
  4. 1   2   3
  5. 1   2   3
  6. 1   2   3
  7. 1   2   3
  8. 1   2   3
  9. 1   2   3
10. 1   2   3

Write the correct phonetic symbols in the brackets above the boldfaced letters.

          [tʃ]   [ʃ]   [ʃ]
EXAMPLE   Too mu**ch** milk makes mu**sh**y ma**sh**ed potatoes.

       [ ]   [ ]   [ ]
1. The puppy **sh**ouldn't **ch**ew the **sh**oes.

  [ ]   [ ]   [ ]
2. **Sh**ine the furniture with poli**sh**.

   [ ]   [ ] [ ]
3. The **ch**ef prepared a spe**ci**al di**sh**.

      [ ]   [ ]   [ ]

4. We **sh**ould **ch**ange the dirty **sh**eets.

      [ ]   [ ]   [ ]

5. **Ch**oosing a profe**ssi**on is a **ch**allenge.

📖 **Check your answers. Then read the sentences aloud.**

CHECK YOURSELF 3 🎧 **Listen and circle the word used to complete each sentence.**

                           [ʃ]   [tʃ]

EXAMPLE   You sure can (shop / chop).

                         [ʃ]   [tʃ]

1. I didn't see the (dish / ditch).

                       [ʃ]   [tʃ]

2. He hurt his (shin / chin).

                             [ʃ]   [tʃ]

3. Did you hear that (shatter / chatter)?

                       [ʃ]   [tʃ]

4. It's a silly (wish / witch).

                            [ʃ]   [tʃ]

5. It was an endless (marsh / March).

                         [ʃ]   [tʃ]

6. She brought me the (wash / watch).

                       [ʃ]   [tʃ]

7. You have a large (share / chair).

                     [ʃ]   [tʃ]

8. We must fix the (ship / chip).

                          [ʃ]   [tʃ]

9. Does she have a new (crush / crutch)?

                       [ʃ]   [tʃ]

10. You completed the (shore / chore).

📖 **Check your answers. Then read each sentence aloud twice. Use the first word in the first reading and the second word in the second reading.**

CHECK YOURSELF 4 **Circle the words containing the consonant [ʃ] and underline the words containing the consonant [tʃ].**

Richard: Do you have any <u>change</u> for the (washing) (machine)? My wife, Sharon, is

                 visiting her parents in Michigan. I'm watching the children and doing

                 the chores.

Marshall: Watch out! Don't put bleach on those shirts. You'll wash out the color.

Richard: Will you teach me how to wash clothes?

Marshall: Be sure to wash white shirts separately. Don't use too much soap.

Richard: I wish Sharon would return. It's more natural for a woman to wash and shop.

Marshall: You sound like a chauvinist! I don't mind doing chores. I'm great in the kitchen, too!

Richard: Would you like to take charge? I'll cheerfully pay you cash.

Marshall: Listen, old chap, I'm a bachelor and too old to chase after children. I'm in a rush. It's been nice chatting with you, Richard.

Richard: Sure, nice chatting with you, too, Marshall.

Check to make sure you circled the words containing the consonant [ʃ] and underlined the words containing the consonant [tʃ]. Then practice reading the dialogue with a partner.

More Practice

EXERCISE A

Read the words aloud. You will see them again in Exercise B.

[tʃ]	[ʃ]
creature	sugar
children	shutters
porch	should
chimney	Dasher
kerchief	flash
miniature	sash
	shouted
	dash

EXERCISE B

Read aloud these lines from the poem "The Night Before Christmas." Pay attention to the boldfaced words with the consonants [ʃ] and [tʃ].

'Twas the Night Before Christmas
Clement Clark Moore

'Twas the night before Christmas, when all through the house
Not a **creature** was stirring, not even a mouse;
The stockings were hung by the **chimney** with care,
In hopes that St. Nicholas soon would be there;
The **children** were nestled all snug in their beds,
While visions of **sugar**-plums danced in their heads;
And Mamma in her **'kerchief** and I in my cap,
Had just settled down for a long winter's nap,
When out on the lawn there arose such a clatter,
I sprang from my bed to see what was the matter.

Away to the window I flew like a **flash**,
Tore open the **shutters** and threw up the **sash**.
When what to my wondering eyes **should** appear,
But a **miniature** sleigh, and eight tiny reindeer
With a little old driver, so lively and quick,
I knew in a moment it must be St. Nick.
More rapid than eagles his coursers they came,
And he whistled, and **shouted**; and called them by name;
"Now, **Dasher**! now, Dancer! now, Prancer and Vixen!
On, Comet! on, Cupid! on, Donner and Blitzen!
To the top of the **porch**, to the top of the wall!
Now **dash** away! **dash** away! **dash** away all!"

Lesson 31 Contrast and Review of [s], [ʃ], [t], and [tʃ]

EXERCISE

🎧 **Listen and repeat the words and sentences.**

	[s]	[ʃ]	[t]	[tʃ]
1.	Sue	shoe	too	chew
2.	sear	sheer	tear	cheer
3.	sip	ship	tip	chip
4.	sin	shin	tin	chin
5.	mass	mash	mat	match

6. Did **S**ue **ch**oose her new **sh**oes?
    [s]   [tʃ]   [ʃ]

7. There's a **ch**ip on the **t**ip of the **sh**ip.
    [tʃ]   [t]   [ʃ]

8. **C**ass paid **c**a**sh** for the **c**at**ch** of the day.
    [s]   [ʃ]   [tʃ]

9. **T**erry made a **ch**erry pie for **Sh**erry.
    [t]   [tʃ]   [ʃ]

10. **Sh**e's eating a **ch**eese sandwi**ch**.
    [ʃ]   [tʃ]   [tʃ]

Lesson 32 [ʒ] as in *measure*, *vision*, and *rouge*

PRONOUNCING [ʒ]

Tongue tip: In the same position as for [ʃ]
Airstream: Continuous without interruption
Vocal cords: Vibrating

Possible Pronunciation Problems

Pronunciation problems occur because of similarities between [ʒ] and other sounds.

EXAMPLES   If you say [ʃ] instead of [ʒ]:   **vision** will sound like **vishion**.
If you say [dʒ] instead of [ʒ]:   **pleasure** will sound like **pledger**.

Be sure your vocal cords are vibrating when you say [ʒ]. Put your hand on your throat to feel the vibration!

It will be a plea*s*ure to pronounce [ʒ]!

Practice

EXERCISE A   🎧 **Listen and repeat.**

[ʒ] In the Middle of Words			[ʒ] At the End of Words		
Asia	measure	decision	rouge	garage	prestige
usual	pleasure	division	beige	corsage	camouflage
vision	occasion	television	mirage	massage	entourage
leisure					

In English, [ʒ] does not occur at the beginning of words.

[ʒ] Spelled		
si	*su*	*gi* or *ge*
lesion	closure	beige
vision	unusual	regime
explosion	casual	massage
conclusion	composure	negligee
collision		camouflage
illusion		

156

EXERCISE B

🎧 **Listen and repeat. Pay attention to the boldfaced words containing the consonant [ʒ].**

1. color **television**
2. long **division**
3. That's **unusual**!
4. big **decision**
5. What's the **occasion**?
6. It's a **pleasure** to meet you.
7. A **mirage** is an **illusion**.
8. The **azure** skies are **unusual**.
9. She bought a **beige negligee**.
10. We **usually** watch **television**.
11. Get a **massage** at your **leisure**.
12. The **excursion** was a **pleasure**.
13. I heard an **explosion** in the **garage**.
14. The **collision** caused great **confusion**.
15. She received a **corsage** for the **occasion**.

CHECK YOURSELF 1

🎧 **Listen and circle the word in each group that does NOT contain the consonant [ʒ]. (For answers to Check Yourself 1–3, see Appendix II, pages 293–294.)**

EXAMPLE	composure	exposure	enclosure	(position)
1.	leisure	pleasure	sure	measure
2.	Asia	Asian	Parisian	Paris
3.	huge	beige	rouge	prestige
4.	passion	collision	occasion	decision
5.	massage	mirage	message	corsage
6.	confusion	conclusive	contusion	conclusion
7.	lesion	profession	explosion	aversion
8.	vision	version	television	visible
9.	seizure	seize	azure	division
10.	treasury	treasurer	treason	treasure

🔊 **Listen and write the phonetic symbol [ʒ] or [ʃ] to represent the consonant sound of the boldfaced letters. Refer back to Lesson 30, practicing [ʃ] as needed.**

[ʃ]   [ʒ]

EXAMPLE   We will va**c**ation in **A**sia.

[ ]   [ ]

1. The commi**ss**ion made a deci**si**on.

          [ ]   [ ]

2. The class learned divi**si**on and addi**ti**on.

[ ]   [ ]

3. Mea**s**ure the gara**ge**.

     [ ]   [ ]

4. Your profe**ss**ion has presti**ge**.

    [ ] [ ]   [ ]

5. That's an unu**su**al **sh**ade of rou**ge**.

🔊 **Listen to the newscast, and circle all words pronounced with the [ʒ] sound.**

Good evening. This is Frazier White with the 10:00 p.m. television news. Tonight we have some most unusual stories. Here are the headlines:

- Tourists on a pleasure trip discovered valuable Persian rugs. The rugs dated back to ancient Persia.

- An explosion took place in a garage on First Avenue. Seizure of a bomb was made after much confusion.

- Asian flu is spreading. Asian flu vaccinations will be available to those with exposure to the germ.

- Today was the Parisian fashion show. Everything from casual leisure clothes to negligees was shown. Beige is the big color. Hemlines measure two inches below the knee.

- Carry your raincoat. Occasional showers are due tomorrow. Hope your evening is a pleasure.

This is Frazier White saying GOOD NIGHT!

🔊📖 **Listen again to make sure you circled all words containing the consonant [ʒ]. Then pretend to be a newscaster and read the newscast aloud yourself.**

📖 **Read the limerick aloud. Be sure to pronounce the boldfaced words correctly.**

A **Delusion**?

A man woke up in **confusion**.
In a dream he'd reached the **conclusion**
    That he would have **treasure**,
    Luxury and **pleasure**.
He asked himself, "Truth or **delusion**?"

It will be a plea*s*ure to pronounce [ʒ]!

Lesson 33 [dʒ] as in *jam*, *magic*, and *age* and [j] as in *you* and *yes*

PRONOUNCING [dʒ]

Tongue tip: Firmly pressed against gum ridge behind upper front teeth

Airstream: Stopped (as for [d]) and then released (as for [ʒ])

Vocal cords: Vibrating

Possible Pronunciation Problems

Confusing English spelling patterns and similarities between [dʒ] and other sounds cause your pronunciation problems with [dʒ].

EXAMPLES   If you say [j] instead of [dʒ]:   **Jell-O** will sound like **yellow**.

If you say [ʒ] instead of [dʒ]:   **legion** will sound like **lesion**.

If you say [tʃ] instead of [dʒ]:   **badge** will sound like **batch**.

If you say [h] instead of [dʒ]:   **jam** will sound like **ham**.

Remember to start [dʒ] with your tongue in the same place as for the sound [d]. Be sure your tongue is pressed against your upper gum ridge and that your vocal cords are vibrating when you say [dʒ].

Just keep practicing! It will be a *joy* to say [dʒ]!

Practice

EXERCISE A   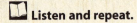 **Listen and repeat.**

[dʒ] At the Beginning of Words		[dʒ] In the Middle of Words		[dʒ] At the End of Words	
jam	jar	agent	enjoy	age	edge
joy	gym	adjust	angel	cage	badge
job	gem	magic	injure	large	ridge

[dʒ] Spelled

j	*g*	*dg*
jaw	giant	fudge
joke	gentle	budge
major	ranger	wedge

Practice

EXERCISE B

🎧 **Listen and repeat. Remember, [dʒ] is a voiced sound; your vocal cords should vibrate! (And be sure to prolong any vowel BEFORE the sound [dʒ].)**

[dʒ]	[tʃ]
joke	choke
gin	chin
badge	batch
ridge	rich
age	"H"

EXERCISE C

🎧 **Listen and repeat. Pay attention to the pronunciation of [dʒ] in the boldfaced words.**

1. **Just** a moment.
2. **Enjoy** yourself!
3. **pledge** of **allegiance**
4. Fourth of **July**
5. **college education**
6. **Jack** of all trades
7. **Jim** is **just joking**.
8. **Jane enjoys jogging**.
9. The **major joined** the **legion**.
10. **George graduates** from **college** in **June**.
11. The **passengers** were **injured** in the **Jeep**.
12. **John** mailed a **large package** to **Virginia**.
13. Do you like **fudge, Jell-O**, or **gingerbread**?
14. The **engineer** lost his **job** in **January**.
15. The **agent** took a **jet** to **Japan**.

Imagine you are taking a jet around the world! You will stop at all the places with names that contain the sound [dʒ]. Circle the names of these places. (For answers to Check Yourself 1 and 2, see Appendix II, page 294.)

(Java)	Luxemburg	Guatemala	Jerusalem
Greece	England	Germany	Algeria
Hungary	Japan	Greenland	China
Egypt	Belgium	Argentina	Jamaica

Read aloud the names of the places you circled. Then practice saying them to complete the following sentence:

I'm taking a **jet** to _____!

Listen and circle the word in each group of four that does NOT contain the consonant [dʒ].

EXAMPLE	(get)	gym	gypsy	jet
1.	badge	bulge	bug	budge
2.	captain	general	major	soldier
3.	hen	gentle	gem	intelligent
4.	juice	age	angel	angle
5.	huge	hug	jug	July
6.	giraffe	gill	giant	gin
7.	duck	cordial	educate	graduate
8.	large	lounge	lung	lunge
9.	Gary	Joe	Jill	Gene
10.	Virginia	Georgia	Germany	Greenland

More Practice

Read the dialogue aloud with a partner. Pay attention to your pronunciation of [dʒ] in the boldfaced words.

Uncle Jack: Hi, **Jill**, how is my favorite **college** student?

Jill: Hi, Uncle **Jack**. I'm a **junior** at **Jackson** University.

Uncle Jack: What are you **majoring** in?

Jill: Well, first I **majored** in **engineering**. But I wasn't a **genius**.

Uncle Jack: So you **changed majors**.

Jill: Right. Then I **majored** in **journalism**. But I was **just** an **average** writer, so I **changed** again.

Uncle Jack: **Jill**, you are a "**Jack**-of-all-trades." But did you finally pick the right **subject**?

Jill:	Yes. Now I'm **enjoying** myself at the **gym** every day!
Uncle Jack:	I'm disappointed in you, **Jill**! You are at **college** for an **education**, not **just** for **enjoyment**.
Jill:	But I am in **education**! I'm **majoring** in physical **education** and I have a **job** at the **gym** to help pay my **college** tuition. I'm **graduating** next **June** with honors!
Uncle Jack:	I **apologize**, **Jill**. To make up for it, I'll give you a **large** gift for **graduation**.
Jill:	I never hold a **grudge**, Uncle **Jack**. You are an **angel**. **Just** come to my **graduation** and I'll be happy!

PRONOUNCING [j]

Tongue tip: In the same position as for the vowel [i]
Airstream: Continuous without interruption
Vocal cords: Vibrating

Possible Pronunciation Problems

The sound [j] may be a difficult sound for you to pronounce. You may confuse it with the similar sound [dʒ] or omit it completely.

EXAMPLE If you say [dʒ] instead of [j]: **yet** will sound like **jet**.
If you omit [j]: **year** will sound like **ear**.

To pronounce [j] correctly, be sure the tip of your tongue is against the back of your lower front teeth and NOT touching the roof of your mouth.

You'll get *your* [j] sound *yet*!

Practice

EXERCISE A

🎧 **Listen and repeat.**

[j] At the Beginning of Words

yes	use	young
you	year	youth
yell	yard	yesterday

[j] In the Middle of Words

onion	beyond	backyard
canyon	values	formula
lawyer	regular	unusual

In English, [j] does not occur at the end of words.

[j] Spelled

y	i	u
yet	union	amuse
your	junior	music
yawn	senior	united
yolk	million	usual
yellow	familiar	university

note

The most common spelling pattern for [j] is *y* followed by a vowel.

yeast   **y**ou   can**y**on   farm**y**ard

hint

When *y* is the first letter in a word, it is ALWAYS pronounced [j]; it is never pronounced [dʒ].

Distinguish between the vowel [u] and the consonant/vowel combination [ju].

[u]	[ju]
food	feud
booty	beauty
fool	fuel

Some English speakers add [j] after [n], [t], [d], or [s] in certain words: *news*, *Tuesday*, *duty*, *suit*. We will not practice that pronunciation of [j] in this book.

EXERCISE B

Listen and repeat. Be sure to differentiate between the boldfaced consonants in each word.

[j]	[dʒ]	[tʃ]
year	jeer	cheer
you	Jew	chew
yolk	joke	choke
yellow	Jell-O	cello

EXERCISE C

Listen and repeat. Pay attention to your pronunciation of the boldfaced words containing the consonant [j].

1. Nice to see **you**.
2. How are **you**?
3. **Yes** or no?
4. Help **yourself**.
5. **You** look great!
6. in my **opinion**

7. Did **you** get **your** car fixed?

8. The **view** of the **canyon** is **beautiful**.

9. Did **you** eat **yams** or **yellow** rice?

10. **Your** senior class **reunion** is this **year**.

11. **You** shouldn't **yell** at **young** children.

12. **Your lawyer** is **brilliant**!

13. The New **York** City **mayor** was **young**.

14. Have **you** had some **yogurt yet**?

15. **Yesterday** we sailed on a **millionaire's yacht**.

CHECK YOURSELF 1 📖 **Read each of the sentences aloud. Complete the words that start with *ye-*; these words all contain the [j] sound. (For answers to Check Yourself 1 and 2, see Appendix II, page 295.)**

EXAMPLE The young man proposed. She said **ye**s_____.

1. The youth left. He hasn't come back **ye**_____.

2. The player ran 50 yards. The crowds began to **ye**_____.

3. Today is Monday. **Ye**_____ was Sunday.

4. Egg yolks should be **ye**_____.

5. You should go to the doctor to get a checkup once

   a **ye**_____.

CHECK YOURSELF 2 🎧 **Listen. Circle SAME if both sentences in each pair are the same. If they are not the same, circle DIFFERENT.**

EXAMPLES *You hear* He is young./He is young. *You circle* (SAME) DIFFERENT

  You hear I heard yes./I heard Jess. *You circle* SAME (DIFFERENT)

1. SAME DIFFERENT

2. SAME DIFFERENT

3. SAME DIFFERENT

4. SAME DIFFERENT

5. SAME DIFFERENT

EXERCISE 📖 **Read aloud the paragraph about New York. Pay attention to your pronunciation of the boldfaced words containing the [j] sound.**

New **York**

New **York** may be one of the most **unique** cities in the world. The largest city in the **United** States, New **York** has a **population** of over eight **million**. People **commute** to the city **regularly**, and visitors come from all over to **view** New **York's beauty** and **confusion**. Come to New **York**! Ride the ferry to the **Statue** of Liberty. Enjoy **museums** of every kind. **You'll** see **huge** skyscrapers. **You** can attend Broadway **musicals** and **previews**. **You** don't need an **excuse** to shop on Fifth Avenue. Help **yourself** to the **unusual** ethnic foods in Chinatown and Little Italy. There are even more **amusements** in the five boroughs. Visit some of the fine **universities**. **Young** or old, **you** will be impressed with the diversity of the city.

LESSON REVIEW: [dʒ] AND [j]

EXERCISE A 🎧 **Listen and repeat. Remember, your tongue tip should touch the upper gum ridge for [dʒ] and touch the back of your lower front teeth for [j].**

[dʒ]	[j]
jell	yell
Jell-O	yellow
joke	yolk
jeer	year
major	mayor

EXERCISE B 🎧 **Listen and repeat. Pay attention to the [dʒ] and the [j] sounds in the boldfaced words.**

[dʒ]	[j]
1. Did they come by **jet**?	Did they come by **yet**?
2. It has no **juice**.	It has no **use**.
3. He became a **major**.	He became a **mayor**.
4. We went to **jail**.	We went to **Yale**.
5. The **jam** is sweet.	The **yam** is sweet.

🎧 **Listen and repeat. Be careful to pronounce the [dʒ] and the [j] sounds correctly.**

              [j]   [dʒ]
1. Do you like **y**ellow **J**ell-O?

  [dʒ]   [j]
2. **J**ess said **y**es.

        [dʒ]   [j]
3. Did the **j**et leave **y**et?

            [dʒ]   [j]
4. The crowds **j**eered this **y**ear.

  [dʒ]   [dʒ]   [j]
5. **J**im found a **j**ar in his **y**ard.

CHECK YOURSELF 1

🎧 **Listen. One word in each sentence will be said INCORRECTLY. On the line to the right of each number, write the CORRECT word for the sentence. (For answers to Check Yourself 1 and 2, see Appendix II, page 295.)**

EXAMPLES   *You hear*   I heard a funny **yolk**.   *You write* _____ joke _____

               You hear   Please don't **jell** so loud.   *You write* _____ yell _____

1. _____
2. _____
3. _____
4. _____
5. _____
6. _____
7. _____
8. _____
9. _____
10. _____

CHECK YOURSELF 2

🎧 **Listen. Then circle all words pronounced with [dʒ] and underline all words pronounced with [j].**

Do you know what <u>YANKEE</u> means? People from the United States are sometimes called Yankees. Soldiers from the northern (region) were called Yankees during the Civil War. George M. Cohan wrote a stage hit called "Yankee Doodle Dandy." Jealous baseball fans waged war over the New York Yankees and Dodgers for years. Whether you are from Georgia or New Jersey, you should enjoy being called a Yank!

📖 **Check your answers. Then practice reading the paragraph aloud.**

EXERCISE A

Read aloud the following selection, written by William Shakespeare. Pay attention to the consonant [dʒ] in the word *age* and the consonant [j] in *young* and *youth*. Be sure to keep your tongue tip against your upper gum ridge for [dʒ] and in back of your lower front teeth for [j].

A Madrigal

Crabbed **Age** and **Youth**
Cannot live together.
Youth is full of pleasance,
Age is full of care
Youth like summer morn,
Age like winter weather,
Youth like summer brave,
Age like winter bare:
Youth is full of sport,
Age's breath is short,
Youth is nimble, **Age** is lame:
Youth is hot and bold,
Age is weak and cold,
Youth is wild, and **Age** is tame:
Age, I do abhor thee,
Youth, I do adore thee;
O! my Love, my Love is **young**!
Age, I do defy thee—
O sweet shepherd, hie thee,
For methinks thou stay'st too long.

EXERCISE B

Read aloud the following story about George Washington. The story contains words pronounced with many of the consonants you have practiced so far. Be sure to pronounce all the [ʃ], [tʃ], [ʒ], [dʒ], and [j] sounds correctly.

George Washington

[dʒ] [dʒ]　[ʃ]　　　　　　　　　　　　　　　　　[j]
Geor**g**e Wa**sh**ington was the first president of the **U**nited States. He
[dʒ]　　　　　　　　[tʃ]　　[dʒ]　　　　　[ʃ]
was a **j**ust man with mu**ch** **c**ourage. His contribu**ti**ons can never be
[ʒ]　　　[ʃ]　　　　　　　　　　[j]　　　　　[dʒ]　　[dʒ]
mea**s**ured. Wa**sh**ington was born in the **y**ear 1732 in Vir**g**inia. A le**g**end
　　　　　　[ʃ]　　　　　　　[tʃ]　　　　　　[tʃ]
about his boyhood **sh**ows his honesty. He **ch**opped down a **ch**erry tree,
　　　　　　[ʃ]　　　　　[dʒ]
but wouldn't lie to his father. Wa**sh**ington was a **g**eneral during the
　　[ʃ]　　　[ʃ]　　　[ʒ]　　　[ʃ]　　　　　[dʒ]
American Revolu**ti**on. He **sh**owed unu**s**ual compa**ss**ion to his sol**di**ers at

        [dʒ]   [tʃ]   [ʃ]   [ʃ]
Valley Forge. He was in **ch**arge at the Constitu**ti**onal Conven**ti**on. Finally,

                               [j]   [ʃ]
he was elected as the first president of the **U**nited States. Wa**sh**ington was

         [tʃ]   [ʒ]
a commander-in-**ch**ief whose deci**si**ons helped make America a great

    [ʃ]   [tʃ] [dʒ]   [ʃ] [ʃ]   [dʒ]   [ʃ]
na**ti**on. Past and fu**tu**re **g**enera**ti**ons **sh**all remember **G**eorge Wa**sh**ington

as the father of our country.

EXERCISE C   **Expressions of greeting often include words containing the consonant [j]. Work with a partner. Create mini-conversations practicing such phrases as "Nice to see *you*," "How are *you*?" and "Say hello to *your* wife."**

***You*'ll en*j*oy saying [dʒ] and [j]!**

CONGRATULATIONS! You've just completed the section with some of the most difficult consonants to say. To help perfect your pronunciation of the consonants you have studied so far, we've prepared a series of review activities for you. Please continue to Lesson 34.

34 Contrast and Review of [tʃ], [dʒ], and [j]

🎧 **Listen and repeat the words and sentences.**

[tʃ]	[dʒ]	[j]
1. **ch**ess	Jess	yes
2. **ch**oke	joke	yolk
3. **ch**eer	jeer	year
4. **c**ello	Jell-O	yellow
5. **ch**ew	Jew	you

          [tʃ]   [j]
6. Don't **choke** on the **yolk**.

  [dʒ]   [j]   [tʃ]
7. **Jess** said, "**Yes**, I will play **chess**."

     [j]   [tʃ]   [dʒ]
8. For **years** there were **cheers** and **jeers**.

    [dʒ] [tʃ]   [tʃ]   [j]
9. **Joe's child chose yellow**.

    [j]   [tʃ] [j]
10. **You** should **chew your** food.

Lesson 35 Additional Contrasts

EXERCISE A

🎧 **Listen and repeat.**

1. [θ]   [ʃ]
   - **th**ank   **sh**ank
   - **th**in   **sh**in
   - **th**igh   **sh**y

2. [z]   [dʒ]
   - **z**oo   **J**ew
   - head**s**   he**dge**
   - **z**one   **J**oan

3. [ð]   [dʒ]
   - **th**ey   **J**ay
   - **th**an   **J**an
   - **th**ough   **J**oe

4. [z]   [ʒ]
   - bay**s**   bei**g**e
   - ru**s**e   rou**g**e
   - Cae**s**ar   sei**z**ure

5. [ʒ]   [dʒ]
   - ver**s**ion   vir**g**in
   - le**s**ion   le**g**ion
   - plea**s**ure   ple**dg**er

🎧 **Listen and repeat.**

    [dʒ]   [j]   [ð] [z]
1. **Jan** is **younger than Zach**.

    [dʒ][ʃ]   [j]   [ʒ]   [ʃ]
2. **Magicians** use **illusions** in their **shows**.

    [z]   [dʒ]   [dʒ]
3. The **zipper** on my **jeans** is **jammed**.

    [ʃ] [θ]   [θ]   [ʃ]
4. **She thinks Thelma** is **shy**.

       [ʒ]   [z]   [ʒ]
5. The **seizure** of **Caesar** was in **Asia**.

PRONOUNCING [p]

Lips: Pressed together
Airstream: Stopped and then exploded
Vocal cords: Not vibrating

Possible Pronunciation Problems

This consonant is familiar to speakers of most languages. However, [p] is much more explosive in English than it is in other languages. When speaking English, [p] at the beginning of words must be produced with strong aspiration or it might sound like [b].

EXAMPLES If you forget to aspirate [p]: **pear** will sound like **bear**.

pat will sound like **bat**.

When *p* follows *s* (as in *spot*, *spend*, *spy*), it is NOT aspirated. Practice saying [p] by loosely holding a tissue in front of your lips. If you aspirate [p] correctly, releasing a puff of air, the tissue will flutter.

So *p*uff, *p*uff, *p*uff, and you'll *p*ronounce a *p*erfect [p]!

Practice

EXERCISE A 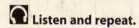 **Listen and repeat.**

[p] At the Beginning of Words			[p] In the Middle of Words			[p] At the End of Words		
pen	pay	pain	open	happy	supper	top	map	pipe
put	pig	past	apart	pepper	airport	cap	stop	jump
pet	pot	person	apple	paper	people	lip	soap	camp

Listen and repeat. The boldfaced words in the following phrases and sentences should be pronounced with [p].

1. **Stop** it!
2. **pencil** and **paper**
3. a **piece** of **pie**
4. **proud** as a **peacock**
5. **Open up**!
6. **Practice** makes **perfect**!
7. The **apples** and **pears** are **ripe**.
8. The **ship** will **stop** in **Panama**.
9. Wash the **pots** and **pans** with **soap**.
10. Her **purple pants** are **pretty**.

CHECK YOURSELF 1

Choose the correct word from the box to complete each of the sentences. Then practice reading the sentences aloud. (For answers to Check Yourself 1 and 2, see Appendix II, pages 295–296.)

peacock	peanuts	people	peeled	peach
Pete	peace	peeve	peak	*P*

1. A nickname for **Peter** is _____.
2. The **opposite** of war is _____.
3. **Pam** bought _____ to feed the elephants.
4. The **top** of a mountain is called a _____.
5. The **plural** of "**person**" is "_____."
6. A **popular** fruit is a _____.
7. A bird with bright feathers is a _____.
8. The **potatoes** should be washed well if they are not going to be _____.
9. The letter **preceding** *Q* is _____.
10. Something that annoys you is called a "**pet** _____."

CHECK YOURSELF 2

Listen to the dialogue. Circle the words that contain the consonant [p].

Peter: (Paulette), I have a (surprise!) We're taking a (trip) tonight!

Paulette: I'm very happy. But I need more time to prepare.

Peter: That's simple. I'll help you pack.

Paulette: Who will care for our pet poodle?

Peter:	Your parents!
Paulette:	Who will pick up the mail?
Peter:	Our neighbor, Pat.
Paulette:	Who will water the plants?
Peter:	We'll put them on the patio.
Paulette:	Who will pay for the trip?
Peter:	The company is paying every penny!
Paulette:	Peter, you've really planned this.
Peter:	Of course! I'm dependable, superior, and a perfect . . .
Paulette:	"Pain in the neck!" Don't get carried away!

Check to make sure you circled the words containing the consonant [p]. Then practice reading the dialogue with a partner.

More Practice

EXERCISE A

Read the nursery rhyme aloud. Pay attention to the boldfaced words containing the consonant [p].

Peter, Peter, Pumpkin Eater

Peter, **Peter**, **pumpkin** eater
Had a wife but couldn't **keep** her;
Put her in a **pumpkin** shell,
And there he **kept** her very well.

EXERCISE B

Work with a partner. Take turns reading the tongue twister. Pay attention to the boldfaced words containing the consonant [p].

Peter Piper

Peter Piper picked a **peck** of **pickled peppers**.
A **peck** of **pickled peppers Peter Piper picked**.
But if **Peter Piper picked** a **peck** of **pickled peppers**,
Where's the **peck** of **pickled peppers Peter Piper picked**?

Remember to *p*uff, *p*uff, *p*uff, and you'll *p*ronounce a *p*erfect [p]!

Lesson 37 [b] as in *boy*, *rabbit*, and *tub*

PRONOUNCING [b]

Lips: Pressed together (as for [p])
Airstream: Stopped and then exploded
Vocal cords: Vibrating

Possible Pronunciation Problems

1. Although the consonant [b] is a simple sound to pronounce, you may confuse it with the sound [v].

EXAMPLE   If you say [v] instead of [b]:   **boat** will sound like **vote**.

2. When [b] is the last sound in a word, many speakers forget to make their vocal cords vibrate. This will make [b] sound like [p] and confuse your listeners.

EXAMPLES   If you say [p] instead of [b]:   **robe** will sound like **rope**.

  cab will sound like **cap**.

The consonant [b] will be easy to say if you make your vocal cords vibrate and firmly press your lips together.

*B*e sure to say [b] with a *b*oom and you'll *b*e at your *b*est!

Practice

EXERCISE A   Listen and repeat.

[b] At the Beginning of Words			[b] In the Middle of Words			[b] At the End of Words		
be	best	boat	obey	rubber	label	cab	rib	crib
but	bone	begin	baby	lobby	ribbon	cub	rob	bulb
bat	bank	borrow	table	cabin	neighbor	rub	knob	robe
back			habit			tub		

The letter *b* is almost always pronounced [b]. Exception: When *b* follows *m* in the same syllable, it is NOT pronounced; it is silent.

com**b**   bom**b**   lam**b**   plum**b**er

EXERCISE B

🎧 **Listen and repeat. Make certain that your lips are pressed together and that you add voicing when saying [b].**

[b]	[p]
robe	rope
mob	mop
tab	tap
rib	rip
stable	staple
symbol	simple

EXERCISE C

🎧 **Listen and repeat. Pay attention to the consonant [b] in the boldfaced words.**

1. **bread** and **butter**
2. **above** and **below**
3. **baseball** game
4. **black** and **blue**
5. the **bigger**, the **better**
6. I'll **be back**.
7. **Bad habits** can **be broken**.
8. **Bill** is in the **lobby**.
9. **Bob bought** a **blue bathrobe**.
10. **Betty** was **born** in **Boston**.

CHECK YOURSELF

📖 **Circle the word that correctly completes each sentence. Then read the sentences aloud. Pay attention to the boldfaced words containing the consonant [b]. (For answers, see Appendix II, page 296.)**

EXAMPLE   **Ben's bicycle** needs new (**brakes**/ breaks).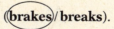

1. I like rye (**bread** / **bred**).
2. Don't walk in your (**bear** / **bare**) feet.
3. **Bob** has (**been** / **bin**) here **before**.
4. Please store the **beans** in the (**been** / **bin**).
5. The wind (**blew** / **blue**) my **bag** away.
6. **Betty's** (**blue** / **blew**) **bonnet** is **becoming**.

7. (**Buy** / **By**) a **box** of **black buttons**.

8. The dog will (**berry** / **bury**) its **bone** in the **backyard**.

9. My **brother** watches **baseball** when he's (**bored** / **board**).

10. The **builder** needs a **bigger** (**bored** / **board**).

More Practice

EXERCISE A

📖 **Read the paragraph aloud. Pay attention to the boldfaced words containing the consonant [b].**

The Heart

The heart is a powerful organ in the chest directly under the **breastbone**. It pumps **blood** around the **body**. **Beating** is an automatic **ability** of the heart. It **begins beating** in **embryonic** development **before** the **baby** is **born**. All **body** tissues need oxygen, which is carried to them **by** the circulating **blood**. If a person's heart stops **beating**, death will occur. In 70 years, a human's heart **beats about** 2 **billion** times. The heart is **able** to **beat** after its nerves have **been** cut. In fact, if it is kept in the proper type of liquid, it will **beat** even when removed from the **body**.

EXERCISE B

👥 **Read the dialogue. Then work with a partner. Carefully pronounce the [b] in the boldfaced word.**

Betty: **Ben**, I **bet** you forgot my **birthday**!

Ben: I **bet** I didn't. I **bought** you a **birthday** present.

Betty: I can't **believe** it. What did you **bring**?

Ben: It **begins** with the letter **B**.

Betty: Oh, **boy**! It must **be** a **bathrobe**. You **buy** me one every **birthday**.

Ben: It's not a **bathrobe**!

Betty: Is it a **bowling ball**?

Ben: No, it's not a **bowling ball**.

Betty: It must **be** a **book about boating**, your favorite **hobby**.

Ben: **Betty**, you're way off **base**. I **bought** you a **bracelet**. A **ruby bracelet**!

Betty: Wow! This is the **best birthday** present I ever got. You didn't **rob** a **bank**, did you?

Ben: Don't worry. I didn't **beg**, **borrow**, or steal. Just don't expect any more presents for a long time. I'm **broke**!

Work with a partner. Take turns reading the tongue twister aloud. Pay attention to the boldfaced words containing the consonant [b].

Betty Botta bought some **butter**
"**But**," said she, "This **butter's bitter**.
If I put it in my **batter**, it will make my **batter bitter**.
But a **bit** o' **better butter** will make my **batter better**."
So she **bought** a **bit** o' **butter better** than the **bitter butter**.
It made her **bitter batter better**.
So, 'twas **better Betty Botta bought** a **bit** o' **better butter**.

Say [b] with a *b*oom and you'll *b*e at your *b*est!

PRONOUNCING [f]

[f]

Upper teeth: Touching lower lip
Airstream: Continuous, without interruption
Vocal cords: Not vibrating

Possible Pronunciation Problems

The sound [f] should be produced with the upper teeth touching the lower lip. Some students tend to keep their lips apart and produce a sound similar to [h]. Others completely close their lips and make the sound [p].

EXAMPLES   If you say [h] instead of [f]:   **fat** will sound like **hat**.

If you say [p] instead of [f]:   **cuff** will sound like **cup**.

Feel your upper teeth touching your lower lip and your [f] will be perfectly fine!

Practice

EXERCISE A   🎧 **Listen and repeat. Be sure to feel your upper teeth touching your lower lip as you produce [f].**

[f] At the Beginning of Words		
for	fast	five
far	from	face
few	free	funny

[f] In the Middle of Words		
sofa	awful	before
offer	office	coffee
after	afraid	telephone

[f] At the End of Words		
if	leaf	laugh
off	half	cough
life	safe	graph

[f] Spelled

f	*ph*	*gh*
fat	phone	rough
fine	phrase	tough
foot	Philip	laugh
first	nephew	cough
stiff	physical	enough
effect	phonetics	
careful	telegraph	

180

The letter *f* is usually pronounced [f]. Exception: The *f* in the word **of** is pronounced [v].

The letters *ph* are usually pronounced [f].

photo tele**ph**one gra**ph**

EXERCISE B

🎧 **Listen and repeat. Pay attention to the pronunciation of the consonant [f] in the boldfaced words.**

1. **half** past **four**
2. **before** or **after**
3. **face** the **facts**
4. I'm **feeling fine**.
5. Do me a **favor**.
6. Answer the **phone**.
7. Are you **free** on **Friday afternoon**?
8. The **office** is on the **first floor**.
9. That **fellow** has a **familiar face**.
10. Do you **prefer fish** or **fowl**?

CHECK YOURSELF 1

📖 **Read the words in the box. Then read the numbered instructions, and write the appropriate word from the box on each line. (For answers to Check Yourself 1 and 2, see Appendix II, pages 296–297.)**

graph	photograph	phone	phonetics	philosopher
pharmacy	nephew	phonograph	physician	prophet

1. **Find** another name **for** a drugstore. _____
2. **Find** another name **for** a doctor. _____
3. **Find** another name **for** a snapshot. _____
4. **Find** the name **for** a person who studies **philosophy**. _____
5. **Find** the short **form** of the word **telephone**. _____
6. **Find** another name **for** a record player. _____
7. **Find** the name **for** a person who predicts the **future**. _____
8. **Find** the name **for** the study of sounds. _____
9. **Find** the term that **refers** to your sister's son. _____
10. **Find** the name **for** a chart showing **figures**. _____

🗣 **Take turns reading aloud the instructions and responses. Pay attention to your pronunciation of the boldfaced words containing the consonant [f].**

📖 **Read aloud the paragraph about Florida. Circle the words that contain the consonant [f]. Be sure your upper teeth touch your lower lip as you say [f].**

(Florida)

(Florida) was (founded) by Ponce de Leon in 1513. This famous explorer from Spain was searching for a fountain of youth. He named the land *Florida*, which means "full of flowers" in Spanish. He failed in his efforts to find the fountain. He finally died after fighting the Indians. Unfortunately, no one has ever found the fountain in Florida or the formula for eternal youth. However, the fun and sun in Florida are enough to attract folks from every hemisphere to this famous state.

Check your answers. Then read the paragraph aloud again. Be sure your upper teeth touch your lower lip as you say [f].

More Practice

📖 **Read the horoscope aloud. Pay attention to your pronunciation of the boldfaced words containing [f].**

Horoscope

If you were born on **February 15th**, this is your **fortune for** today . . . You are destined to **find fame** in the near **future**. Your **failures** will be **few** thanks to the help of loving **friends** or **family** members. **Unfortunately**, a **frail** neighbor **falls** and **fractures** a **foot**. Your social **life** revolves around **food**. In **February** you will attend an important **function** in a **far-off** land. A **favorite nephew forgives** you **for forgetting** to **fulfill** a **favor**. You will receive **flowers** and a **fax from** a **friend** in a **foreign** country.

♟ **List five characteristics of your favorite friend. Be sure your list includes words containing the consonant [f]. Then work with a partner. Take turns asking each other about your favorite friend.**

EXAMPLE   **A:** Tell me about your **favorite friend**.

　　　　　　 B: My **favorite friend** <u>laughs</u> at my jokes even when they are not <u>funny</u>.

Keep practicing and your [f] will be *f*ine!

Lesson 39 [v] as in *very*, *over*, and *save*

PRONOUNCING [v]

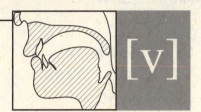

[v]

Upper teeth: Touching the lower lip (as for [f])
Airstream: Continuous, without interruption
Vocal cords: Vibrating

Possible Pronunciation Problems

1. Students frequently substitute [b] for [v] when speaking English. This can greatly confuse the listener!

EXAMPLES If you say [b] instead of [v]: **very** will sound like **berry**.
vest will sound like **best**.

2. When [v] is the last sound in a word, many speakers forget to vibrate their vocal cords. This will make [v] sound like [f] and confuse your listeners.

EXAMPLES If you say [f] instead of [v]: **save** will sound like **safe**.
leave will sound like **leaf**.

The sound [v] will be easy for you to say if you concentrate on placing your upper teeth over your bottom lip. Look in the mirror as you practice the consonant [v], and remember to make your vocal cords vibrate.

Your [v] will be *very* good!

Practice

EXERCISE A

Listen and repeat. Remember that you should feel your upper teeth touch your lower lip when you pronounce the consonant [v].

[v] At the Beginning of Words			[v] In the Middle of Words			[v] At the End of Words		
vine	very	valley	even	cover	movie	of	move	leave
vase	voice	vowel	over	river	clever	love	drive	carve
vote	visit	vacuum	every	heavy	eleven	live	stove	brave
vest			seven			have		

The letter *v* in English is always pronounced [v]. A less common spelling for [v] is the letter *f*.

of

EXERCISE B

🎧 **Listen and repeat. Remember to place your upper teeth over your bottom lip and add voicing for [v]. Be sure to prolong any vowel before the sound [v].**

	[v]	[b]		[v]	[f]
1.	vest	best	8.	vest	fest
2.	vow	bow	9.	leave	leaf
3.	very	berry	10.	very	ferry
4.	marvel	marble	11.	believe	belief
5.	vase	base	12.	vase	face
6.	veil	bail	13.	veil	fail
7.	van	ban	14.	van	fan

EXERCISE C

🎧 **Listen and repeat. The boldfaced words should be pronounced with the consonant [v].**

1. **very** good
2. **very** nice
3. **very** truly yours
4. **Move over!**
5. **over** and **over**
6. **rivers** and **valleys**
7. Please **vacuum** the **living** room.
8. **Have** you **ever** been to **Venice**?
9. The **vase** is **very heavy**.
10. Did **everyone leave** at **seven**?
11. **Eve** has a **severe fever**.
12. **Move** the **TV over** here.
13. **Vera never** eats **liver**.
14. **Steve** was **five** in **November**.
15. The **movie** got **rave reviews**!

Listen and indicate whether you hear the [v] sound at the *beginning* **(B),** *middle* **(M), or** *end* **(E) of the word. (For answers to Check Yourself 1–3, see Appendix II, page 297.)**

EXAMPLES *You hear* saving   *You hear* value

          You circle B Ⓜ E   *You circle* Ⓑ M E

1. B   M   E
2. B   M   E
3. B   M   E
4. B   M   E
5. B   M   E
6. B   M   E
7. B   M   E
8. B   M   E
9. B   M   E
10. B   M   E

CHECK YOURSELF 2 **Read the sentences aloud. Circle the word that correctly completes the sentence. Be sure your vocal cords are vibrating and you feel your top teeth touch your bottom lip as you produce [v]. Then check your answers.**

EXAMPLES (calves)/ calfs / caves)   My _____ are sore from walking.

1. (clever / clover / cover)   **Van** is a _____ student.

2. (clever / clover / cover)   I bought a **velvet** _____.

3. (berry / very / ferry)   **Vera** is _____ pretty.

4. (leaf / leave / live)   The train will _____ at **seven**.

5. (leaves / loves / lives)   **Vicky** _____ her sons, **Victor** and **Vance**.

6. (off / of / if)   My **vest** is made _____ leather.

7. (alive / arrive / live)   The plane will _____ at **five**.

8. (belief / believe / bereave)   I _____ **Vinny** will be **eleven** in **November**.

9. (several / severe / seventh)   **Eve** has _____ **TVs** in her **living** room.

10. (oven / over / overt)   He left before the **movie** was _____.

📖 **Read aloud the poem by Emily Dickinson. Circle the words that should be pronounced with the consonant [v].**

I (Never) Saw a Moor
Emily Dickinson

I never saw a moor,

I never saw the sea;

Yet know I how the heather looks,

And what a wave must be.

I never spoke with God,

Nor visited in Heaven;

Yet certain am I of the spot

As if the chart were given.

Check your answers. Read the poem aloud again. Be sure to feel your top teeth touching your bottom lip as you pronounce the [v] words.

More Practice

📖 **Read the joke aloud. Be sure to pronounce all the boldfaced [v] words correctly.**

Two **weevils** named **Vic** and **Van** grew up in a **village** in **Virginia**. **Vic moved** to Hollywood and became a **very** famous **television** actor. The other one, **Van**, stayed behind in **Virginia** and **never** amounted to much **of** anything. **Van**, naturally, became known as the lesser **of** two **weevils**!

Everyone likes to be complimented or praised! Work with a partner. Write a dialogue in which you compliment or praise each other. Use the expressions "very good," "very nice," "You look very well," "You have a very pretty sweater," or other expressions that include words containing the consonant [v].

Keep practicing *e*very day and your [v] will be *v*ery good!

Lesson 40 [h] as in *hat* and *behind*

PRONOUNCING [h]

Tongue: Glides into position for whichever vowel follows [h]
Airstream: Continuous
Vocal cords: Not vibrating

Possible Pronunciation Problems

The sound [h] is a familiar sound for many. However, in some languages it is silent, and you may omit it when speaking English. Some speakers substitute [f] or [ʃ] for [h] before the vowels [u] and [i].

EXAMPLES   If you omit [h]:   **hat** will sound like **at**.
                hand will sound like **and**.

If you say [f] instead of [h]:   **Hugh** will sound like **few**.

If you say [ʃ] instead of [h]:   **heat** will sound like **sheet**.

Relax your throat and tongue when you pronounce [h]. Gently let out a puff of air as if you were sighing.

Work *h*ard and you'll be *h*appy with [h]!

Practice

EXERCISE A   🎧 **Listen and repeat. Remember to let out a gentle puff of air as you say [h].**

[h] At the Beginning of Words			[h] In the Middle of Words		
he	here	home	ahead	inhale	perhaps
how	heat	hello	behind	anyhow	inherit
who	have	heart	behave	unhappy	rehearse

The consonant [h] does not occur at the end of words in English.

note   A less frequent spelling pattern for [h] is *wh*.

who   **wh**om   **wh**ose   **wh**ole

The letter *h* is silent when it follows *g*, *k*, or *r* at the beginning of words.

   ghost   **kh**aki   **rh**ubarb

The letter *h* is always silent in the words *honest*, *heir*, *honor*, *hour,* and *herb.*

EXERCISE B

🎧 **Listen and repeat. Be sure to distinguish between the words in each column and to pronounce the consonant [h] with a puff of air.**

Initial Vowel	[h]	[f]	[ʃ]
eat	heat	feet/feat	sheet
ear	hear/here	fear	sheer
air	hair	fare/fair	share
Ed	head	fed	shed
all	hall	fall	shawl
ease	he's	fees	she's

EXERCISE C

🎧 **Listen and repeat. Pay attention to your pronunciation of the consonant [h] in the boldfaced words.**

1. **Hurry** up!
2. **Who** is it?
3. **hand** in **hand**
4. What **happened**?
5. **How**'ve you been?
6. **Henry hit** a **home** run.
7. **Helen has** brown **hair**.
8. **Hank helped Herbert** carry the **heavy** box.
9. I **hate hot** and **humid** weather.
10. **Heaven helps** those **who help** themselves.

CHECK YOURSELF 1

📖 **Guess what? You're having a holiday! You're visiting places with names that contain the consonant [h]! Read the list aloud and circle the names of places containing [h]. (For answers to Check Yourself 1 and 2, see Appendix II, page 298.)**

(Ohio)	Michigan	Oklahoma	Houston
Idaho	Massachusetts	Washington	New Hampshire
Chicago	Hartford	Hawaii	Tallahassee

👤 **Check your answers. With a partner, practice the names of these places by using them in the sentence, "I'm having a holiday in _____."**

Read the dialogue aloud with a partner. Circle the words that contain the consonant [h].

Helen: (Hi), Mom. Welcome (home).

Mother: Hi, honey.

Helen: How was Holland?

Mother: Like a second honeymoon! I'm as happy as a lark. How are you?

Helen: Not so hot! Henry is in the hospital with a broken hip.

Mother: That's horrible. How did that happen?

Helen: He heard a noise outside. He went behind the house and fell over a hose.

Mother: How are my handsome grandsons?

Helen: They won't behave. And my housekeeper had to quit.

Mother: Perhaps you'd like me to help at home.

Helen: Oh, Mom, I was hoping you'd say that. Hurry to the house as soon as possible.

Mother: I guess the honeymoon is over. Here we go again!

Check your answers. Then change roles and read the dialogue aloud again.

More Practice

Read the paragraph aloud. Remember that all the boldfaced words should be pronounced with a clear, audible [h] sound.

From **Harrison** to **Hawaii**

Author Unknown

Someday, I **hope** to **have** a **happy home** in **Honolulu**, **Hawaii**. As I **rehash** my **hectic childhood** days, I **have** fond memories of our **household**, especially during the **holidays**. **However**, social life in the one-**horse** town of **Harrison** was not so **hot**. **Who** wants to live permanently amid **herds** of **heifers**? So it's with a not too **heavy heart** that I **head** for the surf. **Here's hoping** I like **Honolulu**!

Read aloud the lines from the poem. Be sure to aspirate the consonant [h] in each boldfaced word.

My **Heart's** in the **Highlands**

Robert Burns

My **heart's** in the **Highlands**, my **heart** is not **here**.
My **heart's** in the **Highlands**, a-chasing the deer—
A Chasing the wild deer, and following the roe;
My **heart's** in the **Highlands**, wherever I go.

Farewell to the **Highlands**, farewell to the North
The birth place of Valour, the country of Worth;
Wherever I wander, wherever I rove,
The **hills** of the **Highlands** for ever I love.

List the names of five things you have that contain the consonant [h]. Then work with a partner. Take turns asking each other what you have.

EXAMPLE   **A:** What do you **have**?
B: I **have** <u>two</u> **hamsters**.

Now list five things you have to do this week. Make sure the items on your list contain the consonant [h]. Work with your partner again. Take turns asking each other about the things you have to do.

EXAMPLE   **A:** What do you **have** to do this week?
B: I **have** to <u>get a</u> **haircut**.

Many expressions of greeting include words containing the consonant [h]. Work with a partner. Look at the expressions below.

EXAMPLES   Hi
Hello

Can you think of expressions to add to the list? Write a short dialogue containing some of the expressions. Practice the dialogue with a partner. Pay attention to your pronunciation of the words containing the consonant [h].

Do your *h*omework and you'll be *h*appy with [h]!

PRONOUNCING [w]

Lips: Rounded and in the same position as for the vowel [u]

Airstream: Continuous

Vocal cords: Vibrating

Possible Pronunciation Problems

1. It is easy to confuse [w] with [v]. If you make this error, it can completely change the meaning of the word you are saying.

EXAMPLES   If you say [v] instead of [w]:   **went** will sound like **vent**.

wheel will sound like **veal**.

2. Speakers of other languages sometimes omit [w] before the vowels [u] or [ʊ].

EXAMPLES   If you omit [w]:   **wool** will sound like **ool**.

wood will sound like **ood**.

As you start to produce the consonant [w], remember to completely round your lips as for [u]. Be sure your lower lip does NOT touch your upper teeth or you'll make a [v] instead.

Don't *w*orry! Keep *w*orking a*w*ay and your [w] *w*ill be *w*onderful!

Practice

EXERCISE A   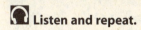 **Listen and repeat.**

[w] At the Beginning of Words			[w] In the Middle of Words		
we	word	wool	away	anyway	someone
was	work	would	awake	beware	quick
want	wait	women	always	between	choir

The consonant sound [w] does not occur at the end of words in English.

hint

The letter *w* is always pronounced [w] when followed by a vowel in the same syllable.

wood   **w**ill   back**w**ard   high**w**ay

The letter *w* at the end of a word is always silent.

how   sew   law   know

hint

Some English speakers use [hw] when pronouncing words spelled with *wh*, such as *when*, *where*, *white*, *wheel*, *awhile*, *somewhat*. They use aspiration and sound as if they are saying [h] before the [w]. Both [hw] and [w] are acceptable pronunciations of the letters *wh*.

EXERCISE B

🔊 **Listen and repeat. Pay attention to the boldfaced words containing the consonant [w].**

1. **What** do you **want**?
2. You're **welcome**.
3. **Where will** you be?
4. **Walk quickly**.
5. **Where** is it?
6. **Waste** not, **want** not!
7. **Which one** do you **want**?
8. **What was** the **question**?
9. The **women** are **wearing white**.
10. **Walt always works** on **Wednesday**.

EXERCISE C

🔊 **Listen and repeat. Be sure to distinguish between the [w] and [w]-blends in each pair.**

[w]	[tw]		[w]	[kw]		[w]	[sw]
1. win	twin	6. white	quite	11. wheat	sweet
2. wine	twine	7. wire	choir	12. wine	swine
3. wig	twig	8. wit	quit	13. wet	sweat
4. week/ weak	tweak	9. west	quest	14. well	swell
5. witch/ which	twitch	10. wick	quick	15. war	swore

CHECK YOURSELF 1 🎧 **Listen and repeat. Circle the words that are pronounced with [w]. (For answers to Check Yourself 1 and 2, see Appendix II, page 298.)**

(week)	someone	queen	write
while	who	wrong	worry
whose	waiter	reward	square
guilt	unwilling	saw	worthy
west	lawyer	anywhere	low

CHECK YOURSELF 2 📖 **Read aloud the paragraph about Woodrow Wilson. Circle all words that should be pronounced with [w].**

(Woodrow) (Wilson)

Woodrow Wilson was the twenty-fifth president of the United States. He will always be remembered for his work to establish world peace. Wilson was born in 1865 and went to Princeton University. He became president in 1913 and stayed in the White House for two terms. His first wife died while he was in office, and he later married a Washington widow. When the United States entered World War I in 1917, Wilson quickly provided the needed wisdom. After the war, Wilson made a nationwide tour to win support for the League of Nations. Wilson was awarded the Nobel Prize for his worthwhile work for peace. He died in 1924. Everywhere in the world, Wilson was thought of as a wise and wonderful leader.

Check your answers. Read the paragraph aloud again.

More Practice

EXERCISE A 📖 **Read the poem aloud. Pay attention to your pronunciation of the consonant [w] and [w]-blends in the boldfaced words.**

When I Was One-and-Twenty
A. E. Housman

When I **was one**-and-**twenty**
    I heard a **wise** man say,
"Give crowns and pounds and guineas
    But not your heart **away**;
Give pearls **away** and rubies
    But keep your fancy free,"
But I **was one**-and-**twenty**,
    No use to talk to me.

When I was **one**-and-**twenty**
    I heard him say again,
"The heart out of the bosom
    Was never given in vain;
'Tis paid **with** sighs a plenty
    And sold for endless rue."
And I am two-and-**twenty**,
    And oh, 'tis true, 'tis true.

EXERCISE B   ![icon] Now work with a partner. Take turns asking and answering the questions about Woodrow Wilson. Refer to the paragraph about Woodrow Wilson in Check Yourself 2, as needed, to complete the answers. Pay attention to the boldfaced words containing the consonant [w].

1. **When was Woodrow Wilson** born?

    Woodrow Wilson was born in _____.

2. How many **wives** did **Wilson** have **while** in the **White** House?

    Wilson had _____ **wives while** in the **White** House.

3. **When** did the United States enter **World War I**?

    The United States entered **World War I** in _____.

4. **Why was Wilson awarded** the Nobel Prize?

    Wilson was awarded the Nobel Prize for his _____.

5. **Where was Wilson** thought of as a **wise** and **wonderful** leader?

    Wilson was thought of as a **wise** and **wonderful**

    leader _____.

EXERCISE C   ![icon] Work with a partner. Ask your partner to tell you something he or she did recently (for example: went on a trip, went shopping, visited a friend, saw a movie). Ask your partner questions beginning with [w].

Keep *w*orking a*w*ay and your [w] *w*ill be *w*onderful!

PRONOUNCING [l]

[l]

Tongue tip: Pressed against gum ridge behind upper front teeth
Airstream: Continuous and passes over both sides of the tongue
Vocal cords: Vibrating

Possible Pronunciation Problems

The consonant [l] may not exist in your language. The differences between [l] and [r] may be difficult for you to hear, causing you to confuse the two sounds.

EXAMPLES If you say [r] instead of [l]: **flight** will sound like **fright**.
                                          late will sound like **rate**.

The consonant [l] will be easier for you to say if you concentrate on feeling your tongue tip press against your upper gum ridge like [t].

***Learn* your *lessons* we*ll*. You wi*ll* say a perfect [l]!**

Practice

EXERCISE A 🎧 **Listen and repeat the words. They should be pronounced with [l]. (When [l] is the last sound in a word, the back of the tongue should be raised higher than for [l] at the beginning or in the middle of words.)**

[l] At the Beginning of Words			[l] In the Middle of Words			[l] At the End of Words		
let	leg	long	only	alone	asleep	all	call	able
late	last	leave	hello	salad	yellow	fill	fool	table
light	little		family	believe		apple	trouble	
learn	live		balloon	alive		people	tell	

hint When an unstressed syllable begins with [t] or [d] and ends in [l], the [l] frequently becomes its own syllable. It is formed by keeping your tongue tip on your upper gum ridge without moving it from the position of the preceding [t] or [d].

      paddle   little   bottle   saddle   noodle

🎧 **Listen and repeat these short sentences. Remember to raise the back of your tongue higher when you say the [l] at the END of the boldfaced words.**

1. He's **ill**.
2. Linda is **tall**.
3. It's not **small**.
4. Don't **yell** at me.
5. I don't want to **fall**.

hint

Speakers of other languages frequently produce [l]-blends incorrectly by inserting a vowel between sounds (for example, *plight* becomes *polite*). When saying words pronounced with [l]-blends, take care not to incorrectly insert a vowel sound before the [l]. Lesson 52, Pronouncing Consonant Clusters (page 236), will give you lots of practice perfecting your pronunciation of various consonant clusters.

EXERCISE C

🎧 **Listen and repeat the phrases and sentences. The boldfaced words should be pronounced with [l].**

1. **telephone call**
2. **Leave** me **alone**.
3. **lots** of **luck**
4. **Light** the **candle**.
5. **Please believe** me.
6. **Learn** your **lesson well**.
7. **Will** you **mail** the **letter?**
8. The **little girl fell asleep**.
9. **Lucy lost** her **locket**.
10. He who **laughs last, laughs** best.
11. Do you **like chocolate** or **vanilla?**
12. The **airplane flight leaves** at **eleven**.
13. His **family lives** in **Maryland**.
14. You can't **fool all** of the **people all** of the time.
15. **Leave** the **umbrella** in the **hall closet**.

Read the dialogue aloud with a partner. Be sure the tip of your tongue touches your gum ridge as you pronounce the [l] sound in the boldfaced words.

Lillian: **Allan**, I just had a **telephone call** from Aunt **Lola**. **Uncle Bill** died.

Allan: **Uncle Bill** the **millionaire**?

Lillian: Yes. He **lived alone** in **Los Angeles**.

Allan: Did he **leave** us any money?

Lillian: **Well**, the **lawyer** is reading the **will** at **11:00**. I **really** don't **believe** he **left** his **family** anything!

Allan: **Uncle Bill** had to **leave** something to a **relative**.

Lillian: He **lived** with **lots** of **animals**. He didn't **like people**.

Allan: **Hold** it! **I'll** answer the **telephone**. (*Allan hangs up the phone.*) **Well**, **Lillian**, you're out of **luck**! **Uncle Bill left all** his "**loot**" to the **Animal Lovers' League**.

Lillian: Do you think **Lulu**, our **poodle**, is **eligible** for a **little**?

Read the sentences aloud. Fill in the blanks with the correct [l] country or state. (For answers to Check Yourself 1–3, see Appendix II, page 299.)

EXAMPLE If you **live** in **Los Angeles**, you **also live** in *California*_____.

1. If you **live** in **Dublin**, you **also live** in _____.
2. If you **live** in **London**, you **also live** in _____.
3. If you **live** in **Lisbon**, you **also live** in _____.
4. If you **live** in **Lucerne**, you **also live** in _____.
5. If you **live** in **Milan**, you **also live** in _____.
6. If you **live** in **Baltimore**, you **also live** in _____.
7. If you **live** in **Brussels**, you **also live** in _____.
8. If you **live** in **Orlando**, you **also live** in _____.
9. If you **live** in **São Paulo**, you **also live** in _____.
10. If you **live** in **New Orleans**, you **also live** in _____.

CHECK YOURSELF 2 Listen to ten pairs of words. ONE word in each pair contains [l]. Circle the number of the word with the consonant [l].

EXAMPLE   *You hear*   lane   rain

            You circle   ①   2

          1.   1   2
          2.   1   2
          3.   1   2
          4.   1   2
          5.   1   2
          6.   1   2
          7.   1   2
          8.   1   2
          9.   1   2
         10.   1   2

CHECK YOURSELF 3 Read the telegram aloud. Circle all words pronounced with [l].

(July)(11th)

Linda,

Leon and I had bad luck.—Luggage was lost while traveling from La Paz, Bolivia, to Honolulu.—Airline personnel were all very helpful.—They told Leon they will certainly locate all, eventually, if we're lucky.—It looks like the luggage landed in Lima.—At least we met lots of lovely people.—Also, we could leave on a later flight.—I'll telephone with new flight schedule.—We should be home for lunch with the family at twelve o'clock.—Hopefully, our arrival won't be delayed.—Talk to you later.—Love you a whole lot,—Lou.

Check your answers. Then read the telegram aloud again. Be sure to press the tip of your tongue against your upper gum ridge as you pronounce [l].

EXERCISE A

Read the dialogue aloud with a partner. Be sure to place your tongue tip on your gum ridge as you pronounce the boldfaced [l] words.

Paulette: Hi, **Elena**. **Let's** meet at **11:00** for a **long** walk.

Elena: OK, **Paulette**. **I'll** meet you by the **lake** at **eleven**.

Paulette: **Please** don't be **late**. I'm **playing golf later** with **Les**. He **likes** me to be **punctual**.

Elena: I can't **believe** you **still love** him. He **always calls** you at the **last** minute.

Paulette: **Well**, that's his **style**. I'm **glad** he **called**.

Elena: **Surely** there are **plenty** of **eligible bachelors** who **like** to **play golf**.

Paulette: You're **probably** right. But **Les** is good-**looking** and he **also** makes me **laugh**.

Elena: **Well**, he is an **excellent lawyer** and has a **lovely family**.

Paulette: You know, **Elena**, I **always** thought you'd make an **ideal sister-in-law**!

EXERCISE B

Everyone loves a compliment. Compliment at least five people you know. Use the following key phrases:

I **like** your _____(new blouse)_____.

You **look lovely** in _____(yellow)_____.

Your ___(leather gloves)___ are **really** nice.

That's a **lovely** _____(necklace)_____ you have on.

Learn your lessons well. You will say a perfect [l]!

43 [r] as in *red*, *marry*, and *far*

PRONOUNCING [r]

[r]

Lips: Rounded

Tongue tip: Curled upward but not touching the roof of the mouth

Airstream: Continuous

Vocal cords: Vibrating

Possible Pronunciation Problems

The sound [r] as it is produced in English may not exist in your language. Some speakers mistakenly produce [w] instead of [r]. Others often substitute the [l] sound. You see, the [r] in many languages is a blend of English [r] and [l] and is produced by rapidly touching your tongue tip to the roof of your mouth. Pronunciation problems occur when you attempt to say the English [r] by touching the roof of your mouth with your tongue. This results in the substitution of [l].

EXAMPLES If you say [l] instead of [r]:   **berry** will sound like **belly**.

rice will sound like **lice**.

If you say [w] instead of [r]:   **red** will sound like **wed**.

right will sound like **white**.

Make sure that the tip of your tongue never touches your upper gum ridge but is curled upward toward the roof of your mouth.

Remember to p*r*actice [r] ca*r*efully and you*r* [r] will be *r*ight on ta*r*get!

Practice

EXERCISE A

🎧 **Listen and repeat. Be sure your tongue does NOT touch your upper gum ridge when you say [r].**

[r] At the Beginning of Words

red	rest	real
run	rich	wrong
row	rain	write
read		

[r] In the Middle of Words

very	sorry	orange
marry	hurry	around
story	carrot	tomorrow
berry		

[r] At the End of Words

or	near	their
are	more	before
far	sure	appear
door		

EXERCISE B

🎧 **Listen and repeat. Each word contains an [r]-blend. Be careful not to insert a vowel before the consonant [r].**

1. **br**ing
2. **cr**y
3. **tr**ee
4. **pr**oud
5. **dr**ink
6. **fr**eeze
7. **gr**ow
8. **pr**ess
9. **br**oke
10. **dr**y

EXERCISE C

🎧 **Listen and repeat. Remember, your tongue should be in the same position as for the vowel [u] when you pronounce the consonant [w], and it should be curled upward toward the roof of your mouth as you pronounce the consonant [r].**

[r]	[w]
round	wound
array	away
rise	wise
rent	went
rest	west

EXERCISE D

🎧 **Listen and repeat. Pay attention to the consonant [r] in the boldfaced words.**

1. **Where are** you?
2. **near** or **far**
3. **Are** you **sure**?
4. See you **tomorrow**.
5. I'm **very sorry**.
6. He'll be **right there**.
7. **Roy returns tomorrow morning**.
8. The **train arrives every hour**.
9. I **already read** that **short story**.
10. **Rose** is **wearing** a **red dress**.
11. **Robert ran around** the **corner**.
12. **Rita** and **Larry are married**.
13. **Remember, never** put the **cart before** the **horse**!*
14. **Mark** couldn't **start** the **car**.
15. I **rented** a **four-room apartment**.

*This phrase means to do things backwards or in reverse order.

The first word in each of the pairs begins with the sound [r]. Write a letter in the blank before the second word to form a new [r]-blend word. (For answers to Check Yourself 1–3, see Appendix II, pages 299–300.)

EXAMPLE   ride   _____bride

1. rave   _____rave

2. right   _____right

3. rip   _____rip

4. ream   _____ream

5. row   _____row

6. rain   _____rain

7. rash   _____rash

8. room   _____room

9. round   _____round

10. race   _____race

📖 **Check your answers. Then read the words aloud. Try using them in your own sentences.**

📖 **Read the hints aloud. Identify the creature described. The names of the creatures all contain the consonant [r].**

1. This **creature** has black and white **stripes**.

   This **creature** is a _____.

2. This **forest creature** has long **ears** and is a **celebrity** at **Easter**.

   This **creature** is a _____.

3. This **creature** has **large antlers** and is **around** at **Christmas**.

   This **creature** is a _____.

4. This **creature** has spots and a **very** long neck.

   This **creature** is a _____.

5. This **creature** lives in the **arctic**, is **large**, and is **very hungry**.

   This **creature** is a **polar** _____.

6. This **forest creature carries her** babies in a pouch.

   This **creature** is a _____.

7. This **friendly creature** "croaks" and says **"ribbit, ribbit."**

   This **creature** is a _____.

8. This **forest creature** is a very talkative bird.

   This **colorful creature** is a _____.

9. This **fierce creature** has black and yellow **stripes**.

   This **ferocious creature** is a _____.

10. This **graceful creature started** as a **caterpillar**.

    This **pretty creature** is a _____.

CHECK YOURSELF 3 📖 **Read the paragraph about Robin Hood. Circle all the words pronounced with the consonant [r].**

(Robin) Hood

The story of Robin Hood has been retold many times. Robin Hood was an outlaw who lived in Sherwood Forest. He lived there with Maid Marion, Friar Tuck, and others. Robin was really a hero rather than a criminal. He robbed the rich and gave to the poor. He was a remarkable marksman with his bow and arrow. The story of Robin Hood has been written about and dramatized since the eleventh century. Robin truly represents a righteous figure opposing cruelty and greed.

Check your answers. Then practice reading the paragraph aloud.

More Practice

EXERCISE A 📖 **Read the paragraph aloud. Pay attention to the boldfaced words containing the consonant [r].**

Rabbits

Rabbits represent some of **our favorite characters** in **literature. Children** enjoy **reading** about **Peter Rabbit** and his **adventures** with **Farmer McGregor.** The white **rabbit** was **featured** in the **remarkable story** of Alice in **Wonderland** by Lewis **Carroll.** The fable about the **tortoise** and the **hare (rabbit) describes** the **rabbit** as a fast **runner** who loses the **race** because he is too **sure** of himself. One of the most **renowned rabbits** is Bugs Bunny, the **cartoon character** who munches on **carrots** and asks, "What's up, Doc?" Bugs Bunny is **smart**, but he **frequently** gets into **trouble.** Even **grown-ups** like **rabbits.** The **Broadway** play *Harvey* was about a man whose pal was an **imaginary rabbit** named **Harvey.** Of **course**, the man was thought to be **crazy**, but in the end **everyone** believed in this **incredible rabbit.** So let's **hear** it for **rabbits**, our good **friends**!

▼ **Work with a partner. List as many expressions and phrases as you can think of using the word *right*.**

EXAMPLES   right away

right of way

just right

Then write a dialogue that includes one or more of the expressions and phrases on your list. Practice reading your dialogue together. Pay attention to the words containing the consonant [r].

Remember to practice [r] carefully and your [r] will be right on target!

Contrast and Review of [l] and [r]

🎧 **Listen and repeat the pairs of words. Be sure the tip of your tongue touches your gum ridge for [l] but not for [r].**

Contrast at the Beginning of Words		Contrast in the Middle of Words		Contrast at the End of Words	
[l]	[r]	[l]	[r]	[l]	[r]
late	rate	elect	erect	tile	tire
led	red/read	collect	correct	stall	star
low	row	believe	bereave	foil	foyer
list	wrist	palate	parrot	pail	pair
lose	ruse	alive	arrive	file	fire

🎧 **Listen and repeat the sentences. Be sure to clearly pronounce the difference between [l] and [r] in the boldfaced words.**

[l]	[r]
1. Move toward the **light**.	Move toward the **right**.
2. There is a **lack** of lamb.	There is a **rack** of lamb.
3. He's on the **long** line.	He's on the **wrong** line.
4. Please don't **lock** it.	Please don't **rock** it.
5. The teacher **collected** the work.	The teacher **corrected** the work.

  　　　　　　　[l]　　　　　　　　[r]
6. Carry that **load** down the **road**.

  　　　　　　　　[l]　　　　　　　　[r]
7. The Versailles **palace** is near **Paris**.

  　　　　　[r]　　　　　　　[l]
8. I lost my **rake** near the **lake**.

  　　　[l]　　　　　　　　　　　[r]
9. He **lied** about taking a long **ride**.

  　　[r]　　　　　[l]
10. **Jerry** likes **jelly** on his bread.

🎧 **Listen and repeat the [l]- and [r]-blend pairs aloud. Remember to produce the blend at the beginning of each word without inserting a vowel.**

EXAMPLE   bloom/broom (NOT baloom/barroom)

	[l]	**[r]**
1.	flea/flee	free
2.	glaze	graze
3.	clue	crew
4.	clam	cram
5.	blues	bruise
6.	They went to **play**.	They went to **pray**.
7.	It will **glow**.	It will **grow**.
8.	I saw her **blush**.	I saw her **brush**.
9.	Did they **clash**?	Did they **crash**?
10.	The **cloud** disappeared.	The **crowd** disappeared.

       [r]   [l]
11. We had a **fright** on the **flight**.

       [r]   [l]
12. That **brand** of food is **bland**.

     [l]   [r]
13. The **clown** was wearing a **crown**.

  [r]   [l]
14. **Fred fled** from the room.

     [l]   [r]
15. I hope **Blake** doesn't **break** his leg.

🎧 **You will hear the sentences using only ONE of the choices. Listen and circle the word used. (For answers to Check Yourself 1–3, see Appendix II, pages 300–301.)**

        [pl]   [pr]
EXAMPLE   We all like (plays /(praise)).

       [gl]   [gr]
1. Don't step on the (glass/grass).

       [l]   [r]
2. Please put this on your (list/wrist).

       [pl]   [pr]
3. The entire family is (pleasant/present).

       [kl]   [kr]
4. It was a terrible (climb/crime).

       [fl]   [fr]
5. Look at the bright red (flame/frame).

       [kl]   [kr]
6. He likes black (clothes/crows).

       [bl]   [br]
7. She has the (blues/bruise).

[bl]   [br]

8. That's a new (bloom / broom).

[l]   [r]

9. I lost the (lock / rock).

[l]   [r]

10. We need new (tiles / tires).

CHECK YOURSELF 2 🎧 **Listen carefully to five sentences. One word in each sentence will be said INCORRECTLY. Write the CORRECT word.**

EXAMPLE   *You hear*   Make a **light** turn at the corner.   *You write* _____ right _____

               You hear   He had a **berry** ache.   *You write* _____ belly _____

1. _____

2. _____

3. _____

4. _____

5. _____

CHECK YOURSELF 3 📖 **Read aloud the sentences about color. Fill in the blank with the correct color selected from the words in the box.**

red	yellow	green	blue	orange	lavender
black	brown	gray	purple	blonde	

EXAMPLE   Valentines are always _____ red _____.

1. The color of Halloween pumpkins is _____.

2. I like bananas that are ripe and _____.

3. Caribbean waters are usually a bright _____.

4. Emeralds should be a clear _____.

5. Fran's lipstick is a deep _____.

6. Formal attire requires _____ tie.

7. People frequently use color when their hair turns _____.

8. "Brunette" describes someone with _____ hair.

9. The color of orchids is often deep _____

    or _____.

10. Many models use lemon juice to give their hair _____

    highlights.

More Practice

📖 **Read aloud the paragraph about Elizabeth Barrett Browning and her famous poem. Be sure to pronounce the boldfaced [r] and [l] sounds correctly.**

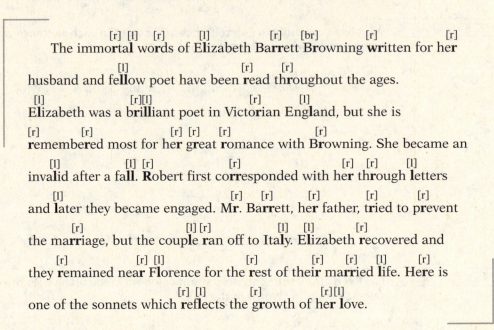

                    [r] [l]   [r]   [l]   [r]   [br]   [r]   [r]
         The immortal words of Elizabeth Barrett Browning written for her
               [l]   [r]   [r]
husband and fellow poet have been read throughout the ages.
    [l]   [r][l]   [r]   [l]
Elizabeth was a brilliant poet in Victorian England, but she is
[r]   [r]   [r] [r]   [r]   [r]
remembered most for her great romance with Browning. She became an
    [l]   [l] [r]   [r]   [r] [r]   [l]
invalid after a fall. Robert first corresponded with her through letters
      [l]   [r]   [r]   [r]   [r]   [r]
and later they became engaged. Mr. Barrett, her father, tried to prevent
      [r]   [l] [r]   [l] [l]   [r]
the marriage, but the couple ran off to Italy. Elizabeth recovered and
    [r]   [r] [l]   [r]   [r] [r] [l] [r]
they remained near Florence for the rest of their married life. Here is
                       [r] [l]   [r]   [r][l]
one of the sonnets which reflects the growth of her love.

How Do I Love Thee?
Elizabeth Barrett Browning

              [l]   [l]
How do I love thee? Let me count the ways.

  [l]   [r]
I love thee to the depth and breadth and height

         [l]   [r]   [l]
My soul can reach, when feeling out of sight

  [r]   [l] [r]
For the ends of Being and ideal Grace.

  [l]   [l] [l]   [r]
I love thee to the level of every day's

                          [l][l]
Most quiet need, by sun and candlelight.

  [l]   [r] [l]   [r]   [r]
I love thee freely as men strive for Right.

[l]   [r][l]   [r] [r]   [r]
I love thee purely, as they turn from Praise;

[l]
I love thee with the passion put to use

      [l] [r]   [l]
In my old griefs, and with my childhood's faith.

    [l]   [l]   [l]
I love thee with a love I seemed to lose

         [l]   [l]   [r]
With my lost saints,—I love thee with the breath,

    [l]   [r]   [l] [l]
Smiles, tears, of all my life! and, if God choose,

    [l]   [l]   [r]
I shall but love thee better after death.

EXERCISE B

📖 **Read the limerick aloud. Pay careful attention to the boldfaced [l] and [r] sounds.**

    [l]   [r]
Ilene and Irene

    [l] [l] [l]   [l]   [l]
A lovely blonde lady named Ilene

    [r]   [r]   [r]
Had a rowdy friend named Irene.

    [r]   [l]
Irene shouted out loud

     [l]   [r]
When alone or in a crowd

  [l] [l]   [r]   [r] [r]   [r]
While Ilene remained proper and serene.

Lesson 45 [k] as in *cake*, *car*, and *book*

PRONOUNCING [k]

Back of tongue: Touching the soft palate
Airstream: Stopped and then exploded
Vocal cords: Not vibrating

Possible Pronunciation Problems

[k] is an easy consonant for you to say. Just remember that [k] is very explosive in English. When it begins a word, it must be said with strong aspiration and a puff of air. When *k* follows *s* (as in *sky*, *skin*, *skate*), however, it is NOT aspirated with a puff of air.

Keep practicing. You *c*an say [k] OK!

More Practice

EXERCISE A   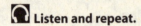 **Listen and repeat.**

[k] At the Beginning of Words

can	come
car	quick
key	could
cold	correct
keep	

[k] In the Middle of Words

cookie	walking
become	because
record	mechanic
jacket	backward
inquire	

[k] At the End of Words

like	make
took	clock
week	speak
sick	black
work	

[k] Spelled

k	*c*	*qu* ([kw])	*x* ([ks])
kite	coat	quit	six
kill	cone	quick	box
lake	acre	quiet	wax
keep	class	quote	exit
bake	crime	square	mixture

note

A less frequent spelling pattern for [k] consists of the letters *ch*.

chorus   **ch**rome   me**ch**anic   **Ch**ristmas

hint

The most common spelling pattern for [k] is *k*.

The letters *qu* are usually pronounced [kw].

    queen   **qu**ite   re**qu**ire

The letter *c* before *a*, *o*, or *u* is usually pronounced [k].

    cap   be**c**ause   **c**omb   be**c**ome   **c**ut

The letter *k* followed by *n* is usually NOT pronounced; it is silent.

    knit [nɪt]   knot [nat]   know [noʊ]

EXERCISE B

📖 **Read the phrases and sentences aloud. Be sure to pronounce any [k] at the beginning of the boldfaced words with a puff of air.**

1. **Keep quiet**.
2. **milk** and **cookies**
3. **Call** it **quits**.
4. **cup** of **coffee**
5. **Can** I **come** in?
6. **Speak clearly**.
7. I **like black coffee**.
8. **Carol** is **working** as a **cook**.
9. **Pack** your **clothes** for the **weekend**.
10. **Can** the **bookkeeper keep accurate records**?

CHECK YOURSELF 1

📖 **Read aloud each four-word series. Circle the ONE word in each group of four that is NOT pronounced with [k]. (For answers to Check Yourself 1 and 2, see Appendix II, page 301.)**

EXAMPLE	(rice)	rack	rake	wreck
1.	course	count	choose	chorus
2.	can't	can	cent	cone
3.	Canada	Texas	Kansas	Massachusetts
4.	key	keep	keen	kneel
5.	celery	corn	carrots	cabbage

Check your answers. Then read aloud each four-word series again.

6. mix	box	explain	xylophone
7. knee	back	ankle	cheek
8. Charles	Carol	Chris	Michael
9. mechanic	much	chrome	Christmas
10. milk	cider	coffee	cream

CHECK YOURSELF 2 📖 **Read the paragraph aloud. Circle all the words that should be pronounced with [k].**

The 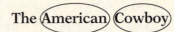 American Cowboy

Americans created the name *cowboy* for the men who cared for cattle. You might recall the typical singing cowboy in the movies. He was kind, courageous, and good-looking. He always caught the cow, colt, and of course the girl! But the real cowboy was a hard worker who had many difficult tasks. He had to take the cattle to market. These lonely cattle drives took many weeks through rough country. The cowboy had to protect the cattle and keep them from running off. In fact or fiction, the cowboy will continue to be a likeable American character. *Ride 'em cowboy*!

Check your answers. Then practice reading aloud "The American Cowboy" once again.

More Practice

EXERCISE A 👤 **Read the dialogue aloud with a partner. Be sure to pronounce all the boldfaced words correctly.**

Ken: Dad, I've been **packing** all **week** for **Camp Keekeekuma**. I **can't** wait to get there. Do you remember your **camping** days?

Dad: You bet. I was a **camper** and then a **counselor** at **Camp Keekeekuma**.

Ken: What **kinds** of **activities** did you **like**?

Dad: I was in charge of **canoeing**. We went out on **Lake Keekeekuma** for swimming, **canoeing**, and **waterskiing**.

Ken: I hope we go **hiking** and **camp** out.

Dad: You **can count** on it. You'll even **cook** hot dogs at **campfires**.

Ken: Did you ever get **homesick**?

Dad: Not really, but don't worry. You'll **make** friends with all the **kids** in your **cabin**. Let's **check** your **suitcase** to be sure you have everything on the **camp** list.

Ken: Dad, you don't have to; I've already **completed** everything.

Dad: Oh, **come** on. Let me see. **Camp** shorts and shirts, **comfortable clothing**. Wait, I see you've got my **camera**.

Ken: I know. I want to take **pictures**.

Dad: **OK**, but **next** time, **ask**! Let's see. You have a **jacket** for the **cool** nights. Plenty of **socks**. Wait a minute, what are these **cookies** and **candies**?

Ken: Dad, please leave those **packages** alone. You know how hungry a **camper can** get.

Dad: **OK**, but what's **covered** up? Why it's your **kitten**, **Katie**! **Ken**, you know you **can't take** pets to **camp**.

Ken: I guess I got **caught**! Oh, well, take good **care** of **Katie** while I'm at **camp**!

EXERCISE B

Ask new people you meet, "What kind of work do you do?" Every time you ask for a "cup of black coffee" or "coffee with milk or cream," carefully pronounce [k]!

Keep pra*c*ticing and . . . you *c*an say [k] O*K*.

[g] as in *go*, *begin*, and *egg*

PRONOUNCING [g]

[g]

Back of tongue: Touching the soft palate
Airstream: Stopped and then exploded
Vocal cords: Vibrating

Possible Pronunciation Problems

[g] should be an easy consonant for you to say. However, when [g] is the last sound in a word, you might forget to add voicing or substitute [k] by mistake. This will change the meaning of your words.

EXAMPLES   If you say [k] instead of [g]:   **bag** will sound like **back**.

If you say [ŋ] instead of [g]:   **rug** will sound like **rung**.

Always make your vocal cords vibrate for [g] at the end of words. Let your [g] GO with an explosion.

Your [g] has got to be good!

Practice

EXERCISE A   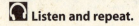 **Listen and repeat.**

[g] At the Beginning of Words

go	guess
get	green
girl	glass
gone	gather
great	

[g] In the Middle of Words

cigar	bigger
agree	hungry
begin	beggar
anger	cigarette
forget	

[g] At the End of Words

beg	dog
pig	egg
bag	drug
rug	flag
log	

[g] Spelled

g		*x* ([gz])	
green	beggar	exact	exhibit
glass	egg	exert	example
hungry	drug	exam	exist

Listen and repeat the pairs of words. Be sure to make your vocal cords vibrate for [g] and to prolong any vowel BEFORE the sound [g].

[g]	[k]
bag	ba**ck**
pig	pi**ck**
log	lo**ck**
dug	du**ck**
tag	ta**ck**

Read the phrases and sentences aloud. The boldfaced words should be pronounced with [g].

1. **good** night
2. I don't **agree**.
3. Where are you **going**?
4. **begin again**
5. a **good girl**
6. a **big dog**
7. **Peggy** is **going** to the **game**.
8. The **dog dug** up his bone **again**.
9. There's a **big bug** on the **rug**.
10. All that **glitters** is not **gold**.

Read aloud the series of words containing [g]. In the blanks provided, write your own sentence using the three [g] words. Be sure to pronounce the [g] words carefully. (For answers to Check Yourself 1 and 2, see Appendix II, pages 301–302.)

EXAMPLE   girl   angry   forgive

    The girl is too angry to forgive her friend.

1. luggage   tag   forget

   _____

2. grow   garden ground

   _____

3. dog   growl   bug

   _____

4. green   grass   log

   _____

5. glad   gift   groom

   _____

📖 **Mr. and Mrs. Green are planning a menu for their guests. Only foods pronounced with [g] will be served. Read the menu aloud and circle all items pronounced with [g].**

Breakfast			
(Grapefruit)	Fried eggs	Grits	Sausage
Lunch			
Hamburgers	Grilled onions	Gelatin	Vinegar dressing
Dinner			
Lasagna	Leg of lamb	Green peas	Chicken gumbo
Dessert			
Angel food cake	Glazed doughnuts	Grapes	Figs

Check your answers. Then practice each circled [g] menu item by saying it in the sentence ,"I'm going to eat _____." Be sure to pronounce all [g] menu items correctly!

More Practice

EXERCISE A   📖 **Read the Aesop fable aloud. Pay attention to the boldfaced words containing the consonant [g].**

The **Goose** That Laid the **Golden Eggs**

One day a farmer was **going** to the nest of his **goose**. He found an **egg** that was all yellow, very **big** and **glittering**. At first, he **guessed** it was the **glow** of the sun reflected on the **egg**. But when he **gazed** at it carefully, he realized that it was an **egg** of pure **gold**. Every morning he would **eagerly go** back to the **goose** and find another **big golden egg**. He **grew** to be very rich and **greedy**. He thought that he could **get** all the **gold** at once if he could only **get** inside the **goose**. So this **greedy** man killed the **goose** and opened it up—only to find nothing!

We have all met individuals who are **greedy** and want more than they are already **getting**. For **example**, when people **bargain** on a purchase, if they **go** too low in their bid, they may **anger** the seller and lose the object. Remember: *"Don't kill the **goose** that lays the **golden eggs**."*

Every time you use the word *good* **in conversation ("Good morning," "You look good," "Did you have a good time?" etc.), be sure to pronounce [g] correctly.**

Work with a partner. List as many expressions and phrases as you can think of using the word *good* **or other [g] words.**

EXAMPLES   Good morning.
You look good.
I had a great time.

Then write a dialogue that includes the expressions on your list. Practice reading your dialogue aloud with a partner. Pay attention to the words containing the consonant [g].

Your [g] has got to be good!

PRONOUNCING [m]

[m]

Lips: Together in a "humming" position
Airstream: Continuous through the nose
Vocal cords: Vibrating

Possible Pronunciation Problems

This is a familiar sound to you; it will be easy to say in the beginning and middle of words. However, you might substitute the more familiar [n] or [ŋ] at the end of words in English.

EXAMPLE   If you say [n] instead of [m]:   **some** will sound like **sun**.
If you say [ŋ] instead of [m]:   **swim** will sound like **swing**.

**Re*m*e*m*ber, *m*ake your lips co*m*e together in a "hu*mm*ing" position for [m].
Say "*mmmmmmmm*" and your [m] will be *m*arvelous!**

Practice

EXERCISE A   🎧 **Listen and repeat.**

[m] At the Beginning of Words		[m] In the Middle of Words		[m] At the End of Words	
me	mean	army	summer	am	time
may	month	among	hammer	him	room
mat	matter	lemon	policeman	them	come
more	minute	animal	something	seem	comb
milk		camera		name	

EXERCISE B   🎧 **Listen and repeat the phrases and sentences. The boldfaced letters should be pronounced as [m]. Remember, keep your lips together as you pronounce [m].**

1. ar**m** in ar**m**
2. le**m**on and li**m**e
3. su**mm**erti**m**e
4. What's your na**m**e?
5. What ti**m**e is it?

6. Don't blame **me**.

7. The poe**m** doesn't rhy**me**.

8. Sa**m** is a co**mm**on American na**me**.

9. What ti**me** is my appoint**m**ent?

10. Tell the**m** to come ho**me**.

11. Ti**m** is from a far**m**.

12. Give Pa**m** some **m**ore ha**m**.

13. The ho**me** team won the ga**me**.

14. The picture fra**me** is **m**ade of chro**me**.

15. **Mom m**akes ho**m**e**m**ade ice crea**m**.

CHECK YOURSELF 1 🎧 **Listen to each three-word series. Only ONE word in each series will have the [m] sound. Circle the number of the word with [m]. (For answers to Check Yourself 1 and 2, see Appendix II, page 302.)**

EXAMPLE

You hear	some	son	sung
You circle	①	2	3

1. 1 2 3   4. 1 2 3

2. 1 2 3   5. 1 2 3

3. 1 2 3

CHECK YOURSELF 2 📖 **Read aloud the paragraphs describing famous people with the initials *M.M.* Fill in the blanks with the correct name from the box below. Be sure to pronounce all [m] sounds correctly.**

Molly Malone	**Mickie Mouse**	**Margaret mitchell**
Mickey Mantle	**Mitchell Martin**	**Marilyn monroe**

1. **Norma** Jean Baker was her real **name**. She **became** a **film** star and a sex **symbol** throughout the world. She **made** over 30 **movies** including **comedies**, **romances**, and **mysteries**. She was **married** to two famous **men**: Joe **DiMaggio**, the baseball player, and the author Arthur **Miller**. Her last **film** was *The Misfits*. Although she died at age 36, she has been **immortalized** in **documentaries**, **movies**, and books.

   She is M_____ M_____.

2. He is a **famous** baseball player. He was a **member** of the New York Yankees. He was inducted into the Baseball Hall of **Fame**. He held the record for the longest **home** run ever hit. **Many** have said that no **man** has had **more** power than this baseball legend.

   He is M_____ M_____.

3. She wrote one of the **most famous** books of all time. Her book was **made** into a **motion** picture about the South. Her **hometown** of Atlanta **became** the focus of that **movie** starring the **handsome** Clark Gable and the **magnificent** Vivien Leigh.

She is **M**_____ **M**_____.

4. He is a **famous** cartoon figure. He has appeared in **many comics**, and **movies made** by Disney. You can **meet him** at Disney World and Disneyland any **time**. His **companion's name** is **Minnie**.

He is **M**_____ **M**_____.

Check your answers.

More Practice

EXERCISE A

Read the poem aloud with a partner. Be sure to put your lips together for all the boldfaced [m] words. (*Abou* is pronounced as [abu] and rhymes with *shoe*.)

Abou Ben **Adhem**
Leigh Hunt

Abou Ben **Adhem** (**may** his tribe increase!)
Awoke one night **from** a deep **dream** of peace,
And saw, within the **moonlight** in his **room**,
Making it rich, and like a lily in **bloom**,
An angel writing in a book of gold:

Exceeding peace had **made** Ben **Adhem** bold,
And to the Presence in the **room** he said,
"What writest thou?" The Vision raised its head,
And with a look **made** of sweet accord
Answered, "The **names** of those who love the Lord."

"And is **mine** one?" said Abou. "Nay, not so,"
Replied the angel. Abou spoke **more** low,
But cheerily still; and said, "I pray thee, then,
Write **me** as one who loves his fellow **men**."

The angel wrote, and vanished. The next night
It **came** again with a great awakening light,
And showed the names **whom** love of God had blessed,
And lo! Ben **Adhem's name** led all the rest.

EXERCISE B

Every time you meet someone new, be sure to use the phrase, "What's your name?" If someone asks your name, be sure to respond, "My name is . . ."

Re*m*e*m*ber to say "*mmmmmmmmmm*" and your [m] will be *m*arvelous!

Lesson 48 [n] as in *no* and *run*

PRONOUNCING [n]

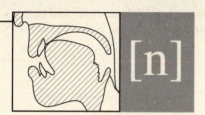

[n]

Tongue: Firmly pressed against gum ridge behind upper front teeth

Airstream: Continuous through the nose

Vocal cords: Vibrating

Possible Pronunciation Problems

Because of the similarity of the nasal consonants [m], [n], and [ŋ], many speakers frequently confuse them in English, particularly at the end of words.

EXAMPLES   If you say [m] instead of [n]:   **sun** will sound like **some**.

If you say [ŋ] instead of [n]:   **ran** will sound like **rang**.

ALWAYS press your tongue tip firmly against the gum ridge behind your upper front teeth as you say [n], especially at the end of words.

Practice this sound again and again; you'll have a fine pronunciation of [n]!

Practice

EXERCISE A   **Listen and repeat. Remember, tongue tip up!**

[n] At the Beginning of Words		[n] In the Middle of Words		[n] At the End of Words	
no	nail	any	dinner	in	fine
new	neck	many	tennis	on	begin
net	need	money	runner	can	again
know	night	window	candle	when	tin
knee		banana		then	

hint

The letter *n* is almost always pronounced [n]. Exception: When *n* follows *m* in the same syllable, it is usually NOT pronounced; it is silent.

column**n**   solem**n**   hym**n**

EXERCISE B

🎧 **Listen and repeat the phrases and sentences. The boldfaced words should be pronounced with [n]. Remember, tongue tip up (especially when [n] is the last sound in a word).**

1. **Answer** the **phone**.
2. Come **again**.
3. **rain** or **shine**
4. I **don't know**.
5. **Open** the **window**.
6. Leave me **alone**.
7. **Dinner** is **between seven and nine**.
8. **Dan** is a **fine man**.
9. The **brown pony** is **in** the **barn**.
10. **Ben** will be **on** the **ten** o'clock **train**.
11. Come **down when** you **can**.
12. **Everyone** has **fun** in the **sun**.
13. I **need** a **dozen lemons**.
14. **Turn on** the **oven** at **noon**.
15. **John** has a **broken bone**.

CHECK YOURSELF 1

🎧 **Listen to the pairs of sentences. Circle S if both sentences in the pair are the SAME. If they are DIFFERENT, circle D. (For answers to Check Yourself 1 and 2, see Appendix II, page 302.)**

EXAMPLES	*You hear*	Is it **Tim**? Is it **tin**?	*You circle*	S	Ⓓ
	You hear	I feel **fine**. I feel **fine**.	*You circle*	Ⓢ	D

1. S   D
2. S   D
3. S   D
4. S   D
5. S   D

📖 **Read the paragraph aloud. Fill in the blanks with one of the words from the list below. Remember to press your tongue tip firmly against your gum ridge when you pronounce [n].**

than	then	on	in	can
can't	into	and	down	

When **John** got home, his wife **Gwen** was _____ the **kitchen**. She was _____ the **phone again**. It was later _____ he realized; it was already **ten** o'clock! **John** was so tired he **went** to his bedroom. _____ he sat _____ **on** his bed **and** took off his shoes _____ socks. "_____ you get off that **phone**," he called to **Gwen**. "Yes, I _____," she yelled back. But by the time **Gwen** walked _____ the room, **John** was fast asleep!

More Practice

📖 **Read the e-mail aloud. Pay attention to all the boldfaced words with the consonant [n].**

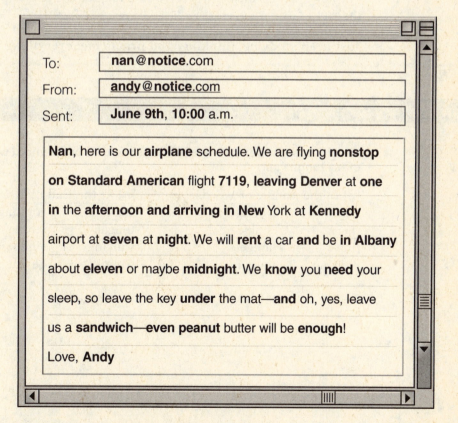

To: nan@notice.com
From: andy@notice.com
Sent: June 9th, 10:00 a.m.

Nan, here is our **airplane** schedule. We are flying **nonstop on Standard American** flight 7119, **leaving** Denver at **one in** the **afternoon and arriving in New** York at **Kennedy** airport at **seven** at **night**. We will **rent** a car **and** be **in Albany** about **eleven** or maybe **midnight**. We **know** you **need** your sleep, so leave the key **under** the mat—**and** oh, yes, leave us a **sandwich**—**even peanut** butter will be **enough**!
Love, **Andy**

Practice this [n] sound again and again!!!

Lesson 49 [ŋ] as in *sing*

PRONOUNCING [ŋ]

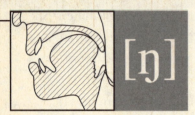

Back of tongue: Raised toward the soft palate
Airstream: Continuous through the nose
Vocal cords: Vibrating

Possible Pronunciation Problems

Many international students are unaccustomed to pronouncing [ŋ] at the end of words. Also, the similarity between [ŋ] and [n] might confuse you.

EXAMPLES   If you say [n] instead of [ŋ]:   **sung** will sound like **son/sun**.

rang will sound like **ran**.

The key to pronouncing [ŋ] correctly is to raise the BACK of your tongue—NOT the TIP!

Just keep study*ing*, think*ing*, and practic*ing*; everythi*ng* will be OK with [ŋ]!

Practice

EXERCISE A   **Listen and repeat the words. They should be pronounced with [ŋ]. Remember, back of the tongue up!**

[ŋ] In the Middle of Words		[ŋ] At the End of Words	
anger	youngest	sting	running
thank	single	tongue	strong
finger	longest	walking	singing
banging	hungry	feeling	belong

The consonant [ŋ] does not occur at the beginning of words in English.

hint

The letters *ng* or *ngue* at the ends of words are always pronounced [ŋ].

wro**ng**   si**ng**   walki**ng**   to**ngue**

The letter *n* before *g* or *k* is usually pronounced [ŋ].

hu**n**gry   si**n**gle   tha**n**k   dri**n**k

EXERCISE B

🎧 **Listen and repeat the phrases and sentences. The boldfaced words should be pronounced with [ŋ]. Remember, the back of the tongue must go up toward the palate.**

1. Good **evening**.
2. I'm **going** home.
3. Is **something wrong**?
4. **ring** on my **finger**
5. **raining** and **snowing**
6. Are you **coming along**?

CHECK YOURSELF 1

🎧 **Listen to the pairs of sentences. ONE sentence in each pair has a word pronounced with [ŋ]. Circle the number of the sentence with the [ŋ] word. (For answers to Check Yourself 1 and 2, see Appendix II, page 303.)**

EXAMPLE	*You hear*	He's a **swinger**.	He's a **swimmer**.
	You circle	①	2

1. 1   2
2. 1   2
3. 1   2
4. 1   2
5. 1   2

CHECK YOURSELF 2

🎧 **Listen and repeat the words. Circle only the words that are pronounced with [ŋ].**

1. (bring)	6. tangerine	11. along	16. engage
2. anger	7. swing	12. talking	17. stinging
3. hang	8. tangle	13. sponge	18. stingy
4. angel	9. danger	14. grin	19. lunch
5. dancing	10. sink	15. running	20. bank

Check your answers. Then read the words aloud again.

EXERCISE   📖 **Read the poem aloud. Pay attention to the boldfaced words with the consonant [ŋ].**

The Cataract of Lodore (*Excerpt*)
Robert Southey

Retreating and **beating** and **meeting** and **sheeting**,
Delaying and **straying** and **playing** and **spraying**,
Advancing and **prancing** and **glancing** and **dancing**,
Recoiling, **turmoiling** and **toiling** and **boiling**,
And **gleaming** and **streaming** and **steaming** and **beaming**,
And **rushing** and **flushing** and **brushing** and **gushing**,
And **flapping** and **rapping** and **clapping** and **slapping**,
And **curling** and **whirling** and **purling** and **twirling**,
And **thumping** and **plumping** and **bumping** and **jumping**,
And **dashing** and **flashing** and **splashing** and **clashing**;
And so never **ending**, but always **descending**,
Sounds and motions for ever and ever are **blending**,
All at once and all o'er, with a mighty uproar,
And this way the water comes down at Lodore.

Keep think*ng* and practic*ing*; everyth*ng* will be OK with [ŋ]!!!

🎧 **Listen and repeat the words and sentences. Feel the movement from the lips to tongue tip to back of throat as you pronounce [m], [n], and [ŋ].**

	[m]	[n]	[ŋ]
1.	whim	win	wing
2.	some	sun	sung
3.	rum	run	rung
4.	ram	ran	rang
5.	Kim	kin	king
6.	Is that a clam?	Is that a clan?	Is that a clang?
7.	He is Kim.	He is kin.	He is king.
8.	The bam was sudden.	The ban was sudden.	The bang was sudden.
9.	They had rum.	They had run.	They had rung.
10.	It was a whim.	It was a win.	It was a wing.

        [n] [ŋ]   [m] [ŋ]
11. My **son sang some songs**.

        [m] [ŋ]   [ŋ]   [n]
12. **Tim thinks** that **thing** is **thin**.

        [m]   [n]   [ŋ]
13. **Kim** is **kin** to the **king**.

        [m]   [n] [m] [ŋ]
14. It's a **whim** to **win** the **wings**.

        [m]   [n] [m] [ŋ]
15. I **seem** to have **seen him sing**.

Listen to the words. Circle the ONE word that you hear from each of the pairs below. (For answers to Check Yourself 1–4, see Appendix II, pages 303–304.)

EXAMPLES	sing	(sin)
	(foam)	phone

1. thin   thing
2. ban   bang
3. sinner   singer
4. comb   cone
5. rum   run
6. seem   scene
7. some   sung
8. hammer   hanger
9. ram   rang
10. gone   gong

CHECK YOURSELF 2 Read the sentences aloud; circle the correct word to complete the sentence. Be sure to pronounce each nasal consonant carefully.

1. **Jean** sat **in** the (sum / sun / sung).
2. The bird hurt his (whim / win / wing).
3. It is **fun** to (rum / run / rung).
4. The **meat needs** to (simmer / sinner / singer).
5. They **removed** the (bam / ban / bang).

CHECK YOURSELF 3 Listen to the sentences. One of the words in parentheses will be used. Circle the word you hear.

                              [n]   [m]

EXAMPLE   Give me the (cone / (comb)).

               [m]   [n]

1. I'll call (them / then).

               [n]   [ŋ]

2. He (ran / rang) twice.

               [n]   [m]

3. That (bun / bum) is old.

               [m]   [n]

4. We got (some / sun) at the beach.

               [m]   [ŋ]

5. I heard a (bam / bang).

               [ŋ]   [n]

6. You shouldn't (sing / sin).

                      [ŋ]   [m]

7. The children like (swinging/swimming).

                    [ŋ] [n]

8. It's a small (ping/pin).

                     [m] [n]

9. Get rid of the (gum/gun).

                     [m]   [ŋ]

10. Buy another (hammer/hanger).

📖 **Check your answers. Then read each of the sentences aloud twice. Use the first word in the first reading and the contrast word in the second reading.**

CHECK YOURSELF 4   👤 **Read the commercial aloud with a partner. In the brackets provided, write the phonetic symbol representing the sound of the boldfaced letters.**

> Pronunciation Key: [m] as in **m**e
>   [n] as in **n**o
>   [ŋ] as in ri**ng**

                         [n]   [ŋ]   [ŋ] [n]   [ŋ]   [n]

Announcer: Is your ski**n** feeli**ng** dry? Are you findi**ng** **n**ew wri**n**kles a**n**d
                        [ ]   [ ]   [ ]   [ ]   [ ]   [ ]   [ ][ ]   [ ]
                 li**n**es? The**n** you **n**eed Po**m**'s Ski**n** Crea**m**. **M**e**n** a**n**d wo**m**e**n**
                                 [ ]   [ ]   [ ]   [ ]   [ ]
                     everywhere are talki**ng** about our crea**m**. Liste**n** to fa**m**ous fil**m**
                               [ ]   [ ]   [ ]   [ ]   [ ]   [ ]   [ ]
                     star **M**olly **M**alone, who has bee**n** acti**ng** for a lo**ng**, lo**ng**, ti**m**e.
                                 [ ]   [ ] [ ]   [ ]

Molly: H**mmm**. Of course, everyo**n**e k**n**ows I started **m**aki**ng**
                [ ]   [ ]   [ ]   [ ]   [ ]   [ ]   [ ]
                 fil**m**s whe**n** I was **n**i**n**e. But I've bee**n** usi**ng** Po**m**'s Crea**m** for
                             [ ]   [ ]   [ ]   [ ]
                 years, a**n**d I thi**n**k it's wo**n**derful. Just put it o**n** every **m**or**n**i**ng**
                        [ ] [ ][ ][ ]   [ ]   [ ]
                 and eveni**ng**, a**n**d i**n** o**n**e week you'll start seei**ng** the difference.
                               [ ]   [ ]   [ ]
                 Your face will glea**m** a**n**d shi**n**e, a**n**d you'll look just fi**n**e!
                 [ ][ ]   [ ]   [ ]   [ ]

Announcer: A**n**d **n**ow for a li**m**ited ti**m**e, you ca**n** get two jars for the price of
                [ ]   [ ]   [ ]   [ ]   [ ][ ]   [ ]
                 o**n**e. Re**m**e**m**ber, use Po**m**'s Ski**n** Crea**m** a**n**d you, too, ca**n** look
                     [ ]
                 like a fil**m** star.

Check your answers. Then practice the commercial again with a partner.

More Practice

📖 Read the joke aloud. Pay attention to the boldfaced words with the consonants [m], [n], and [ŋ].

      [n]   [n]   [n] [m]   [ŋ] [n]   [ŋ]   [m]

One day **seven**-year-old **Norma** was **sitting and watching** her **mother**

                  [n] [ŋ]   [n] [n]

wash the dishes at the **kitchen sink**. She **suddenly noticed** that her

[m]   [n]   [ŋ]   [n]

mother had several **strands** of white hair **sticking** out of her **brunette**

           [m]   [n]   [m]

head. She looked at her **mother and** asked, "Why are **some** of your

       [m] [m]   [m]   [m]

hairs white, **Mommy**?" Her **mother** replied, "Well, every **time** that

       [m]   [ŋ]   [ŋ] [m]   [m] [n]   [n] [n] [m]

you do **something wrong**, it **makes me unhappy**, **and one** of **my** hairs

[n]   [n] [m]   [ŋ] [ŋ]   [m] [n]   [n]

turns white." **Norma** started **thinking** about this for a few **minutes and**

[n]   [m] [m]   [m]   [m]

then said, "**Mommy**, how **come** all of **grandma**'s hairs are white?"

Lesson 51 Pronouncing Final Consonant Sounds

Final Consonants in English

A final consonant is any consonant that is the last sound in a word. Consonant sounds that end words are very important. They can determine grammatical as well as word meaning. Careful production of final consonants is necessary to convey your message correctly and to sound like a native English speaker.

hint

Words pronounced with a final consonant often have *e* as the final letter. When *e* is the last letter in a word, it is usually silent; the consonant is actually the last sound.

ma**d**e   pho**n**e   bi**t**e   ha**v**e

Possible Pronunciation Problems

In your language, the majority of words may end in vowels. Consonants may rarely be found at the ends of words. The opposite is true in English. The majority of words end in consonants. Because you are not used to using final consonants, you may frequently omit them at the end of words in English or add a vowel sound to the end of the word. Without realizing it, you can confuse your listeners, and they will have trouble understanding you.

EXAMPLES

You will not be saying your target word:

place will sound like **play**.

card will sound like **car**.

Your speech will be difficult to understand:

hat will sound like **hato**.

dog will sound like **dogu**.

some will sound like **soma**.

Your listener won't understand you at all:

ca without a final consonant is meaningless. You could be trying to say *case, came, cake, cane, cage, cape,* or *cave*. Your listener would have to guess!

Practice

🎧 **Listen and repeat the words. The words in each row will sound the same if their final consonant sound is omitted.** *Exaggerate* **your pronunciation of the final consonant in each word.**

1. cat   cap   can   cab
2. bowl   bowls   bold   bolt
3. rag   rat   rap   rack
4. coal   colt   cold   coals
5. wrote   robe   rode   rope
6. soon   soup   suit   sued
7. ten   tense   tent   tend
8. sight   side   sign   size
9. bill   bills   build   built
10. cord   corn   court   cork

EXERCISE B

📖 **Read the phrases aloud. Carefully distinguish between the phrases in each row by exaggerating your pronunciation of the final consonants.**

1. I saw.   eyesore   I sawed.
2. Joe knows her.   Joan knows her.   Joan owns her.
3. heat wave   He waved.   He waves.
4. I'll earn it.   I learn it.   I earn it.
5. I sigh.   eyesight   I sighed.

EXERCISE C

🎧 **Listen and repeat the sentences. Exaggerate your pronunciation of the final consonant sound in each boldfaced word.**

1. She **sighed** at the beautiful **sight**.
2. **Bess** is the **best** artist.
3. **Can't** Amy **catch** a **cab**?
4. The thief **stole** the **stove**.
5. **Ben** couldn't **bend** his knees.
6. The **coal** is very **cold**.
7. We **paid** for the **pane** of glass.
8. **I'm** sure **I'll** go.
9. **Would** he like a **wool** coat?
10. She **sat** on the **sack** full of **sap**.

232 Part 3: Consonants

🎧 **Listen and repeat the pairs of words. Be sure to keep your vocal cords vibrating as you pronounce the voiced final consonants of the words.**

Voiceless	Voiced
ha**t**	ha**d**
sigh**t**	si**de**
mo**p**	mo**b**
ro**pe**	ro**be**
ra**ck**	ra**g**
bu**s**	bu**zz**
hal**f**	ha**ve**

👥 **Read the dialogue aloud with a partner. Be sure to *exaggerate* your pronunciation of the final consonant sound in each boldfaced word.**

Patrick: Hi, **Pam**. **Have** you **had** dinner at the **Old Inn**?

Pam: No, **Pat**. But Bea said their **beef** can't be **beat**.

Patrick: And **Hal** told me to **have** the **ham**.

Pam: **Doug** said the **duck** was **done** just **right**.

Patrick: And Sue thought the **soup** would **suit** a **king**!

Pam: **Kate raved** about the **cake**.

Patrick: I'd say the **inn** was **it**! **Pam**, will you be ready at **eight**?

Pam: Oh, **Pat**, I already **am**! I thought you'd never **ask**!

(The exciting story of Pam and Pat at the Old Inn continues in Check Yourself 4.)

🎧 **Listen to the 10 three-word series. Write the number 1, 2, or 3 on the line next to each word in the order you hear it. *Listen carefully* for the final consonant sound in each word. (For answers to Check Yourself 1–4, see Appendix II, pages 304–305.)**

EXAMPLE   *You hear*   half   hat   had
   You write   __2__ hat   __3__ had   __1__ half

1. _____ hot   _____ hog   _____ hop
2. _____ wrote   _____ rope   _____ robe
3. _____ save   _____ safe   _____ same
4. _____ right   _____ ride   _____ ripe
5. _____ mad   _____ mat   _____ map
6. _____ fade   _____ fate   _____ fake
7. _____ wipe   _____ white   _____ wife
8. _____ peg   _____ pen   _____ pet
9. _____ prize   _____ prime   _____ pride
10. _____ bit   _____ big   _____ bid

📖 **Read the sentences aloud. Circle one word to complete each sentence.** *Exaggerate* **the pronunciation of the final consonant sound of each word you choose to fill in the blanks.**

1. The key opens the _____. (lock/log/lot)
2. The _____ is in the fire. (lock/log/lot)
3. _____ the dirty dishes. (soak/soap/sole)
4. Wash your hands with _____. (soak/soap/sole)
5. He _____ the letter. (wrote/rose/rode)
6. He _____ the bicycle. (wrote/rose/rode)
7. The _____ landed. (plague/plane/plate)
8. The _____ is broken. (plague/plane/plate)
9. Send a birthday _____. (cart/card/carve)
10. The bags are in the _____. (cart/card/carve)

🎧 **Listen to the sentences. Circle the ONE word in parentheses that is used. Listen carefully for the final consonant sound.**

EXAMPLE The (ⓒab/cat) is lost.

1. I can't find the (belt/bell).
2. My son is (five/fine).
3. I think he's (dead/deaf).
4. Tim bought another (car/card).
5. The (guild/guilt) is ours.
6. The (pack/pact) was sealed.
7. There's a (lake/lane) near the house.
8. I (can/can't) go.
9. The (den/dent) is very small.
10. The (coal/colt) is black.

📖 **Check your answers. Then read each of the sentences aloud twice. Use the first word in parentheses in the first reading and the contrast word in the second reading. Exaggerate your pronunciation of the final consonant sounds.**

♟ **Read the dialogue aloud with a partner. Fill in the blanks with the final consonant sound that completes the word.**

Ann: Hi, Pam! How was your da__e last nigh__ with Pat?

Pam: Nothing went righ__ last nigh__. Pa__ had a flat tire and came la__e!

Ann: How was the foo__ at the Ol__ Inn?

Pam: It was ba__. The soup was col__. My stea__ was tough. They ra__ out of chocola__e ca__e.

Ann: What about the dinner Pa__ a__e?

Pam: His duc__ was overdo__e. His garli__ brea__ was sta__e!

Ann: Did it cos___ a lot of money?

Pam: Yes! And Pat didn't ha___e enough to pay the bi___.

Ann: I guess you won'___ go ou___ with him agai___!

Pam: Why do you say tha___? We're going for a b___ke ri___e this afternoon. He's so handso___e!

Check your answers. Then change roles and read this dialogue aloud again. Exaggerate your pronunciation of all final consonant sounds.

More Practice

EXERCISE A

Read the following poem aloud. Be sure to pronounce all of the final consonant sounds; pay particular attention to those in boldface.

State of Mind
Author Unknown

If you thin**k** you are beat**en**, you are.
If you thin**k** you dare not, you don'**t**.
If you'**d** li**k**e to wi**n**, but you thin**k** you can'**t**,
It's almos**t** a cin**ch** tha**t** you won'**t**.

If you thin**k** you'll lose, you've los**t**;
For ou**t** **in** the worl**d** you'll fin**d**
Succe**ss** begin**s** with a person'**s** wi**ll**.
It's a**ll** **in** the state of min**d**!

Fu**ll** many a race is lost
Before eve**n** a ste**p** is run.
An**d** many a cowar**d** fall**s**
Before eve**n** hi**s** wor**k** is begun.

Thin**k** high an**d** your deed**s** wi**ll** grow.
Thin**k** low an**d** you'll fa**ll** behind.
Thin**k** tha**t** you ca**n** an**d** you wi**ll**.
It's a**ll** **in** the state of min**d**.

If you thin**k** you're outclasse**d**, you are.
You have to thin**k** high to rise.
You have to be su**re** of yoursel**f**
Before you ca**n** wi**n** a prize.

Life'**s** battle**s** don'**t** alway**s** go
To the stronger or faster man,
But sooner or later the o**ne** who win**s**,
Is the o**ne** who think**s** he can!

EXERCISE B

Tape-record yourself while talking on the telephone. After you hang up, play the recording back. Analyze your speech and listen for final consonants. Make a list of words you didn't pronounce carefully and practice them.

Lesson 52 — Pronouncing Consonant Clusters

Consonant Clusters in English

Consonant clusters are two or more consonant sounds grouped together in a word. They are pronounced with no vowels between them. Careful production of consonant clusters is necessary to convey your message correctly and to sound like a native speaker of English.

Possible Pronunciation Problems

Consonant clusters are difficult for many international speakers of English to pronounce. Often, English speakers pronounce groups of consonants and one vowel as a single syllable. Because this is different from most other languages, you might omit one of the consonant sounds in the cluster or insert a vowel sound between two of the consonants in the cluster. This will confuse your listeners and they may not understand you.

EXAMPLES

You will not be saying your target word:	**asks** will sound like **ax**. **fact** will sound like **fat**.
Your speech or grammar will be difficult to understand:	**asked** will sound like **ask it**. **sport** will sound like **support**.

Practice

EXERCISE A

Consonant clusters generally consist of two or three consonant sounds. The following words contain the most common three-member consonant clusters in English. Listen and repeat them.

Consonant Clusters at the Beginning of Words

[spr]	[spl]	[skr]	[skw]	[str]
spry	splash	screen	squad	strap
spray	split	scream	square	stray
sprout	splice	scratch	squash	strain
spring	splinter	scrape	squint	street
sprinkle	splatter	scrawl	squeeze	stripe

Consonant Clusters in the Middle of Words

display	astray	conclusion
sparkling	complete	widespread
astride	complain	

Consonant Clusters at the End of Words

[sps], [lps]	[spt], [lpt]	[skt], [lkt], [kst]	[sks]	[rks], [rkt]
wasps	gasped	asked	asks	sparks
gasps	lisped	risked	risks	parks
lisps	clasped	milked	masks	sparked
gulps	grasped	waxed	desks	parked
helps	helped	fixed	tasks	worked

EXERCISE B

🎧 **Listen and repeat the words. Be sure to distinguish between the words in each row.**

	[ks]	[kt], [skt]	[kit], [ksit], [ktit]
1.	likes	liked	like it
2.	asks	asked	ask it
3.	fix	fixed	fix it
4.	checks	checked	check it
5.	ax	act	act it

	Consonant Cluster	Consonant + Vowel
6.	plight	polite
7.	Clyde	collide
8.	prayed	parade
9.	sport	support
10.	claps	collapse

EXERCISE C

🎧 **Listen and repeat the sentences. Carefully pronounce all the consonant clusters or consonant + vowel combinations in the boldfaced words.**

1. I **fixed** the **cracked masks**.
2. **Spray** the **strong** perfume **sparingly**.
3. The **squirrel** had a **splinter** in its foot.
4. The **strong** man **worked** at the **factory**.
5. The public **supports** many **sports** teams.
6. He **prayed** that they wouldn't cancel the **parade**.
7. We **parked** the car and **strolled through** the **streets**.
8. I hope that **Clyde** and I don't **collide** during the race.
9. I **scream**, you **scream**, we all **scream** for **ice cream**!
10. A **strange insect crawled through** a hole in the **screen**.

Read the dialogue aloud with a partner. Be sure to carefully pronounce the boldfaced words containing consonant clusters.

Stuart: Hello, Mrs. **Springer**. How do you want your hair **fixed** today?

Mrs. Springer: **Stuart**, I need a new **hairstyle**. Do you **think** I need a **permanent**, or should my hair be **straight**? What really **helps** the **most**?

Stuart: I've been **praying** for the **moment** to **try** something new. **First**, **let's start** with your hair color. How about **Sunburst** Red? You'll look like that **screen star Stella Sloan**.

Mrs. Springer: I really **don't** like taking **risks**, but I **trust** your **judgment**.

Stuart: **Splendid**! How about **blonde streaks** as well?

Mrs. Springer: **Slow** down a little, **Stuart**. I **don't want strangers staring** at me.

Stuart: **Next**, we'll **style** your hair in the **latest** fashion . . . very very **short**. You'll look **just** like a **youngster**. How about **bangs**? Everyone **likes bangs**!

Mrs. Springer: I **asked** you for a new look, but I **didn't plan** on such an **extreme**! I **don't want** to **complain** but . . .

Stuart: Now, Mrs. **Springer**, **close** your eyes and **relax**. Your **husband** will **gasp** when he sees how **fantastic** you look.

Mrs. Springer: He'll **gasp** all right . . . at how much I've **spent**. But I'm in your **hands**, so **spray** away!

Listen and repeat the sentences. Circle the two- or three-member consonant cluster contained in each boldfaced word. (For answers to Check Yourself 1–3, see Appendix II, pages 305–306.)

EXAMPLES	[spr]	([skr])	[skt]	[spt]	I play **Scrabble** with my friends.
	[sks]	[rks]	([kst])	[sps]	He **faxed** the documents to Spain.

1. [kt]   [kst]   [sks]   [ks]   Sam **liked** to swim when he was young.

2. [kt]   [kst]   [sks]   [ks]   Stella **walks** home from school.

3. [skr]   [sk]   [sks]   [sk]   Please don't **scream**; I can hear you!

4. [skr]   [kt]   [ks]   [sk]   Our teacher is very **strict**.

5. [skr]   [st]   [sks]   [sk]   My cat **scratched** me.

6. [spl]   [spr]   [str]   [sts]   How did you **sprain** your ankle?

7. [skr]   [sk]   [sks]   [sts]   Try not to take unnecessary **risks**.

8. [skr]   [sk]   [skt]   [kt]   The firefighters **risked** their lives to save us.

9. [skr]   [kst]   [skt]   [ks]   Bob washed and **waxed** his car.

10. [spr]   [spl]   [sp]   [sl]   Many flowers bloom in the **spring**.

Look at the scrambled words. Write the correct word in the blank. Use the clues below each word to help you figure out the scrambled word.

1. E A L S T

   It's a crime to _____.

2. I P R A S E

   To _____ someone is to pay them a compliment.

3. S K A

   To make a request is to _____.

4. S P W A

   A _____ is an insect that stings.

5. S P I R E P E R

   To _____ means to sweat.

6. P L M P U

   The opposite of skinny is _____.

7. U S T E R C L

   Be sure to pronounce each consonant _____ clearly.

8. R P S H A

   Be careful when using an object with a _____ point.

9. S T R A M E

   The children went swimming in the _____.

10. E A S K S Q U

    Squeals, shrieks, screeches, and _____ are all annoying

    sounds.

📖 **Check your answers. Then practice reading each word and clue aloud. Be sure to pronounce all the consonant clusters correctly.**

🎧 **Listen to the audio. A word will be pronounced, used in a sentence, and pronounced again. Circle the three-member consonant cluster that you hear in each word.**

EXAMPLES   [spr]   [spl]   (skr)   [str]   (**screen**; The **screen** has a hole; **screen**)

   [spr]   (sps)   [skt]   [sks]   (**wasps**; Stay away from **wasps**; **wasps**)

1. [spr]   [spl]   [skr]   [str]

2. [spr]   [spl]   [skr]   [str]

3. [spr]   [spl]   [skr]   [str]

4. [spr]   [spl]   [skr]   [str]

5. [spr]   [spl]   [skw]   [str]

6. [sps]   [spt]   [skt]   [kst]

7. [sps]   [spt]   [skt]   [rks]

8. [sps]   [spt]   [skt]   [sks]

9. [sps]   [spt]   [kst]   [sks]

10. [sps]   [spt]   [spl]   [rks]

More Practice

EXERCISE A

📖 **Read the poem aloud. Be sure to carefully pronounce the boldfaced consonant clusters.**

If

Rudyard Kipling

If you can keep your head when all about you
Are losing thei**rs** and **bl**aming it on you;
If you can **tr**u**st** your**self** when all men doubt you,
But make allowa**nce** for their doubting too;
If you can wait and not be ti**red** by waiting,
Or, being lied about, do**n't** deal in lies,
Or, being hated, do**n't** give way to hating,
And yet do**n't** look too good, not talk too wise;

If you can **dr**eam—and not make **dr**eams your ma**st**er;
If you can thi**nk**—and not make though**ts** your aim;
If you can meet with **Tr**iu**mph** and Disa**st**er
And **tr**eat those two impo**st**ers ju**st** the same;
If you can bear to hear the **tr**uth you've **sp**oken
Twi**st**ed by kna**ves** to make a **tr**ap for foo**ls**,
Or watch the thi**ngs** you gave your life to, **br**oken,
And **st**oop and bui**ld** them up with wo**rn**-out too**ls**;

If you can make one heap of all your winni**ngs**
And ri**sk** it on one tu**rn** of pitch-and-toss,
And lose, and **st**art again at your beginni**ngs**
And never **br**eathe a wo**rd** about your loss;
If you can fo**rce** your hea**rt** and ne**rve** and sinew
To se**rve** your tu**rn** long after they are gone,
And so ho**ld** on when there is nothing in you
Ex**cept** the will which says to them: "Ho**ld** on!"

If you can talk with **cro**w**ds** and keep your virtue,
Or walk with ki**ngs**—nor lose the common touch,
If neither foes nor loving **friends** can hu**rt** you,
If all men cou**nt** with you, but none too much;
If you can fill the unforgiving minute
With si**xt**y seco**nds**' wo**rth** of di**st**ance run—
You**rs** is the Ea**rth** and everything tha**t's** in it,
And—which is more—you'll be a Man, my son!

EXERCISE B

Think of ten words that contain with three-member consonant clusters. Then try to use as many of those words as you can in the same sentence. Practice saying your original sentences with a partner.

EXAMPLES   scream, split, pants

When I **split** my **pants**, I started to **scream**.

Lesson 53 Pronouncing Past Tense Verbs

When writing English, we add the ending -ed to form the past tense of regular verbs. That's easy to remember! However, when you are *speaking* English, the -ed ending can have three different pronunciations. Sometimes -ed sounds like [t], as in *stopped* [stapt]; sometimes it sounds like [d], as in *lived* [lɪvd]; sometimes it sounds like a new syllable, [ɪd], as in *loaded* [loudɪd].

Possible Pronunciation Problems

As discussed in Lesson 51, many consonants may not be found at the end of words in your language. Consequently, you may not be used to saying final consonants in English. This might make you omit or mispronounce past tense verb endings.

EXAMPLES	Past tense verbs will sound like present tense verbs:	**washed** will sound like **wash**. **played** will sound like **play**.
	A new syllable will be incorrectly added to a past tense verb:	**lived** [lɪvd] will sound like **live-id** [lɪvɪd]. **tapped** [tæpt] will sound like **tap-id** [tæpɪd].
	You will not be saying your target past tense verb:	**played** [pleɪd] will sound like **plate** [pleɪt]. **tied** [taɪd] will sound like **tight** [taɪt].

This might seem confusing, but don't worry! We have good news! In this chapter we will teach you three EASY rules to help you pronounce past tense regular verbs correctly. You will learn when -ed sounds like [t], [d], or [ɪd]. Study the rules and *you've got it made*!

-ed PRONOUNCED [t]

The ending -ed will always sound like [t] when the last sound in the present tense verb is voiceless.

EXAMPLES   talk**ed** [tɔkt]   cross**ed** [krɔst]   laugh**ed** [læft]

EXERCISE

🎧 Listen and repeat the verbs. Be sure to pronounce the *-ed* in the past tense verbs like [t]. (Do NOT add a new syllable to any word!)

Present Tense (last sound is voiceless)	Past Tense (*-ed* = [t])
look	looked
miss	missed
stop	stopped
work	worked
pick	picked
wash	washed
drip	dripped
pass	passed
place	placed
laugh	laughed

-ed PRONOUNCED [d]

The ending *-ed* will always sound like [d] when the last sound in the present tense verb is a vowel or voiced consonant.

EXAMPLES   lived [lɪvd]   turned [tɜ˞nd]   played [pleɪd]

Practice

EXERCISE

🎧 Listen and repeat the verbs. Be sure to pronounce *-ed* like [d]. (Do NOT add a new syllable to the words!)

Present Tense (last sound is voiced)	Past Tense (*-ed* = [d])
love	loved
stay	stayed
fill	filled
burn	burned
rain	rained
live	lived
clean	cleaned
stare	stared
study	studied
follow	followed

-ed PRONOUNCED [ɪd]

The ending -ed will always sound like the new syllable [ɪd] when the last sound in the present tense verb is [t] or [d].

EXAMPLES   wanted [wantɪd]   rested [rɛstɪd]   ended [ɛndɪd]

Practice

EXERCISE A

🎧 **Listen and repeat the verbs. NOW you should pronounce -ed like the new syllable [ɪd].**

Present Tense (end in *t* or *d*)	Past Tense (-*ed* = the new syllable [ɪd])
end	ended
add	added
hunt	hunted
want	wanted
need	needed
fold	folded
start	started
print	printed
sound	sounded
count	counted

EXERCISE B

🎧 **Listen and repeat the sentences. Be sure to pronounce the -ed ending in the past tense verbs correctly.**

-*ed* = [t]	-*ed* = [d]	-*ed* = [ɪd]
1. She cook**ed** dinner.	We play**ed** a game.	He avoid**ed** his boss.
2. The boy danc**ed** all night.	He mov**ed** again.	I rest**ed** at home.
3. The bus stopp**ed** in the road.	Ted stay**ed** out late.	The car start**ed**.
4. Mom bak**ed** a pie.	I mail**ed** a letter.	Mike need**ed** money.
5. She finish**ed** early.	We open**ed** a window.	Our house was paint**ed**.

       [t]   [ɪd]

6. Sue **packed** her suitcase and **waited** for a taxi.

       [t]   [ɪd]

7. Tim **cashed** a check and **deposited** the money.

8. The children **played** games and **jumped** rope.
                    [d]   [t]

9. I **studied** hard and **passed** the test.
       [d]   [t]

10. He **listened** while I **showed** photos and **talked** about my trip.
   [d]   [d]   [t]

CHECK YOURSELF 1

📖 **Read the sentences aloud. Choose the correct past tense verb from the box to fill in the blanks. In the brackets, write either [t], [d], or [ɪd] to represent the -ed sound in the verb. Check your answers. (For answers to Check Yourself 1–4, see Appendix II, pages 306–307.)**

EXAMPLE   I _____ locked _____ the door. [t]

painted	mailed	danced	washed	waited
lived	deposited	asked	walked	talked

1. We _____ the rumba and tango. [ ]

2. She _____ on the phone for an hour. [ ]

3. Dad _____ the fence green. [ ]

4. The student _____ three questions. [ ]

5. They _____ fifteen minutes for the bus. [ ]

6. I've _____ in the same house for four years [ ].

7. My father _____ a letter. [ ]

8. The man _____ five miles. [ ]

9. I _____ my check in the bank. [ ]

10. He _____ his car with a hose. [ ]

CHECK YOURSELF 2

🎧 **Listen to five sentences. Some of the -ed verb endings will be said INCORRECTLY. Circle C for Correct or I for Incorrect to indicate whether the past tense verb in each sentence is pronounced properly.**

EXAMPLES   *You hear* She **baked** [beɪkɪd] a pie. *You circle* C   (I)

                  You hear I **liked** [laɪkt] the book. *You circle* (C)   I

    1. C   I

    2. C   I

    3. C   I

    4. C   I

    5. C   I

Listen and repeat each three-word series. Circle the ONE word in each group that has a different *-ed* sound than the others.

EXAMPLE   (placed)   pleased   played

1. stopped   started   stated
2. finished   followed   phoned
3. loved   looked   liked
4. tasted   traded   taped
5. cooked   cleaned   baked
6. packed   pasted   passed
7. ironed   sewed   mended
8. whispered   shouted   screamed
9. skipped   hopped   lifted
10. pushed   pulled   raised

Check your answers. Then read the verbs aloud. Try using one verb from each series in a sentence.

Read the following dialogue with a partner. In the brackets above each past tense verb, write the phonetic symbol representing the sound of the -ed ending.

                                    [ɪd]   [d]
Roberta: Karl, have you **started** your diet? I hope you haven't **gained** any weight.
                     [ ]   [ ]
Karl: I **boiled** eggs and **sliced** celery for lunch.
                              [ ]
Roberta: Have you **exercised** at all?
                     [ ]   [ ]
Karl: I **walked** five miles and **jogged** in the park.
                              [ ]   [ ]
Roberta: Have you **cleaned** the house? Calories can be **worked** off that way.
                     [ ]   [ ]   [ ]
Karl: I **washed** and **waxed** the floors. I even **painted** the bathroom.
                     [ ]   [ ]
Roberta: Who **baked** this apple pie? Who **cooked** this ham?
                         [ ]   [ ]   [ ]
Karl: When I **finished** cleaning, I was **starved**. I **prepared** this food for dinner.
                                                          [ ]
Roberta: Oh, no! I'll take this food home so you won't be **tempted**.
                         [ ]
              I really **enjoyed** being with you. Your diet is great!
                         [ ]   [ ]
Karl: What **happened**? Somehow, I **missed** out on all the fun.

Check your answers. Change roles and read the dialogue aloud again. Be sure to carefully pronounce all past tense endings.

More Practice

EXERCISE A

👥 **Read the dialogue aloud with a partner. Be sure to pronounce all the past tense endings correctly.**

Mr. West: Why are you **interested** [ɪd] in working for Westfield stores?

Ed: The company has **earned** [d] the admiration of the retail industry.

Mr. West: Are you **experienced** [t]?

Ed: I am well **educated** [ɪd] and have **worked** [t] for **respected** [ɪd] retail shops in Europe.

Mr. West: I see you've **traveled** [d] extensively. Have you **studied** [d] other languages?

Ed: I **lived** [d] in Japan for six months and **attended** [ɪd] an intensive program where I **learned** [d] Japanese.

Mr. West: Our company is service **oriented** [ɪd] and has **maintained** [d] high standards.

Ed: I'm **impressed** [t] by your management style.

Mr. West: Your interest in our company is **appreciated** [ɪd]. I'm sure you will be **offered** [d] a position with Westfield.

Ed: Thanks, Dad!

EXERCISE B

👥 **Think of a response to the question, "What happened to you today?" Be sure your response contains many past tense verbs. When you complete your response, work with a partner and ask him or her the same question. Use a chart like the one below to categorize the verbs according to the sound of their –ed endings.**

EXAMPLE **A:** What **happened** to you today, Claude?

B: I **pulled** into my driveway, **lifted** the garage door, **backed** in, **knocked** over the bicycle, **parked** the car, **opened** the door, and was **shocked** to see my house had been **robbed**!

-ed = [t]	-ed = [d]	-ed = [ɪd]
backed	pulled	lifted
knocked	opened	
parked	robbed	
shocked		

54 Pronouncing Plurals, Third-Person Verbs, Possessives, and Contractions

When you are writing English, the letter *s* at the end of words serves many different purposes. The letter *s* is used to form plural nouns (*hats*, *dogs*); third-person present tense regular verbs (*he likes*; *she eats*); possessive nouns (*my friend's house*; *the dog's collar*); and contractions (*it's late*; *he's here*). As you can see, *s* is a very versatile letter in English. It is important to learn its many different sounds!

When you are speaking English, the *-s* ending can have three different pronunciations. It can sound like [s], as in *hats* [hæts]; [z], as in *tells* [tɛlz]; or like a new syllable, [ɪz], as in *roses* [roʊzɪz].

Possible Pronunciation Problems

Once again, the tendency to drop final consonants results in omissions or incorrect pronunciations of *-s* at the ends of words. This will make you difficult to understand and confuse your listeners.

EXAMPLES

Plural nouns will sound like singular nouns:	**Two books** will sound like **two book**.
Third-person present tense verbs will be incorrect:	**He eats** will sound like **he eat**. **She sings** will sound like **she sing**.
Possessives and contractions will be omitted:	**Bob's house** will sound like **Bob house**. **He's right** will sound like **he right**.
You will not be saying your target word:	**My eyes** will sound like **my ice**. **Sue sings** will sound like **Sue sinks**.

You are probably wondering if there are any rules to help you correctly pronounce *s* in all these different situations. The answer is YES! In this lesson, you will learn how to pronounce *s* when it forms plurals, third-person present tense verbs, possessives, and contractions. Study the rules and listen to the CD carefully. You will soon notice a big improvement in your pronunciation!

-s PRONOUNCED [s]

The *-s* forming the plural always sounds like [s] when the last sound in the singular noun is voiceless.

EXAMPLES   hats [hæts]   lips [lɪps]   sticks [stɪks]

The -s forming the third-person present always sounds like [s] when the last sound in the base form of the verb is voiceless.

EXAMPLES   he likes [laɪks]   she talks [tɔks]   it floats [floʊts]

The -s forming the possessive always sounds like [s] when the last sound in the noun is voiceless.

EXAMPLES   Pat's [pæts] car   the book's [bʊks] binding

The -s forming contractions always sounds like [s] when the last sound in the word being contracted is voiceless.

EXAMPLES   It's [ɪts] true.   That's [ðæts] my house.

Practice

EXERCISE   🎧 **Listen and repeat the phrases. The final -s will sound like [s]. (Do NOT add a new syllable to any word!)**

Plural Noun Phrases	Third-Person Verb Phrases	Possessive/Contraction Phrases
Bake the cakes.	He smokes too much.	the cat's milk
Wash the plates.	She sleeps late.	Ralph's friend
Stack the cups.	It tastes good.	the plant's leaf
Clean the pots.	My mother makes tea.	Let's eat now.
Darn the socks.	The dog eats.	What's wrong?
Feed the cats.	He jumps high.	It's time to go.

-s PRONOUNCED [z]

The -s forming the plural always sounds like [z] when the last sound in the singular noun is voiced.

EXAMPLES   floors [flɔrz]   bags [bægz]   cars [karz]

The -s forming the third-person present always sounds like [z] when the last sound in the base form of the verb is voiced.

EXAMPLES   He swims [swɪmz].   The bird flies [flaɪz].   She sings [sɪŋz].

The -s forming the possessive always sounds like [z] when the last sound in the noun is voiced.

EXAMPLES   Tim's [tɪmz] house   My friend's [frɛndz] cat

The -s forming a contraction always sounds like [z] when the last sound in the word being contracted is voiced.

EXAMPLES   She's [ʃiz] my sister.   He's [hiz] leaving.

EXERCISE

🎧 **Listen and repeat the phrases. Remember, the -s ending must sound like [z].**

Plural Noun Phrases	Third-Person Verb Phrases	Possessive/Contraction Phrases
Close your eye**s**.	He save**s** money.	Sue**'s** pencil
Kill the flea**s**.	The man live**s** here.	the baby**'s** milk
Sing the song**s**.	Dad read**s** books.	our teacher**'s** desk
lost 30 pound**s**	The boy listen**s**.	my friend**'s** house
Open the letter**s**.	It smell**s** good.	Here**'s** a pencil.
Buy some shoe**s**.	She see**s** me.	There**'s** a note.

-s (or -es) PRONOUNCED [ɪz]

The -s or -es forming the plural always sounds like the new syllable [ɪz] when the last sound in the singular noun is [s], [z], [ʃ], [tʃ], [ʒ], or [dʒ].

EXAMPLES   wish**es** [wɪʃɪz]   church**es** [tʃɝtʃɪz]   plac**es** [pleɪsɪz]

The -s or -es forming the third-person present always sounds like the new syllable [ɪz] when the last sound in the base form of the verb is [s], [z], [ʃ], [tʃ], [ʒ], or [dʒ].

EXAMPLES   He watch**es** [watʃɪz].   The bee buzz**es** [bʌzɪz].

The -s or -es forming the possessive always sounds like the new syllable [ɪz] when the last sound in the noun is [s], [z], [ʃ], [tʃ], [ʒ], or [dʒ].

EXAMPLES   the rose**'s** [rouzɪz] stem   the church**'s** [tʃɝtʃɪz] altar

Practice

EXERCISE A

🎧 **Listen and repeat the phrases. NOW you should pronounce -s or -es like the new syllable [ɪz].**

Plural Noun Phrases	Third-Person Verb Phrases	Possessive Phrases
two new dress**es**	He wish**es**.	the church**'s** steeple
Trim the hedg**es**.	She watch**es** him.	the witch**'s** broom
Buy the watch**es**.	He judg**es** the contest.	Mr. Jones**'s** pen
Win the priz**es**.	Mother wash**es** clothes.	the mouse**'s** cheese
in the cag**es**	The bee buzz**es**.	the bus**'s** tires

📖 **Read the sentences aloud. Be sure to pronounce the plurals, verbs, possessives, and contractions correctly.**

s = [s]	*s* = [z]	*s* = [ɪz]
1. He want**s** to leave.	Blow out the candle**s**.	The speech**es** are boring.
2. My sister like**s** gum.	The hen laid egg**s**.	Please turn the pag**es**.
3. I read many book**s**.	Gun**s** are dangerous.	Mary danc**es** well.
4. Mother ironed shirt**s**.	Here**'s** some money.	I won many priz**es**.
5. Jack**'s** not coming.	The girl**'s** dress is old.	You have three choic**es**.

     [z]   [z]   [z]   [z]   [z]   [z]
6. **Boys** play **cowboys** and **Indians** and **use** toy **guns** and **knives**.

         [z]   [ɪz]   [z]   [s]   [z]   [z]
7. The store **sells watches**, **rings**, **bracelets**, **diamonds**, and **rubies**.

         [z]   [ɪz]   [ɪz]   [z]
8. My **sister's dresses**, **blouses**, and **shoes** are new.

         [z]   [z]   [z]   [z]
9. Our **teacher's** favorite saying **is**, "Where **there's** a will, **there's** a way."

    [z]   [z]   [z] [s]   [z]   [s]
10. **Tim's friend's** house **has lots** of **rooms** with oriental **carpets**.

👤 **Read the dialogue aloud with a partner. Be sure to pronounce all -s endings correctly.**

               [z]   [s]
Charles: Hi, Jame**s**. What**'s** new?

                 [z]   [z]   [s]
James: Nothing, Charle**s**. All the guy**s** have date**s** for the prom except me!

            [s]   [ɪz]
Charles: That**'s** all right. You can take Bess**'s** sister Nancy.

          [s]
James: What**'s** she like?

             [z]   [ɪz]   [z]   [z]
Charles: She measure**s** about 5 feet 2 inch**es**, has blue eye**s**, and weigh**s**

         [z]   [s]
102 pound**s**. She look**s** like a model.

                   [s]   [z]
James: Then she probably dislike**s** her studie**s**.

          [s]   [z]   [z]   [s]
Charles: That**'s** not true. She enter**s** law school after final**s**. She get**s**

          [z]
good grade**s**.

                [z]   [s] [s]
James: What are her hobbie**s**? She probably hate**s** sport**s**!

         [s]   [z]   [z]   [ɪz]
Charles: She golf**s**, play**s** tennis, and swim**s**. She also dance**s** very well.

          [z]
James: There**'s** got to be SOMETHING wrong! She probably has no

      [s]
date**s**.

Charles: She has lot$\overset{[s]}{s}$ of boyfriend$\overset{[z]}{s}$. In fact, let'$\overset{[s]}{s}$ make some change$\overset{[ɪz]}{s}$. I'll

take Bess'$\overset{[ɪz]}{s}$ sister! You can take Mary.

James: NO WAY! There will be no exchange$\overset{[ɪz]}{s}$! Nancy sound$\overset{[z]}{s}$ great. I

just hope she like$\overset{[s]}{s}$ me!

CHECK YOURSELF 1   🎧 **Listen to the sentences. Circle the ONE word in parentheses that you hear. (For answers to Check Yourself 1–3, see Appendix II, pages 307–308.)**

EXAMPLE   Did you pay for the ((blouse)/blouses)?

1. The men cut the (tree/trees).

2. He repaired the (watch/watches).

3. The (book/book's) cover is red.

4. Did they finally make (peace/peas)?

5. Did you see the little (cups/cubs)?

📖 **Check your answers. Then read each sentence aloud twice. Use the first word in parentheses the first time and the contrast word the second time.**

CHECK YOURSELF 2   🎧 **Listen and repeat the three-word groups. Circle the ONE word in each group of three that has an -s ending sound different from the others.**

EXAMPLE	belts	hats	(ties)
1.	talks	walks	runs
2.	dishes	gates	pages
3.	pears	apples	oranges
4.	eyes	noses	toes
5.	saves	makes	cooks
6.	newspapers	magazines	books
7.	dogs	birds	cats
8.	tables	chairs	couches
9.	dentists	doctors	lawyers
10.	lunches	beaches	chimes

📖 **Read the passages from William Shakespeare's plays. Circle all words with *-s* endings and write them under the phonetic symbol representing the sound of their *-s* ending. Use the chart at the bottom of the page.**

From (As) *You Like It*

All the (world's) a stage,
And all the men and women merely players;
They have their exits and their entrances;
And one man in his time plays many parts,
His acts being seven ages.

From *Othello*

Good name in man and woman, dear my lord,
Is the immediate jewel of their souls;
Who steals my purse steals trash; 'tis something, nothing;
'Twas mine, 'tis his, and has been slave to thousands;
But he that filches from me my good name
Robs me of that which not enriches him
And makes me poor indeed.

From *The Merchant of Venice*

Hath not a Jew eyes?
Hath not a Jew hands, organs, dimensions, senses, affections, passions?
Fed with the same food,
Hurt with the same weapons,
Subject to the same diseases,
Healed by the same means,
Warmed and cooled by the same winter and summer, as a Christian is?

[s]	[z]	[ɪz]
	world's	

More Practice

EXERCISE A

📖 **Read the poem aloud. Be sure to pronounce all the plural endings correctly.**

> ### The Pied Piper of Hamelin (*Excerpt*)
> *Robert Browning*
>
>   [ɪz]   [s]
> And out of the hous**es** the rat**s** came tumbling.
>   [s]   [s]   [s]   [s]
> Great rat**s**, small rat**s**, lean rat**s**, brawny rat**s**,
>   [s]   [s]   [s]   [s]
> Brown rat**s**, black rat**s**, gray rat**s**, tawny rat**s**,
>   [z]   [z]
> Grave old plodder**s**, gay young frisker**s**,
>   [z]   [z]   [z]   [z]
> Father**s**, mother**s**, uncle**s**, cousin**s**,
>   [z]   [z]
> Cocking tail**s** and pricking whisker**s**,
>   [z]   [z]   [z]
> Familie**s** by ten**s** and dozen**s**,
>   [z]   [z]   [z]   [z]
> Brother**s**, sister**s**, husband**s**, wive**s** . . .
>   [z]
> Followed the Piper for their live**s**.

EXERCISE B

⚒ **Work with a partner and think of at least ten different categories of things, for example, vehicles, fruits, flowers, items of clothing. Think of related questions to ask each other. Responses should contain at least four plural nouns related to that category.**

EXAMPLE   **A:** What **types** of **flowers** do you like?

            B: I like yellow **roses**, **tulips**, **daisies**, and **carnations**.
               What **types** of **flowers** do YOU like?

            A: I like **gardenias**, red **roses**, **lilies**, and **orchids**.

EXERCISE C

Every time you go to the cleaners practice the plural endings of words that identify clothing. Use phrases such as "*I have two dresses to clean,*" "*These shirts need to be laundered,*" "*Can you clean these ties?*"

Appendices

Appendix I: To the Teacher

Welcome to the challenge! You recommended *English Pronunciation Made Simple* to your students because you are committed to helping them improve their pronunciation of English. This is a difficult task, but it's *not* impossible. Teaching and learning English pronunciation can be difficult, tedious work. It can also be more fun than you ever imagined possible. (In our accent-reduction classes, there have been countless occasions when we, along with our students, have laughed long and hard enough for tears to roll!)

Some of you are already experienced teachers of English for nonnative speakers or speech instructors and/or speech pathologists involved in teaching foreign-accent–reduction classes, and you already employ a variety of effective techniques with your students. Please: Share some of your most successful ones with us. We invite you to let us know how you like our suggestions. We truly look forward to hearing from you!

Some of you are new at teaching English pronunciation to nonnative speakers. Don't worry. An enthusiastic attitude and genuine desire to learn with your students will be more valuable than years of experience. As you'll quickly realize, the *English Pronunciation Made Simple* program provides you with an easy-to-follow, systematic approach to teaching English pronunciation.

Breaking the Ice

Teaching foreign-accent reduction can and should be fun for all concerned. At first, students will invariably be apprehensive and self-conscious about taking such a course and "exposing" their speech patterns in front of you and their peers. The time you spend trying to alleviate their initial concerns will be time well spent. We recommend that you:

- Use the first class meeting to discuss the positive aspects of "accents" in general. Elaborate on the information presented on page ix in "To the Student."

- Emphasize that accent reduction is not the losing of one's culture or heritage, but the improvement of a skill—such as the ability to play the piano, guitar, or tennis! Our students relate well to such analogies.

- Describe your own embarrassing mistakes or those of other native English speakers when speaking a foreign language. Our students laugh heartily at our examples and are comforted by the thought that we, too, experience pronunciation difficulties when speaking our second language.

Hearing the Sounds

Advise your students that their initial difficulty in hearing the various vowel sounds is perfectly normal. Nonnative speakers of English frequently have difficulty recognizing sounds absent in their native language. (Studies have found that the sound system of one's native language will influence one's perception of English phonemes.) Your students will overcome this initial "deafness" to specific sounds after directed auditory discrimination practice. If possible, ask your school nurse, speech pathologist, or local public health department to administer a quick, routine hearing screening to each of your students. This will dissolve their concerns (and yours) about any possibility of hearing loss.

Accent Analysis

The Accent Analysis should be used at the beginning of the *English Pronunciation Made Simple* program. Record each student (or have them record themselves at home) reading the **Accent Analysis Sentences** (Vowels on page 261 and Consonants on page 264). Each sentence pair is designed to survey the students' pronunciation of a specific target vowel or consonant. Encourage them to read the sentences in a natural, conversational voice. The Accent Analysis should be used again when your students complete the program. This will help you (and them) measure their progress.

Now you are ready to listen to your students' tapes and do a written survey of their pronunciation difficulties with vowels, diphthongs, consonants, and word stress. Use the **Summary of Errors** forms (Vowels form on page 263 and Consonants form on page 267) to record the results. The pairs of Accent Analysis Sentences are numbered to correspond to the phonetic symbols.

As each group of sentences is read, listen only to the pronunciation of the *target* sound. Ignore all other errors. While a student is reading, follow along sentence by sentence on the **Teacher's Record Form** (see pages 262 and 265). Circle all target words that are mispronounced. On the line above the mispronounced target word, record the error. Use any marking (e.g., phonetic symbols) that is meaningful to you. You can then complete the Summary of Errors forms (pages 263 and 267) at your leisure.

For example, your student substitutes [aʊ] (as in *out*) for [ɔ] in sentence 9's target words *author* and *audience*, and [oʊ] (as in *no*) in *office* and *boring*. You might record the errors as follows:

[aʊ]	[oʊ]	[aʊ]		[oʊ]

9. The (author) gave a **long talk** in the (office). The **small** (audience) **thought** it was (boring).

On the Summary of Errors form, you might make the following notations:

Vowels	Correct	Error	Comments
9. [ɔ] as in *all*	____	[aʊ], [oʊ] for [ɔ]	Errors seem related to spelling patterns.

Accent Analysis Sentences: Vowels

1. Please believe that sweet peas and beans are good to eat. Eat them at least twice a week.
2. Tim's sister swims a little bit. It keeps her fit, slim, and trim.
3. Ten times seven is seventy. Seven times eleven is seventy-seven.
4. Many animals inhabit Africa. Africa has camels, giraffes, parrots, and bats.
5. Doctors say jogging is good for the body. Lots of starch causes heart problems.
6. Who flew to the moon? Numerous lunar flights are in the news. We'll soon put a person on Jupiter and Pluto.
7. Would you look for my cookbook? It should be full of hints for good cookies and pudding.
8. The southern governor is Republican. The public election was fun. She won by one hundred votes.
9. The author gave a long talk in the office. The small audience thought it was boring.
10. Nurses do worthy work. They certainly deserve a word of praise.
11. Labor Day is in September. Workers are honored.
12. Maine is a state in the northern United States. It's a great place for a vacation.
13. The North Pole is close to the Arctic Ocean. It's known for polar bears, snow, and severe cold.
14. Owls are now found throughout the world. They avoid crowds and make loud sounds.
15. Eyesight is vital for a normal life. I prize mine highly.
16. The auto industry is a loyal employer in Detroit. People enjoy their choice of cars.

Word Stress

17. Africa, Asia, Australia, South America, and Europe comprise five of the continents. North America is another continent.
18. I have televisions in the bedroom, living room, and dining room. The programs about detectives and hospitals are my favorites.

Target Vowels

[i] 1. **Please believe** that **sweet peas** and **beans** are good to **eat**. **Eat** them at **least** twice a **week**.

[ɪ] 2. **Tim's sister swims** a **little bit**. It keeps her **fit**, **slim**, and **trim**.

[ɛ] 3. **Ten** times **seven** is **seventy**. **Seven** times **eleven** is **seventy-seven**.

[æ] 4. Many **animals inhabit Africa**. **Africa has camels**, **giraffes**, **parrots**, and **bats**.

[a] 5. **Doctors** say **jogging** is good for the **body**. **Lots** of **starch** causes **heart problems**.

[u] 6. **Who flew to** the **moon**? **Numerous lunar** flights are in the **news**. We'll **soon** put a person on **Jupiter** and **Pluto**.

[ʊ] 7. **Would** you **look** for my **cookbook**? It **should** be **full** of hints for **good cookies** and **pudding**.

[ʌ] 8. The **southern governor** is **Republican**. The **public** election **was fun**. She **won** by **one hundred** votes.

[ɔ] 9. The **author** gave a **long talk** in the **office**. The **small audience thought** it was **boring**.

[ɝ] 10. **Nurses** do **worthy work**. They **certainly deserve** a **word** of praise.

[ɚ] 11. **Labor** Day is in **September**. **Workers** are **honored**.

[eɪ] 12. **Maine** is a **state** in the northern United **States**. It's a **great place** for a **vacation**.

[oʊ] 13. The North **Pole** is **close** to the Arctic **Ocean**. It's **known** for **polar** bears, **snow**, and severe **cold**.

[aʊ] 14. **Owls** are **now found throughout** the world. They avoid **crowds** and make **loud sounds**.

[aɪ] 15. **Eyesight** is **vital** for a normal **life**. **I prize mine highly**.

[ɔɪ] 16. The auto industry is a **loyal employer** in **Detroit**. People **enjoy** their **choice** of cars.

Word Stress

[ə] 17. **Africa**, **Asia**, **Australia**, South **America**, and **Europe comprise** five of the **continents**. North **America** is **another continent**.

18. I have **tel**evisions in the **bed**room, **liv**ing room, and **din**ing room. The **pro**grams a**bout** de**tec**tives and **hos**pitals are my **fav**orites.*

* The boldface letters indicate the syllable that should receive primary stress. If the student errs on a target word, circle the incorrectly stressed syllable.

Student's Name: _____ Date: _____

Summary of Errors: Vowels

Vowels	Correct	Error	Comments
1. [i] as in *me*	_____	_____ for [i]	_____
2. [ɪ] as in *it*	_____	_____ for [ɪ]	_____
3. [ɛ] as in *egg*	_____	_____ for [ɛ]	_____
4. [æ] as in *at*	_____	_____ for [æ]	_____
5. [a] as in *hot*	_____	_____ for [a]	_____
6. [u] as in *you*	_____	_____ for [u]	_____
7. [ʊ] as in *cook*	_____	_____ for [ʊ]	_____
8. [ʌ] as in *up*	_____	_____ for [ʌ]	_____
9. [ɔ] as in *all*	_____	_____ for [ɔ]	_____
10. [ɝ] as in *first*	_____	_____ for [ɝ]	_____
11. [ɚ] as in *father*	_____	_____ for [ɚ]	_____

Diphthongs

	Correct	Error	Comments
12. [eɪ] as in *ate*	_____	_____ for [eɪ]	_____
13. [oʊ] as in *no*	_____	_____ for [oʊ]	_____
14. [aʊ] as in *out*	_____	_____ for [aʊ]	_____
15. [aɪ] as in *my*	_____	_____ for [aɪ]	_____
16. [ɔɪ] as in *boy*	_____	_____ for [ɔɪ]	_____

Word stress	Correct	Error	Comments
17. [ə] as in *soda*	_____	_____ for [ə]	_____

18. Is stress placed on the wrong syllable of words of more than one syllable?

Errors: _____

Other Observations

Accent Analysis Sentences: Consonants

1. The United States started with thirteen small states. Now there are fifty states spread from east to west.
2. Lazy cows graze in the fields of New Zealand. The pleasant breeze blows from the seas.
3. *A Tale of Two Cities* was written by Charles Dickens. Today it is taught throughout the world.
4. Dad had a bad cold. He stayed in bed all day Monday and Tuesday.
5. Is there a threat of World War Three? After a third war, many think there will be nothing left on Earth. We must be thankful for peace.
6. My mother and father loathe northern weather. They prefer the climate of the southern states.
7. Sherry took a short vacation to Washington. She went fishing and found shells along the ocean shore.
8. Chuck ate lunch in the kitchen. He had a cheese sandwich and peach pie.
9. I made a decision to paint the garage beige. I usually paint or watch television in my leisure time.
10. George is majoring in education. He will graduate from college in June.
11. Year after year, millions of people visit New York. Young and old enjoy familiar sights.
12. Pick up a pack of ripe apples. Mom will bake apple pie for supper.
13. Bob built a big boat. He finds lobster and crab and cooks them in the cabin below.
14. The elephant is friendly and full of life. It's a fact that an elephant never forgets!
15. Leave the veal and gravy in the oven. Vicky wants to keep it very hot. She will serve everyone at seven.
16. Kathy can't bake a cake for the card party. She is working at the bank until six o'clock.
17. Gambling is legal in Las Vegas. Gamblers go for the big win!
18. We would like to see the Seven Wonders of the World. We will just have to wait awhile!
19. Roads are rough in rural areas. Be very careful when you drive your car.
20. I like the cooler climate in the fall. The gold and yellow colors of the leaves are beautiful.
21. Heaven helps those who help themselves. Anyhow, hard work never hurt anyone.
22. I'm coming home for Christmas. As the poem says, "Wherever you may roam, there's no place like home."
23. Now you can learn to pronounce the consonants. Practice them again and again on your own.
24. The strong young men are exercising this morning. They are running long distances.
25. Mother washed, cooked, and cleaned. After she finished, she rested.
26. Put the shoes and boots in the boxes. Hang the dresses and pants on the hangers.

Teacher's Record Form

Target Consonants

[s] 1. The United **States started** with thirteen **small states**. Now there are fifty **states spread** from **east** to **west**.

[z] 2. **Lazy cows graze** in the **fields** of New **Zealand**. The **pleasant breeze blows** from the **seas**.

[t] 3. *A Tale of Two Cities* was **written** by Charles Dickens. **Today it** is **taught throughout** the world.

[d] 4. **Dad had** a **bad cold**. He **stayed** in **bed** all **day Monday and Tuesday**.

[θ] 5. Is there a **threat** of World War **Three**? After a **third** war, many **think** there will be **nothing** left on **Earth**. We must be **thankful** for peace.

[ð] 6. My **mother** and **father loathe northern weather**. **They** prefer **the** climate of **the southern** states.

[ʃ] 7. **Sherry** took a **short vacation** to **Washington**. **She** went **fishing** and found **shells** along the **ocean shore**.

[tʃ] 8. **Chuck** ate **lunch** in the **kitchen**. He had a **cheese sandwich** and **peach** pie.

[ʒ] 9. I made a **decision** to paint the **garage beige**. I **usually** paint or watch **television** in my **leisure** time.

[dʒ] 10. **George** is **majoring** in **education**. He will **graduate** from **college** in **June**.

[j] 11. **Year** after **year, millions** of people visit New **York. Young** and old enjoy **familiar** sights.

[p] 12. **Pick up** a **pack** of **ripe apples**. Mom will bake **apple pie** for **supper**.

[b] 13. **Bob built** a **big boat**. He finds **lobster** and **crab** and cooks them in the **cabin below**.

[f] 14. The **elephant** is **friendly** and **full** of **life**. It's a **fact** that an **elephant** never **forgets**!

[v] 15. **Leave** the **veal** and **gravy** in the **oven. Vicky** wants to keep it **very** hot. She will **serve everyone** at **seven**.

[k] 16. **Kathy can't bake** a **cake** for the **card** party. She is **working** at the **bank** until six **o'clock**.

[g] 17. **Gambling** is **legal** in Las **Vegas. Gamblers go** for the **big** win!

[w] 18. **We would** like to see the Seven **Wonders** of the **World. We will** just have to **wait awhile**!

[r] 19. **Roads** are **rough** in **rural areas**. Be **very careful** when you **drive your car**.

(Continued)

[l]   20.   I **like** the **cooler climate** in the fall. The **gold** and **yellow colors** of the **leaves** are **beautiful**.

[h]   21.   **Heaven helps** those who **help** themselves. **Anyhow**, **hard** work never **hurt** anyone.

[m]   22.   **I'm coming home** for **Christmas**. As the **poem** says, "Wherever you **may roam**, there's no place like **home**."

[n]   23.   **Now** you **can learn** to **pronounce** the **consonants**. Practice them **again and again on** your **own**.

[ŋ]   24.   The **strong young** men are **exercising** this **morning**. They are **running long** distances.

Past Tense

25.   Mother wash**ed**, cook**ed**, and clean**ed**. After she finish**ed**, she rest**ed**.

Plurals

26.   Put the shoe**s** and boot**s** in the box**es**. Hang the dress**es** and pant**s** on the hanger**s**.

Summary of Errors: Consonants

Consonants	Correct	Error	Comments
1. [s] as in *see*	_____	_____ for [s]	_____
2. [z] as in *zoo*	_____	_____ for [z]	_____
3. [t] as in *too*	_____	_____ for [t]	_____
4. [d] as in *dog*	_____	_____ for [d]	_____
5. [θ] as in *think*	_____	_____ for [θ]	_____
6. [ð] as in *them*	_____	_____ for [ð]	_____
7. [ʃ] as in *shoe*	_____	_____ for [ʃ]	_____
8. [tʃ] as in *chair*	_____	_____ for [tʃ]	_____
9. [ʒ] as in *rouge*	_____	_____ for [ʒ]	_____
10. [dʒ] as in *jaw*	_____	_____ for [dʒ]	_____
11. [j] as in *you*	_____	_____ for [j]	_____
12. [p] as in *pay*	_____	_____ for [p]	_____
13. [b] as in *boy*	_____	_____ for [b]	_____
14. [f] as in *foot*	_____	_____ for [f]	_____
15. [v] as in *very*	_____	_____ for [v]	_____
16. [k] as in *key*	_____	_____ for [k]	_____
17. [g] as in *go*	_____	_____ for [g]	_____
18. [w] as in *we*	_____	_____ for [w]	_____
19. [r] as in *red*	_____	_____ for [r]	_____
20. [l] as in *look*	_____	_____ for [l]	_____
21. [h] as in *hat*	_____	_____ for [h]	_____
22. [m] as in *me*	_____	_____ for [m]	_____
23. [n] as in *no*	_____	_____ for [n]	_____
24. [ŋ] as in *ring*	_____	_____ for [ŋ]	_____

Past Tense	Correct	Error	Comments
25. a. [t] as in wash**ed**	_____	_____	_____
b. [d] as in clean**ed**	_____	_____	_____
c. [ɪd] as in rest**ed**	_____	_____	_____

Plurals

	Correct	Error	Comments
26. a. [z] as in shoe**s**	_____	_____	_____
b. [s] as in boot**s**	_____	_____	_____
c. [ɪz] as in dress**es**	_____	_____	_____

Are Final Consonants Clear? _____

Other Observations

Using the Manual for Classroom Instruction

Whether you are an instructor of English for speakers of other languages, speech, or accent reduction, or a speech pathologist, you will find *English Pronunciation Made Simple* completely adaptable for classroom or clinical use. The exercises and Check Yourself sections have been tested in the classroom and proven to be effective with nonnative speakers of English striving to improve their American English pronunciation. The manual is so complete that it eliminates the need for you to spend endless hours preparing drill materials. The following are some suggestions to help you use the manual effectively.

- **To the Student:** Read this section first to familiarize yourself with the organization and content of the manual.

- **Sequence of Material Presentation:** The order of sound presentation is flexible. The integrity of the program will remain intact if you assign the lessons in a sequence of your own choosing. Your personal teaching philosophy, available time, and students' specific needs should dictate what you teach first. Many students will not have difficulty with all the sounds. Consequently, you may wish to skip some lessons completely and spend more time on the real "trouble makers" (like [ɪ] as in *it* or [ʊ] as in *cook*)!

- **A Key to Pronouncing the Vowels and Consonants of American English:** These sections introduce the International Phonetic Alphabet. Don't be concerned if you are currently unfamiliar with the phonetic symbols. Each symbol is introduced and explained one at a time. You will learn each one easily and gradually as you progress through the program with your students. Refer back to the Key to Pronouncing the Vowels of American English (page 3) and the Key to Pronouncing the Consonants of American English (page 117) when you need to refresh your memory.

- **Adaptation of Material:** The material presented in each lesson can be adapted easily. If your students require more drill at the sentence level before progressing to dialogues or paragraphs, focus your attention on the appropriate exercises; defer presentation of more difficult activities to a later time.

- **Check Yourself:** The Check Yourself exercises can be used in a variety of ways: (1) You can present the exercises to evaluate your students' progress; (2) you can use them as both pre- and post-tests to more precisely measure students' gains; (3) you can divide your students into teams to complete the exercises as a group rather than individually; or (4) you can assign the exercises as homework to encourage out-of-class practice.

- **More Practice:** These sections have a variety of additional readings and conversational and communicative activities to encourage further practice with the target sound or feature of English pronunciation emphasized in the lesson. The activities can easily be expanded for classroom use. The diversity of these assignments will certainly liven up the regular classroom routine. For example, in lesson 2 on [i] and [ɪ], students are asked to make several social introductions using phrases pronounced with the target sounds. This activity could be employed in the classroom by having students introduce themselves to each other.

Additional Communicative Practice Activities

As an extra bonus, here are some additional in-class activities to vary your presentation of the material and encourage further communicative practice.

Objective: To increase students' ability to produce the target sound in connected speech.

Activity 1: Have students role-play using the communicative activity at the end of each lesson.

Activity 2: Play a memory game using word lists. Ask one student to complete a sentence with a word containing the target sound. The next student must repeat the sentence and add another word with the target sound.

Example for target consonant [v]: "I'm going on **vacation** and **I've** packed a **vest, vase, stove,** ____, . . ."

Example for target vowel [ɪ]: "I'm going on a **trip** and I **will bring** a **pin, winter** coat, **guitar,** ____, . . ."

Activity 3: Assign students a topic for a list. List topics might include Grocery List, Laundry List, List of Daily Chores, List of Phone Calls to Make, List of Famous People to Invite to a Party, List of Things to Pack for a Trip. Have them list at least five items loaded with the target sound. When the lists are completed, ask students to share their responses with you and their classmates. You'll be delighted with their creativity.

Example for target consonant [r]: (1) **Remind Florist** to **Deliver Roses** to Aunt **Roda,** (2) **Grocery** Shop for **Bread, Oranges, Radishes, Rolls,** and **Carrots**.

Activity 4: Ask students to write their own personal ads describing their ideal mate. Assign this either for homework or as an in-class activity. They should use as many words with the target sound as possible. Instead of having students read their own "personal ads," collect all of them and redistribute to the class. Each student gets a turn reading one of the ads. In this way, authors remain anonymous!

Example for target consonant [m]: I'm looking for a **manly, muscular male**. He **must** be **smart, handsome,** and like **music**. He should be **multi**-talented and **most important,** be **marriage-minded**.

Activity 5: Ask students to create their own tongue twisters with the target sound in the initial position of words. Encourage them to use the dictionary to find as many words with the target sound as possible.

Example for target sound [l]: "**L**arge **L**arry **l**istened as **L**aura **l**ectured **l**oudly" or "**L**ovely **l**adies **l**ove **l**ovely **l**acy **l**ingerie."

Objective: To increase students' ability to correctly pronounce past tense and plural endings.

Activity 1: Play a question-and-answer game using regular present and past tense verbs. Ask one student to respond in a complete sentence to your question; then ask a yes/no question of another student. The next student must respond to the question, pronouncing the verb correctly in the past tense, and ask a question of his or her own.

Example: "When did you stop smoking?" "I **stopped** smoking last year!"
"Did you wash your car today?" "No, I **washed** it yesterday."

Activity 2: Present a variety of 3-verb series aloud. One past tense verb in each series should have a different *-ed* sound than the other two. Ask the students to identify the verb with the different *-ed* sound.

Example: You say **baked, cleaned, cooked;** the students select **cleaned.**

Activity 3: Ask students to prepare a two- to three-minute talk about a personal experience they have had as an adult or child. Encourage them to relate their experiences in a conversational manner and to use as many past tense verbs as possible. Ask the "listeners" to make a list of all the regular past tense verbs used by each speaker. After each presentation, ask for a volunteer to read his or her list aloud, being careful to pronounce the *-ed* endings of the past tense verbs correctly.

Examples of possible experiences:

An Embarrassing Moment	A Sad Experience
A Scary Experience	A Happy Experience
My First Pet	The Time I Was Lost
My First Car	My First Airplane Trip
My Most Memorable Birthday	An Exciting Experience

Activity 4: Play a "bragging" game using various noun categories such as vehicles, foods, items of clothing, types of footware, school supplies, items of furniture.

Example: One student asks, "What types of **vehicles** do you have?" The second student responds, "I have three **cars**, two **boats**, and four **airplanes**"or "What **vegetables** did you eat?" "I ate two **tomatoes**, three **cucumbers**, and nine **olives**."

Objective: To increase the students' ability to use appropriate American English stress, rhythm, and intonation patterns.

Activity 1: Have students write *wh*-question-and-answer pairs using complete sentences. They should underline the word in the answer that provides the desired information. Have them read their pairs aloud, being sure to emphasize the new information in the answer.

Examples: "What's your favorite fruit?" "**Apples** are my favorite fruit." "Who will drive you home?" "My **sister** will drive me home." "Where do you live?" "I live in **Miami**."

Activity 2: Ask students to work in pairs and to take turns interviewing their assigned partners. Encourage them to learn at least five "tidbits" about each other. Have them share what they learn with the rest of the class. Their goal is to use at least one contraction in each sentence.

Example: Sergio**'s** from Brazil. He**'ll** be here for a year. He**'s** currently looking for a job. He does**n't** want to be a busboy, but he**'d** like to be a waiter.

Activity 3: Ask students to formulate short yes/no questions. Students take turns asking their questions and choosing classmates to answer them. Remind the students to use a rising intonation pattern at the end of the yes/no question, to pause after the *yes* or *no* response, and to end their declarative statement with a falling intonation.

Examples: "Do you like school?" ↗ "Yes →, I like it a lot." ↘ "Will you buy a new dress?" ↗ "No →, I don't have any money." ↘ "Is your friend going to drive you?" ↗ "Yes →, he'll pick me up here."↘

With all of these suggestions and the activities, your students will be kept occupied and learning throughout the course!

Additional Auditory Discrimination Practice Activities

Here are some additional in-class activities to vary your presentation of the material and further enhance your students' ability to discriminate aurally between correct and incorrect pronunciation patterns.

Objective: To increase students' ability to recognize the target sound aurally.

Activity 1: Read aloud Exercise A words in mixed order. Have students identify the target sound as occurring in either the beginning, middle, or end position.

Activity 2: Read phrase and sentence exercises orally. Have students list all the words containing the target sound.

Objective: To increase students' ability to discriminate between the target sound and his or her error.

Activity 1: Use minimal pairs exercises/Check Yourself exercises (for example, Exercise A on page 12). Create word pairs such as *sit-sit* and *seat-sit*. Have students identify the words in each pair as being the *same* or *different*.

Activity 2: Read aloud from the minimal pairs/Check Yourself exercises (such as Check Yourself 2 on page 13). Vary the order of the words (*bit, beat; sheep, ship*) or sentences (*Will he leave? Will he live?*). Have students indicate whether they heard the target vowel in the first or second word or sentence.

Activity 3: Give a "spelling test." Read individual words from the minimal pairs exercises (such as the exercise on page 33). Have students write the words as you say them (for example, *aid, Ed, add, odd*). This is a sure way to determine if they are hearing the target sound.

Activity 4: Read aloud the phrase and sentence exercises (for example, Exercise C on page 49). Alternate between imitating a student's typical error and pronouncing the target sound correctly. (*"Dun't [don't] go."* or *"Hold the fun [phone]."*). Have students determine whether or not the words in the phrases and sentences have been produced accurately.

Appendix II:
Check Yourself Answer Key

Check Yourself, Page 8

1. bead (great) leave tea
2. (eight) either believe niece
3. scene (women) these even
4. need (been) sleep thirteen
5. police thief machine (vision)
6. (pretty) wheat sweet cream
7. people (bread) deal east
8. (tin) teen steam receive
9. leave (live) leaf lease
10. steep Steve easy (still)

Check Yourself, Page 11

1. (1) 2 3 (sit seat seat)
2. 1 2 (3) (feet feet fit)
3. 1 (2) 3 (feast fist feast)
4. 1 2 (3) (eat eat it)
5. (1) 2 3 (list least least)
6. 1 2 (3) (beat beat bit)
7. 1 (2) 3 (neat knit neat)
8. (1) 2 3 (hit heat heat)
9. 1 (2) 3 (sheep ship sheep)
10. (1) 2 3 (bin bean bean)

Check Yourself 1, Page 12

1. (field) filled
2. (bean) bin
3. neat (knit)
4. deal (dill)
5. beat (bit)
6. (team) Tim
7. sleep (slip)
8. (green) grin
9. heel (hill)
10. week (wick)

Check Yourself 2, Page 13

1. They cleaned the ((ship)/ sheep).

2. Will he ((leave)/ live)?

3. The boy was (beaten /(bitten)).

4. His clothes are ((neat)/ knit).

5. She has plump ((cheeks)/ chicks).

6. I like low ((heels)/ hills).

7. The children will (sleep /(slip)).

8. I heard every ((beat)/ bit).

9. They stored the ((beans)/ bins).

10. Everyone talks about the ((heat)/ hit)

Check Yourself 3, Page 13

Jim: Hi (Tina!) Do you have a <u>minute</u>?

Tina: Yes, <u>Jim</u>. What <u>is</u> <u>it</u>?

Jim: My <u>sister</u> <u>is</u> <u>in</u> the <u>city</u> on <u>business</u>. (We) will (eat) dinner out tonight. Can you recommend a place to (eat?)

Tina: There <u>is</u> a fine (seafood) place on <u>Fifth</u> (Street). The <u>fish</u> <u>is</u> fresh and the <u>shrimp</u> <u>is</u> great. But <u>it</u> <u>isn't</u> (cheap)!

Jim: That's OK. <u>It</u> <u>will</u> (be) "(feast) today, <u>famine</u> tomorrow!" I'll just have to (eat) "(beans)" the rest of the (week!)

Check Yourself 1, Page 16

1. (steak)	lettuce	(pastry)	cereal
2. bread	(raisins)	melon	bananas
3. (cake)	(tomatoes)	(bacon)	(baking soda)
4. (potatoes)	crackers	peas	ice cream
5. (grapes)	celery	(gravy)	carrots
6. (toothpaste)	peas	squash	(paper plates)

Check Yourself 2, Page 17

1. ① 2 3 (Kate cat cot)   6. ① 2 3 (rate rat rot)

2. 1 ② 3 (can cane con)   7. 1 ② 3 (ran rain wren)

3. 1 2 ③ (pen pan pain)   8. ① 2 3 (late let lot)

4. 1 ② 3 (foot fate fat)   9. 1 ② 3 (calm came comb)

5. ① 2 3 (mate mat met)   10. ① 2 3 (wait what wet)

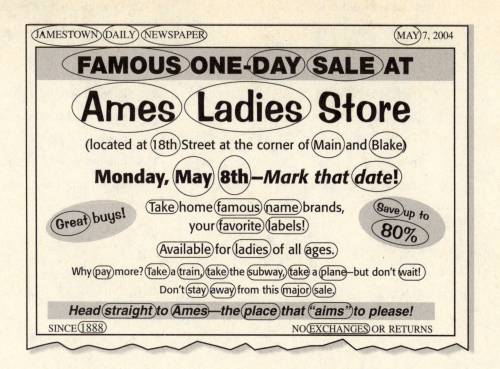

1. any	(crazy)	anywhere	many
2. (paper)	letter	send	pencil
3. seven	eleven	(eight)	twenty
4. health	(wreath)	breath	wealth
5. (reading)	ready	already	head
6. present	precious	(previous)	president
7. November	February	September	(April)
8. guess	guest	(cruel)	question
9. thread	threat	fresh	(theater)
10. (mean)	meant	mental	met

1. C (I)   (He was tired and went to **bad**.)

2. (C) 1   (She is my **best** friend.)

3. C (I)   (The opposite of east is **waste** / **waist**.)

4. C (I)   (My **pan** has no ink.)

5. C ① (Please **sand** the letter.)
6. Ⓒ 1 (Did you **sell** your car?)
7. C ① (My favorite color is **raid**.)

8. C ① (Put salt and **paper** on the salad.)
9. Ⓒ I (Can you **guess** the right answer?)
10. Ⓒ I (This is the **end** of the test!)

Check Yourself 1, Page 24

1. ① 2 3 (rack rock wreck)
2. 1 2 ③ (lake lock lack)
3. ① 2 3 (add aid Ed)
4. 1 ② 3 (pot pat pet)
5. 1 2 ③ (top tape tap)

6. ① 2 3 (laughed left loft)
7. 1 2 ③ (sneak snake snack)
8. 1 ② 3 (paste past pest)
9. ① 2 3 (hat hot hate)
10. 1 ② 3 (made/maid mad mod)

Check Yourself 2, Page 25

1. ⓐn i m a l
2. Ⓐf r i c a
3. C ⓐl i f o r n i a
4. f ⓐs c i n a t e
5. A l ⓐs k a

6. a t t ⓐc k
7. S ⓐt u r d a y
8. C ⓐn a d a
9. D ⓐl l a s
10. p ⓐc k a g e

Check Yourself 3, Page 25

1. The ⟨Titanic⟩ was ⟨traveling⟩ to New York across the ⟨Atlantic⟩ in 1912.
2. This ⟨grand⟩ and ⟨elaborate⟩ ship ⟨had⟩ over 2,200 ⟨passengers⟩.
3. It ⟨crashed⟩ into an iceberg and ⟨sank⟩ in about two and a ⟨half⟩ hours.
4. ⟨Telegraph⟩ warnings reached the ⟨Titanic⟩ too late.
5. ⟨After⟩ the ⟨crash⟩, upper and lower ⟨class⟩ ⟨passengers⟩ ⟨ran⟩ about in a ⟨panic⟩.
6. Women and children ⟨had⟩ a ⟨chance⟩ to ⟨cram⟩ into small boats ⟨at⟩ the ⟨last⟩ minute.
7. The ⟨captain⟩ and other ⟨passengers⟩ could not ⟨abandon⟩ the ship.
8. ⟨Actors⟩ and ⟨actresses⟩ ⟨re-enacted⟩ the ⟨accident⟩ in an ⟨academy⟩ award movie.
9. The story of the ⟨Titanic⟩ remains a ⟨sad⟩ and ⟨tragic⟩ ⟨chapter⟩ in our ⟨past⟩.

Check Yourself 1, Page 29

1. 1 ② 3 (rub rob robe)
2. ① 2 3 (hot hat hut)
3. 1 2 ③ (pope pup pop)
4. 1 ② 3 (gut got goat)
5. 1 ② 3 (note not nut)

6. ① 2 3 (fond fund phoned)
7. 1 ② 3 (stack stock stuck)
8. ① 2 3 (cot cut caught)
9. 1 ② 3 (cup cop cope)
10. ① 2 3 (mod mud mowed)

Check Yourself 2, Page 29

1. ⟨condor⟩ ⟨collie⟩ leopard ⟨llama⟩
2. cat ⟨crocodile⟩ elephant ⟨sea otter⟩

3. (fox)   tiger   (hippopotamus)   (dolphin)

4. (iguana)   kangaroo   (lobster)   (octopus)

5. parrot   (rhinoceros)   (opossum)   lion

Check Yourself 3, Page 29

Donna: (Bob), I (want) to talk to you.

Bob: (Are) you all right, (Donna?)

Donna: Don't be (alarmed). I saw Dr. (Johnson) at the (hospital). You're going to be a (father!) Our new baby will be born in (October).

Bob: I'm in (shock). How do you feel?

Donna: I'm feeling (on) (top) of the world. I've (got) a list of names for the baby.

Bob: If it's a girl, let's call her (Donna) after her (mom).

Donna: ("Donna") is fine for a middle name. How about (Connie) or (Barbara) for her first name?

Bob: Fine. If it's a boy, we'll name him (Don).

Donna: Better yet, it it's a boy, let's call him (Bob) after his (father.) If it's a girl, we'll call her (Barbara).

Bob: (Donna), maybe you want to name her (Rhonda) after your (father's) sister. Then, if it's a boy, we can name him (Ron.)

Donna: We don't want to forget your mother (Carla). So, let's call him (Carl) if it's a boy.

Bob: I think we ought to (stop). This could go (on) and (on).

Donna: It's (not) really a (problem). Now we have names for our first four (darling) babies.

Bob: (Donna), you've (gone) too far. One at a time is enough for this (mom) and (pop.) (Donna) or (Don) is a good (start) for now!

Check Yourself, Page 36

1. 1 2 ③   (look look Luke)

2. 1 ② 3   (cook kook cook)

3. ① 2 3   (fool fall full)

4. ① 2 3   (mood mud made)

5. ① 2 3   (suit sat soot)

6. ① 2 3   (wooed wade would)

7. ① 2 3   (stewed stood stayed)

8. 1 ② 3   (toll tool tall)

9. 1 2 ③   (pull pole pool)

10. 1 ② 3   (skull school scale)

Check Yourself, Page 38

1. C ①   (You **shooed** drive carefully.)

2. © I   (I like chocolate chip **cookies**.)

3. C ①   (He **stewed** on the ladder.)

4. C ①   (The carpenter sawed the **wooed**.)

5. C ①   (The pool was **fool** of water.)

6. © I   (The police caught the **crook**.)

7. © I   (The gun has **bullets**.)

8. C ①   (Please don't **pool** my hair.)

9. © I   (I like coffee with **sugar**.)

10. © I   (He broke his left **foot**.)

   [u]   [ʊ]   [u]
1. **Too** many **cooks** spoil the **soup**!

      [ʊ]   [ʊ] [u]
2. There **should** be a **full moon**.

     [ʊ]   [ʊ]   [ʊ]
3. Mr. **Brooks** is **good looking**.

  [u]   [ʊ]   [u]
4. **June** is a **good** month to **move**.

     [ʊ]   [ʊ]   [u]
5. The **butcher cooked** a **goose**.

       [u] [ʊ]   [ʊ]
6. The **news bulletin** was **misunderstood**.

      [u]   [u]   [u]   [u]
7. Did **you choose** a pair of **new shoes**?

  [u]   [u]   [u]   [ʊ]
8. **Lucy** had a **loose tooth pulled**.

       [u]   [ʊ]   [ʊ]   [ʊ]
9. **Students should** read **good books**.

      [u]   [ʊ]   [u]   [u]
10. The **room** is **full** of **blue balloons**.

1. 1 2 ③   (look look Luke)

2. 1 ② 3   (cook kook cook)

3. 1 ② 3   (fool full fool)

4. ① 2 3   (pull pool pool)

5. 1 2 ③   (suit suit soot)

6. 1 2 ③   (wooed wooed would)

7. ① 2 3   (stewed stood stood)

8. 1 2 ③   (could could cooed)

9. ① 2 3   (wooed wood wood)

10. ① 2 3   (hood who'd who'd)

Houdini

Harry (Houdini) was a magician known (throughout) world. He could (remove) himself from chains and ropes and could walk (through) walls! (Houdini) was born in (Budapest), Hungary. He (moved) to (New) York when he was twelve and (soon) took up magic. (Rumors) spread that (Houdini) had (supernatural) powers. However, he was (truthful) and stated that his tricks could be understood by all (humans). (Houdini) is an idol for all would-be magicians.

1. (cut)   cot   6. (nut)   not

2. (stuck)   stock   7. bum   (bomb)

3. (come)   calm   8. pup   (pop)

4. wonder (wander)   9. (fund)   fond

5. color   (collar)   10. (shut)   shot

1. something   wonder   ugly   (open)

2. trouble   come   (locker)   once

3. color   cups   dozen   (collar)

4. peanut   muddy   (modern)   bunny
5. (stood)   stuff   stump   stuck
6. lucky   brother   just   (lock)
7. Monday   month   (Tuesday)   Sunday
8. (comb)   coming   cutting   country
9. cover   (over)   oven   other
10. rust   must   (rot)   nothing

Check Yourself 3, Page 46

Gus: Hi (Justine)! How's my (fun)-(loving) (cousin)?

Justine: Very worried. I (just) had a (run) of (tough) (luck).

Gus: Why, (what's) (up?)

Justine: My (bus) got (stuck) in the (mud) and I lost (some) (money.) I should carry (something) for (luck)!

Gus: Yes. Here's (some) (other) advice. Never walk (under) ladders, and (run) (from) black cats. They're (nothing) (but) (trouble)!

Justine: Oh, (Gus.) You (must) be a (nut)! Do you really believe (such) (mumbo) (jumbo)?

Gus: Don't make (fun,) (Justine) (Customs) (come) (from) many (countries). You (must) know (some) (others)!

Justine: Well, the (number) 13 is (unlucky.) And, a blister on the (tongue) means (someone) is lying!

Gus: Right! But you can have good (luck,) too. (Discover) a four-leaf clover, or find (bubbles) in your coffee (cup) and you'll get a (sum) of (money.)

Justine: OK, (Gus.) Maybe I'll have (some) (luck) this (month.) Knock on wood!

Check Yourself 1, Page 50

1. (phone)   fun   6. coat   (cut)
2. bone   (bun)   7. (wrote)   rut
3. roam / Rome   (rum)   8. (hole / whole)   hull
4. (boast)   bust/bused   9. rogue   (rug)
5. tone   (ton)   10. (most)   must / mussed

Check Yourself 2, Page 50

1. (toaster)   frying pan   bookcase   freezer
2. clock   (telephone)   faucet   (radio)
3. (stove)   (sofa)   (lawn mower)   table
4. doorknob   (window)   television   (coat rack)
5. (can opener)   (mixing bowl)   (clothes dryer)   iron

Joe: Rose, let's go on a trip. We need to be alone.

Rose: OK, Joe. Where should we go?

Joe: I know! We'll go to Ohio.

Rose: Great! We'll visit my Uncle Roland.

Joe: No, it's too cold in Ohio. We'll go to Arizona.

Rose: Fine. We'll stay with your Aunt Mona!

Joe: No, it's too hot in Arizona. Let's go to Rome.

Rose: Oh, good! You'll meet my Cousin Tony.

Joe: No, no, no!! We won't go to Rome. Let's go to Nome, Alaska. We don't know anyone there!!

Rose: You won't believe it, but I have an old friend . . .

Joe: Hold it, Rose we won't go anywhere! I suppose we'll just stay home.

1. (a) (b) (a. It's in the **hall**. b. It's in the **hull**.)
2. (a) (b) (a. I dropped the **bowl**. b. I dropped the **ball**.)
3. (a) (b) (a. I said **talk**. b. I said **tuck**.)
4. (a) (b) (a. The **stock** is **high**. b. The **stalk** is **high**)
5. (a) (b) (a. He **sawed** it. b. He **sewed** it.)

1. C I (I take long **walks**.)
2. C I (I received a phone **coal**.)
3. C I (The **store** will open at four.)
4. C I (Cats and **dugs** make good pets.)
5. C I (I like to **take** on the phone for hours.)

6. C I (I **boat** a new hat.)
7. C I (My son plays foot**bowl**.)
8. C I (He ate a **small** piece of pie.)
9. C I (The fisherman **coat** ten fish.)
10. C I (Please **call** me tomorrow.)

Audrey: Hi, Paula. Did you hear the awful news? Maude called off her wedding to Claude!

Paula: Why, Audrey? I thought they were getting married in August.

Audrey: Maude kept stalling and decided Claude was the wrong man.

Paula: Poor Claude. He must be a lost soul.

Audrey: Oh no. He's abroad in Austria having a ball!

Paula: I almost forgot. What about the long tablecloth we bought them?

Audrey: I already brought it back. The cost of the cloth will cover the cost of our lunch today.

Paula: Audrey, you're always so thoughtful!

Check Yourself 1, Page 59

1. a l p h (a) b e t
2. u t (i) l i z e
3. d (e) p e n d i n g
4. p h o t (o) g r a p h
5. p a p (a)

6. p r (e) v e n t
7. i m (i) t a t e
8. b r e a k f (a) s t
9. c (o) n t r o l
10. (a) l a r m

Check Yourself 2, Page 59

1. about   oven   (create)   olive
2. minute   second   seven   (leaving)
3. (after)   attend   allow   annoy
4. (something)   support   supply   suppose
5. combine   complete   (camper)   compare
6. Canada   Russia   (Norway)   Columbia
7. lavender   maroon   (yellow)   orange
8. (strawberry)   banana   vanilla   chocolate
9. lettuce   tomato   carrot   (cucumber)
10. giraffe   zebra   (monkey)   camel

Check Yourself 3, Page 60

1. f a v (o) r (i) t e
2. p r i n c (i) p (a) l
3. (a) s s i s t (a) n c e
4. m e d (i) c (a) l
5. (a) t t e n d (a) n c e

6. e v (i) d (e) n c e
7. (o) f f e n d (e) d
8. d (i) p l o m (a)
9. (a) p a r t m (e) n t
10. C a n (a) d (a)

Check Yourself, Page 63

1. The **girl** wore a **purple** __skirt__ .
2. The **Germans** bake good __desserts__ .
3. At Thanksgiving we **serv**e __turkey__ .
4. People **worship** in a __church__ .
5. I heard the **chirping** of the __bird__ .
6. Another **word** for handbag is __purse__ .
7. A **permanent** makes your hair __curly__ .
8. I **prefer** the scent of that __perfume__ .
9. You should **learn** your nouns and __verbs__ .
10. A **person** collects unemployment when he is out of __work__ .

1. return (supper) purple   4. nurse (soldier) (pleasure)
2. (enter) curtain dirty   5. (silver) (weather) (Saturday)
3. third (backward) inform

    [ɚ] [ɝ]
1. silver urn

    [ɚ]   [ɝ]
2. dangerous curve

    [ɝ]   [ɝ]
3. sermon in church

    [ɚ] [ɚ]
4. regular exercise

    [ɚ]   [ɚ]
5. grammar teacher

    [ɚ]   [ɚ] [ɝ]   [ɝ]
6. The grammar teacher worked on verbs.

    [ɝ]   [ɚ]   [ɚ]
7. One good turn deserves another.

    [ɝ]   [ɚ]   [ɚ]
8. Birds of a feather flock together.

    [ɚ]   [ɝ]
9. Actions speak louder than words.

    [ɚ] [ɝ]   [ɚ] [ɝ]   [ɝ]
10. Actors perform better after rehearsing.

Pearls

The <u>pearl</u> is one of the <u>world's</u> most (treasured) gems. <u>Pearls</u> are formed inside the shells of (oysters.) The largest <u>pearl</u> (fisheries) are in Asia. (Cultured) pearls <u>were</u> developed by the Chinese in the twentieth (century.) They are (larger) than (nature's) pearls. A <u>perfect</u> <u>pearl</u> that is round and has great (luster) is <u>worth</u> a lot of money. (Perhaps) a "diamond is a <u>girl's</u> best friend," but <u>pearls</u> will always win a woman's (favor!)

1. brown down (flow) frown
2. foul (group) shout loud
3. (know) how now cow
4. sour hour (tour) our
5. (could) count crown crowd
6. (thought) plough drought thousand
7. ounce out (own) ouch
8. flounder (flood) flour pounce
9. allow about power (arose)
10. noun (consonant) vowel sound

Mr. Brown: You look (out) of sorts. (How) come?

Mrs. Brown: I'm tired (out.) Didn't you hear the (loud) noise (outside) all night?

Mr. Brown: I didn't hear a (sound.) I was (out) like a light!

Mrs. Brown: (Our) neighbors had a big (crowd;) they were (shouting) and (howling!)

Mr. Brown: Why didn't you tell them to stop (clowning) (around?)

Mrs. Brown: I didn't want to (sound) like a (grouch.)

Mr. Brown: Next time I'll go (out.) I'm not afraid to open my (mouth.)

Mrs. Brown: I knew I could (count) on you. Here comes (our) noisy neighbor, Mr. (Crowley,) right now.

Mr. Brown: Sorry dear, I have to go (downtown,) (NOW!!)

Mrs. Brown: Come back, you (coward!)

Check Yourself 1, Page 74

1. price	crime	(pity)	pile
2. mind	kind	(spinning)	finding
3. sign	high	fright	(freight)
4. (list)	cite	aisle	cried
5. (gyp)	bye	cry	reply
6. (niece)	nice	knife	night
7. style	(failed)	filed	fire
8. (pretty)	try	resign	good-bye
9. ice	eye	(aim)	aisle
10. flight	fine	(duty)	dying

Check Yourself 2, Page 75

Mike: (Hi,) (Myra) It's (nice) to see you.

Myra: (Likewise,) (Mike.) How are you?

Mike: (I'm) (tired.) (I) just came in on a (night) (flight) from (Ireland.)

Myra: What (time) did your (flight) (arrive?)

Mike: (I) (arrived) at (five) forty-(five) in the morning.

Myra: (I'm) (surprised) the (airlines) have a late (night) (flight.)

Mike: If you don't (mind,) (Myra) (I) think (I'll) go home and rest for a (while.) (I'm) really (wiped) out!

Myra: (Why) (Mike,) I have a whole (night) (lined) up—(dining) out and going (night)-clubbing!

Mike: (Myra,) are you out of your (mind?)

Myra: (I'm) only joking. You're going (right) home. Sleep (tight!)

Check Yourself 1, Page 78

1. voice	avoid	void	(vows)
2. noise	(nose)	hoist	annoy
3. (towel)	toy	toil	spoil
4. Detroit	Illinois	St. Croix	(New York)

5.	oil	oily	foil	(owl)
6.	boil	broil	(bow)	boy
7.	poison	(pounce)	point	appoint
8.	poise	Joyce	(Joan)	soil
9.	coil	(coal)	coy	coin
10.	(lobster)	sirloin	oyster	moist

Check Yourself 2, Page 78

Mrs. Royce: Hi, Mr. (Lloyd.) Can I help you?

Mr. Lloyd: Yes, Mrs. (Royce,) I'd like a (toy) for my son, (Floyd.)

Mrs. Royce: We have quite a (choice) of (toys.) What about a fire truck?

Mr. Lloyd: That's too (noisy.) Besides, my (boy) would (destroy) it!

Mrs. Royce: Here's an (oil) paint set.

Mr. Lloyd: That's messy. His mother will be (annoyed) if he (soils) anything.

Mrs. Royce: Let me (point) out this electric train.

Mr. Lloyd: Wow! I never had a (toy) like that as a (boy!)

Mrs. Royce: Your (boy) will (enjoy) it. Mr. (Lloyd?) Please turn off the set. Mr. (Lloyd!)

Mr. Lloyd: Did you say something, Mrs. (Royce?) I'm playing with (Floyd's) new (toy!)

Mrs. Royce: I guess you've made your (choice.) I hope you let your (boy) use it once in a while!

Check Yourself 1, Page 87

1. **Juice** made from **oranges** is called orange juice .
2. A **box** used for storing **bread** is called a breadbox .
3. A **store** that sells **books** is called a bookstore .
4. A **ball** you kick with your **foot** is called a football .
5. A **hat** you wear in the **rain** is called a rain hat .
6. A **store** that sells **toys** is called a toystore .
7. A **man** that delivers the **mail** is called a mailman .
8. A **sign** that signals you to **stop** is called a stop sign .
9. When you have an **ache** in your **head**, you have a headache .
10. A **store** that sells **drugs** is called a drugstore .

Check Yourself 2, Page 88

1.	(agent)	annoy	allow	agree
2.	upon	until	undo	(under)
3.	(protect)	program	pronoun	protein
4.	token	toaster	(today)	total
5.	supper	sunken	suffer	(support)
6.	explain	(extra)	excite	exam

7. (deepen) deny devote degree

8. (repair) reason recent reader

9. invite invent inform (instant)

10. open (oppose) over only

Check Yourself 3, Page 88

1. Keep a *record* of your expenses.   ①2

2. The police don't *suspect* anyone.   1②

3. The student will *present* a speech.   1②

4. The *present* was not wrapped.   ①2

5. The *invalid* was in the hospital.   ①2 3

6. Please print your *address* clearly.   ①2

7. I will send a *survey* to all students.   ①2

8. Be sure to *record* your speech.   1②

9. The letter is in the *envelope*.   ①2 3

10. I want to *envelop* the baby in my arms.   1②3

Check Yourself 4, Page 89

①2

Money

①2 ①2
Richard Armour

①2
Workers earn it,

①   2
Spendthrifts burn it,

①   2
Bankers lend it,

①   2
Women spend it,

① 2
Forgers fake it,

①2
Taxes take it,

① 2
Dying leave it,

    1   ②
Heirs receive it,
① 2
Thrifty save it,
① 2
Misers crave it,
① 2
Robbers seize it,
   1 ②
Rich increase it,
① 2
Gamblers lose it . . .

I could use it!

Check Yourself 1, Page 94

1. (Mary) is a (good) (friend.)
2. (Steve) is (tall) and (handsome.)
3. It's (early) in the (morning.)
4. The (baby) (caught) a (cold.)
5. I (ate) a (piece) of (pie.)

6. The (store) (opens) at (nine.)
7. My (shoes) (hurt) my (feet.)
8. (Please) (look) for the (book.)
9. He's (leaving) in a (week.)
10. We (walked) in the (snow.)

Check Yourself 2, Page 94

1. Mary wants ____a____ cup ____of____ coffee.
2. ___The___ show started __at/by__ eight.
3. ___The___ movie __is/was__ very funny.
4. Sue ate __a/the__ slice ____of____ cake.
5. We met ____a____ couple ____of____ friends ____of___ mine.

Check Yourself 3, Page 95

1. Mary is Anna's (friend.) (She isn't her cousin.)

2. John is (married) to Anna. (They aren't engaged anymore.)

3. She's from Washington, (D.C.) (She's not from Washington state.)

4. She lives in the white (house.) (She doesn't live in the White House.)

5. Her house is on First (Street.) (It isn't on First Avenue.)

6. Anna and John got married (three) years ago. (Not five years ago.)

7. They (own) a small home. (They don't rent.)

8. Mary wants to come in a (week.) (She doesn't want to wait a month.)

9. She'll bring her (collie) and snakes. (She's not bringing her poodle.)

10. Mary is opening a (pet) store. (Not a toy store.)

1. __I'm__ a good student. (I am)
2. Lynn __doesn't__ play tennis. (does not)
3. __We've__ seen that movie. (We have)
4. __You're__ quite right. (You are)
5. His brother __can't__ come. (cannot)

1. <u>Meet me at the bus stop // after you're done.</u>
   Meet me at the bus // stop after you're done.
2. Bill Brown the mayor will // speak tonight.
   <u>Bill Brown // the mayor // will speak tonight.</u>
3. <u>Please clean your room // before leaving.</u>
   Please clean your // room before leaving.
4. The truth is I don't // like it.
   <u>The truth is // I don't like it.</u>
5. <u>Cervantes // the famous author // wrote Don Quixote.</u>
   Cervantes the famous author wrote // Don Quixote.
6. <u>He was there // for the first time.</u>
   He was there for // the first time.
7. <u>Where there's a will // there's a way.</u>
   Where there's a // will there's a //way.
8. Do unto others as // you would have them do // unto you.
   <u>Do unto others // as you would have them // do unto you.</u>
9. <u>Patrick Henry said // "Give me liberty // or give me death."</u>
   Patrick Henry // said "Give me // liberty or give me death."
10. When in Rome do // as the Romans do.
    <u>When in Rome // do as the Romans do.</u>

Frances Black: Hello, this is the Black residence. This is Frances Black speaking.

Ellie White: (Howarya) Frannie? (It's) Ellie. (Doyawanna) come over for a (cupacoffee?)

Frances Black: Elinor, I am very sorry I can not visit you. I am going to lunch at the Club.

Ellie White: (That's) OK. (I'm) (gonna) eat at Burger Palace. Why (don't) we go (tathamovies) tonight?

Frances Black: We will not be able to join you. We have tickets for the opera.

Ellie White: My husband Sam (won't) like that. (He's) more of a wrestling fan. (We'll) (meetcha) some other night.

Frances Black: Elinor, I really have to go now. It has been most pleasant speaking with you.

Ellie White: I (hafta) go now too. (It's) been great talking to you. (Hangs up the phone) (Frannie's) a nice girl, but she (hasta) (learnta) relax!

Reduced Forms	Full Form
Howarya?	How are you?
It's	It is
Doyawanna	Do you want to
cupacoffee	cup of coffee
That's	That is
I'm	I am
gonna	going to
don't	do not
tathamovies	to the movies
won't	will not
He's	He is
We'll	We will
meetcha	meet you
hafta	have to
It's	It has
Frannie's	Frannie is
hasta	has to
learnta	learn to

Check Yourself 1, Page 109

		Falling	Rising
1.	When's your birthday?	X	
2.	Did you see my friend?		X
3.	How are you?	X	
4.	I'm fine, thank you.	X	
5.	Why were you absent?	X	
6.	Can you have dinner?		X
7.	How do you know?	X	
8.	I don't like beets.	X	
9.	Where is my pencil?	X	
10.	Will you drive me home?		X

Check Yourself 2, on Page 109

1. We enjoy swimming ↗, hiking ↗, and tennis ↘.

2. Is a barbecue all right ↗ if it doesn't rain? ↗

3. If it rains tomorrow ↗, the game is off ↘.

4. Is he sick ↗? I hope not ↘.

5. Please bring me the hammer ↗, nails ↗, and scissors ↘.

6. Do you like grapes ↗, pears ↗, and plums ↗?

7. May I leave now ↗, or should I wait ↘?

8. He's good at math ↗ but not spelling ↘.

9. Call me later ↗ if it's not too late ↘.

10. Will you visit us ↗ if you're in town ↗?

Check Yourself 3, Page 110

Sam Can't Tell a Joke!

Sam ↗, a convicted **felon** ↗, was sentenced to life in prison ↘. When he arrived at the **prison** ↗, the other inmates were sitting around calling out **numbers** ↘. He heard **Bill** call ↗, "One thousand **twenty**" ↘. Then **Joe** bellowed ↗, "Two hundred **forty**" ↘. "Does anyone know three thousand **two**" ↗? asked **Mark** happily ↘. Each time a number was **called** ↗, the men **roared** with laughter ↘. **Sam** asked ↗, "**What's** so funny ↘? **What** is everyone laughing at" ↘?

Bill explained ↘. "**Well** ↗, we know **thousands** of jokes ↘. It would take **too** long to **tell** each one ↗. So we've **numbered** all of them ↘. When we want to tell a **joke** ↗, we simply call out its **number**" ↘. Sam asked **hopefully** ↗, "Will you guys teach **me** all the jokes ↗ **and** their numbers" ↗?

Bill taught Sam **all** of the jokes **and** their numbers ↘. One **day** ↗, while the inmates were telling **jokes** ↗, **Sam** called "**Five hundred**" ↘. **No** one laughed ↘. He **shouted** ↗, "**Five hundred**" ↘. Still **no** one laughed ↘. "I don't **get** it ↘. **Why** isn't anyone laughing ↘? Isn't number **five hundred** one of our **funniest** jokes" ↗? "**Yes**" ↗, replied **Bill** ↗, "But you didn't **tell** it right" ↘!

Check Yourself, Page 119

1. ⓢu p p o s e
2. Ⓢu s a n
3. d i s a ⓢt e r
4. e a s i e ⓢt
5. p o ⓢt e r s

6. ⓢa l e s m a n
7. ⓢe a s o n
8. r e s i ⓢt
9. p r e s e n t ⓢ
10. b u s i n e ⓢⓢ

Check Yourself, Page 122

1. eyes	nose	(wrist)	ears
2. walls	(waltz)	wells	ways
3. (carrots)	apples	peas	raisins
4. pleasing	pleasant	(pleasure)	please
5. deserve	daisy	(serve)	design
6. (cease)	seize	size	sings
7. Tuesday	Thursday	Wednesday	(Saturday)
8. (east)	ease	easy	tease

9. rose   (rice)   raise   rise

10. (fox)   xylophone   clothes   zero

Check Yourself 1, Page 125

1. 1   2   ③   (peace peace peas)
2. 1   ②   3   (rise rice rise)
3. ①   2   3   (raise race race)
4. 1   ②   3   (Sue zoo Sue)
5. 1   2   ③   (racer racer razor)

6. 1   2   ③   (lose lose loose)
7. ①   2   3   (plays place place)
8. ①   2   3   (phase face face)
9. 1   ②   3   (zeal seal zeal)
10. 1   2   ③   (price price prize)

Check Yourself 2, Page 125

1. **It's** raining **cats** and **dogs**.   [s] [s] [z]
2. Come **as soon as possible**.   [z] [s] [z] [s]
3. **Strike** while the iron **is** hot.   [s] [z]
4. Kill two **birds** with one **stone**.   [z] [s]
5. **Misery loves** company.   [z] [z]

Check Yourself 3, Page 126

1. We finally won the ((race) [s] /raise [z]).
2. I know that ((face) [s] / phase [z]).
3. He gave me a good (price [s] /(prize) [z]).
4. Look at her small ((niece) [s] / knees [z]).
5. We must accept the (loss [s] /(laws) [z]).
6. The sheep have (fleece [s] /(fleas) [z]).
7. Did you hear the (bus [s] /(buzz) [z]).
8. His dog has a large ((muscle) [s] / muzzle [z]).
9. How much is the ((sink) [s] / zinc [z])?
10. 1 can identify the (spice [s] /(spies) [z]).

A Man Named (Stu)

A man from (Texas) named (Stu)
Was <u>crazy</u> about (Silly) (Sue.)
   He <u>proposed</u> twenty <u>times</u>,
      Using (song,) (dance) and <u>rhymes</u>
Until (Sue) (said) to (Stu,) "I do!"

A Girl Named (Maxine)

There <u>was</u> a (slim) girl called (Maxine)
Who loved cooking (Spanish) cuisine.
   She (spent) (days) eating (rice,)
      (Lots) of <u>chicken</u> and (spice.)
Now (Maxine) is no longer lean!

1. (t) r a c t i o n
2. t h a (t)
3. p a t i e n (t)
4. (t) e x t u r e
5. (t) e m p e r a t u r e

6. (t) o o t h
7. p r e s e n (t) a t i o n
8. a r i t h m e (t) i c
9. (t) o g e t h e r
10. s u b (t) r a c t i o n

1. **Tess** had _____too_____ much to **eat**.

2. I **must return** _____two_____ books.

3. "**Two** wrongs **don't** make a ___right___."

4. **Please** ___write___ me a **note**.

5. **Tim's** ___aunt___ is **twenty-two**.

6. **Tie** a **tight** ___knot___.

7. When you go **to** bed, please leave the ___night___ **light** on.

8. **Tony** broke his **little** ___toe___.

9. **What** ___time___ is the **party**?

10. **That** tiger has a **tiny** ___tail___.

1. Ⓒ I   (Mother was **mad** at us.)
2. C Ⓘ   (Be careful when you climb the **lather**.)
3. C Ⓘ   (Plant the **seat** and a flower will grow.)
4. C Ⓘ   (The **bat** children were punished.)
5. Ⓒ I   (The **bride** is very lovely.)

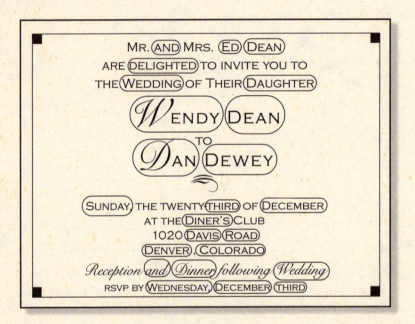

MR. ⒶND MRS. Ⓔd Ⓓean
ARE Ⓓelighted TO INVITE YOU TO
THE Ⓦedding OF THEIR Ⓓaughter

Ⓦendy Ⓓean
TO
Ⓓan Ⓓewey

Ⓢunday, THE TWENTY Ⓣhird OF Ⓓecember
AT THE Ⓓiner's CLUB
1020 Ⓓavis Ⓡoad
Ⓓenver, Ⓒolorado
Reception ⓐnd Ⓓinner following Ⓦedding
RSVP BY Ⓦednesday, Ⓓecember Ⓣhird

Thomas	clothes	ⓉTeeth	feather
ⓇRuth	further	Ⓜmoth	father
although	ⓉThick	other	Ⓕfaith
Ⓣthrow	clothing	breathe	Ⓑbreath
rather	Ⓜmethod	Ⓒcloth	Ⓣthorough

Jim Ⓣhorpe

Do you know Ⓐanything about Jim Ⓣhorpe? He was a Native American Ⓐathlete. He excelled in Ⓔeverything at the Olympics. Ⓣthousands were angry when Ⓣhorpe's medals were taken away because he was called a professional Ⓐathlete. In Ⓐ1973, long after his Ⓓdeath, Ⓣhorpe's medals were restored. Ⓣthroughout the world, Jim Ⓣhorpe is Ⓣthought to be one of the greatest male Ⓐathletes.

1. (This /(These)) shoes are **weatherproof**.
2. **I loathe this** wet ((weather)/whether).
3. ((This)/These) board is **smoother than the other** one.
4. **The** family will be ((there)/their) for **the** wedding.
5. **Mother** told (they /(them)) not to be late.
6. ((They)/Them) are **worthy of the** award.
7. ((Those)/That) **brothers** are **rather** tall.
8. I don't know (weather /(whether)) to buy **this** one or **that** one.
9. ((That)/Those) **lather** is **soothing**.
10. ((Their)/There) **father** likes the **weather** in **southern** Florida.

1. (cloth)   clothing   clothes   clothe
2. though   although   (thought)   those
3. then   them   themselves   (den)
4. feather   father   (faith)   further
5. bathing   (bath)   bathe   breathe
6. (thank)   than   that   then
7. soothe   (sues)   soothing   smooth
8. (dare)   there   their   theirs

(The) Photo Album

Daughter: (Mother,) I like (these) old pictures. Who's (this?)

Mother: (That's) your great (grandmother.)

Daughter: (The) (feathered) hat is funny! Who's (that) man?

Mother: (That's) your (grandfather.) He was from (the) (Netherlands.)

Daughter: I know (these) people! Aren't (they) Uncle Tom and Uncle Bob?

Mother: (That's) right. (Those) are my (brothers.) (They) always (bothered) me!

Daughter: (This) must be (either) (Father) or his (brother.)

Mother: (Neither!) (That's) your (father's) uncle.

Daughter: Why are (there) (other) people in (this) photo?

Mother: (This) was a family (gathering.) We got (together) all (the) time.

Daughter: (Mother,) who's (this) ("smooth")-looking man?

Mother: Shhhhhhhhh! I'd (rather) not say. Your (father) will hear!

Daughter: Is (that) your old boyfriend?

Mother: Well, even (mothers) had fun in (those) days!

Check Yourself, Page 146

1. crush   cash   (catch)   crash
2. chef   (chief)   chute   chiffon
3. machine   parachute   mustache   (kitchen)
4. (China)   Russia   Chicago   Michigan
5. facial   conscience   (science)   conscious
6. pressure   (pressed)   assure   permission
7. (division)   subtraction   addition   multiplication
8. position   action   (patio)   motion
9. Charlotte   Cheryl   Sharon   (Charles)
10. tension   (resign)   pension   mention

Check Yourself, Page 149

1. C (I) (That store has **sheep** prices.)
2. (C) I (I ate **chicken** and rice.)
3. C (I) (My **wash** tells perfect time.)
4. C (I) (He couldn't **cash** the ball.)
5. C (I) (My **choose** hurt my feet.)
6. (C) I (We met the new **teacher**.)
7. (C) I (**March** is a windy month.)
8. (C) I (I can **reach** the top shelf.)
9. C (I) (Please light the **mash**.)
10. (C) I (How many **children** do you have?)

Check Yourself 1, Page 151

1. 1 (2) 3   (chin shin chin)
2. 1 2 (3)   (sheep sheep cheap)
3. (1) 2 3   (chew shoe shoe)
4. (1) 2 3   (dish ditch ditch)
5. 1 2 (3)   (she's she's cheese)
6. 1 (2) 3   (share chair share)
7. 1 2 (3)   (chop chop shop)
8. 1 2 (3)   (mush mush much)
9. 1 2 (3)   (cash cash catch)
10. 1 2 (3)   (witch witch wish)

Check Yourself 2, Page 151

     [ʃ]   [tʃ]   [ʃ]
1. The puppy **sh**ouldn't **ch**ew the **sh**oes.

  [ʃ]   [tʃ]   [ʃ]
2. **Sh**ine the furni**t**ure with poli**sh**.

      [ʃ]   [ʃ]   [ʃ]
3. The **ch**ef prepared a spe**ci**al di**sh**.

      [ʃ]   [tʃ]   [ʃ]
4. We **sh**ould **ch**ange the dirty **sh**eets.

   [tʃ]   [ʃ]   [tʃ]
5. **Ch**oosing a profe**ss**ion is a **ch**allenge.

1. I didn't see the (dish /[ditch]).   6. She brought me the (wash /[watch]).

2. He hurt his (shin /[chin]).   7. You have a large (share /[chair]).

3. Did you hear that ([shatter]/ chatter)?   8. We must fix the ([ship]/ chip).

4. It's a silly ([wish]/ witch).   9. Does she have a new (crush /[crutch])?

5. It was an endless ([marsh]/ March).   10. You completed the (shore /[chore]).

(Each pair is marked with the phonetic symbols [ʃ] over the first word and [tʃ] over the second word.)

Richard: Do you have any <u>change</u> for the (washing) (machine?) My wife, (Sharon,) is visiting family in (Michigan.) I'm <u>watching</u> the children and doing the <u>chores</u>.

Marshall: <u>Watch</u> out! Don't put <u>bleach</u> on those (shirts.) You'll (wash) out the color.

Richard: Will you <u>teach</u> me how to (wash) clothes?

Marshall: Be sure to (wash) white (shirts) separately. Don't use too <u>much</u> soap.

Richard: I (wish) (Sharon) would return. It's more <u>natural</u> for a woman to (wash) and (shop.)

Marshall: You sound like a (chauvinist!) I don't mind doing <u>chores</u>. I'm great in the <u>kitchen</u>, too!

Richard: Would you like to take <u>charge</u>? I'll <u>cheerfully</u> pay you (cash.)

Marshall: Listen, old <u>chap</u>, I'm a <u>bachelor</u> and too old to <u>chase</u> after <u>children</u>. I'm in a (rush.) It's been nice <u>chatting</u> with you, <u>Richard</u>.

Richard: (Sure,) nice <u>chatting</u> with you, too, (Marshall.)

1. leisure	pleasure	(sure)	measure
2. Asia	Asian	Parisian	(Paris)
3. (huge)	beige	rouge	prestige
4. (passion)	collision	occasion	decision
5. massage	mirage	(message)	corsage
6. confusion	(conclusive)	contusion	conclusion
7. lesion	(profession)	explosion	aversion
8. vision	version	television	(visible)
9. seizure	(seize)	azure	division
10. treasury	treasurer	(treason)	treasure

1. The commi**ss**ion [ʃ] made a deci**si**on [ʒ].

2. The class learned divi**si**on [ʒ] and addi**ti**on [ʃ].

3. Mea**s**ure [ʒ] the gara**ge** [ʒ].

4. Your profe**ss**ion [ʃ] has presti**ge** [ʒ].

5. That's an unu**su**al [ʒ] **sh**ade [ʃ] of rou**ge** [ʒ].

Good evening. This is (Frazier) White with the 10:00 p.m. (television) news. Tonight we have some most (unusual) stories. Here are the headlines:

- Tourists on a (pleasure) trip discovered valuable (Persian) rugs. The rugs dated back to ancient (Persia.)

- An (explosion) took place in a (garage) on First Avenue. (Seizure) of a bomb was made after much (confusion.)

- (Asian) flu is spreading. (Asian) flu vaccinations will be available to those with (exposure) to the germ.

- Today was the (Parisian) fashion show. Everything from (casual) (leisure) clothes to (negligees) was shown. (Beige) is the big color. Hemlines (measure) two inches below the knee.

- Carry your raincoat. (Occasional) showers are due tomorrow. Hope your evening is a (pleasure.)

This is (Frazier) White saying GOOD NIGHT!

(Java)	Luxemburg	Guatemala	(Jerusalem)
Greece	England	(Germany)	(Algeria)
Hungary	(Japan)	Greenland	China
(Egypt)	(Belgium)	(Argentina)	(Jamaica)

1. badge · Bulge · (Bug) · Budge
2. (captain) · general · major · soldier
3. (hen) · gentle · gem · intelligent
4. juice · age · angel · (angle)
5. huge · (hug) · jug · July
6. giraffe · (gill) · giant · gin
7. (duck) · cordial · educate · graduate
8. large · lounge · (lung) · lunge
9. (Gary) · Joe · Jill · Gene
10. Virginia · Georgia · Germany · (Greenland)

1. The youth left. He hasn't come back **ye**t.
2. The player ran 50 yards. The crowds began to **ye**ll.
3. Today is Monday. **Ye**sterday was Sunday.
4. Egg yolks should be **ye**llow.
5. You should go to the doctor to get a checkup once a **ye**ar.

Check Yourself 2, Page 165

1. (SAME)　　DIFFERENT　(I had to **yawn**. I had to **yawn**.)
2. SAME　　(DIFFERENT)　(Did you say **yacht**? Did you say **jot**?)
3. SAME　　(DIFFERENT)　(It's not **yellow**. It's not **Jell-O**.)
4. (SAME)　　DIFFERENT　(They left **yesterday**. They left **yesterday**.)
5. SAME　　(DIFFERENT)　(Where is the **mayor**? Where is the **major**?)

Check Yourself 1, Page 167

1. ___Yale___ (**Jail** is a famous university.)
2. ___yam___ (A **jam** is like a sweet potato.)
3. ___yellow___ (**Jell-O** is my favorite color.)
4. ___yolk___ (An egg **joke** is yellow.)
5. ___year___ (There are 365 days in a **jeer**.)
6. ___juice___ (Do you drink apple **use**?)
7. ___jet___ (I travel on **yet** airplanes.)
8. ___yacht___ (We took a cruise on a **jot**.)
9. ___jewel___ (A ruby is a precious **you'll**.)
10. ___jokes___ (People play **yokes** on April Fools Day.)

Check Yourself 2, Page 167

Do <u>you</u> know what <u>YANKEE</u> means? People from the <u>United</u> States are (generally) called <u>Yankees</u>. (Soldiers) from the northern (region) were called <u>Yankees</u> during the Civil War. (George) M. Cohan wrote a (stage) hit called "<u>Yankee</u> Doodle Dandy." (Jealous) baseball fans (waged) war over the New <u>York Yankees</u> and (Dodgers) for <u>years</u>. Whether <u>you</u> are from (Georgia) or New (Jersey,) <u>you</u> should (enjoy) being called a <u>Yank!</u>

Check Yourself 1, Page 174

1. A nickname for **Peter** is ___Pete___.
2. The **opposite** of war is ___peace___.
3. **Pam** bought ___peanuts___ to feed the elephants.
4. The **top** of a mountain is called a ___peak___.
5. The **plural** of "person" is "___people___."
6. A **popular** fruit is a ___peach___.
7. A bird with bright feathers is a ___peacock___.
8. The **potatoes** should be washed well if they are not going to be ___peeled___.
9. The letter **preceding** Q is ___P___.
10. Something that annoys you is called a "**pet** ___peeve___."

Peter: (Paulette), I have a (surprise!) We're taking a (trip) tonight!

Paulette: I'm very (happy). But I need more time to (prepare).

Peter: That's (simple). I'll (help) you (pack).

Paulette: Who will care for our (pet) (poodle)?

Peter: Your (parents!)

Paulette: Who will (pick) (up) the mail?

Peter: Our neighbor, (Pat.)

Paulette: Who will water the (plants?)

Peter: We'll (put) them on the (patio).

Paulette: Who will (pay) for the (trip?)

Peter: The (company) is (paying) every (penny!)

Paulette: (Peter,) you've really (planned) this.

Peter: Of course! I'm (dependable), (superior,) and a (perfect . . .)

Paulette: ("Pain) in the neck!" Don't get carried away!

1. I like rye ((bread)/ bred).
2. Don't walk in your (bear/(bare)) feet.
3. **Bob** has ((been)/ bin) here **before**.
4. Please store the **beans** in the (been /(bin)).
5. The wind ((blew)/ blue) my **bag** away.
6. Betty's (**blew**/(**blue**)) **bonnet** is **becoming**.
7. ((Buy)/ By) a **box** of **black buttons**.
8. The dog will (**berry**/(**bury**)) its **bone** in the **backyard**.
9. My **brother** watches **baseball** when he's ((bored)/ board).
10. The **builder** needs a bigger (**bored**/(**board**)).

1. **Find** another name **for** a drugstore. <u>pharmacy</u>
2. **Find** another name **for** a doctor. <u>physician</u>
3. **Find** another name **for** a snapshot. <u>photograph</u>
4. **Find** the name **for** a person who studies **philosophy**. <u>philosopher</u>
5. **Find** the short **form** of the word **telephone**. <u>phone</u>
6. **Find** another name **for** a record player. <u>phonograph</u>
7. **Find** the name **for** a person who predicts the **future.** <u>prophet</u>
8. **Find** the name **for** the study of sounds. <u>phonetics</u>
9. Find the term that **refers** to your sister's son. <u>nephew</u>
10. **Find** the name **for** a chart showing **figures**. <u>graph</u>

(Florida)

(Florida) was (founded) by Ponce de Leon in (1513.) This (famous) explorer (from) Spain was searching (for) a (fountain) of youth. He named the land (*Florida,*) which means ("full) of (flowers") in Spanish. He (failed) in his (efforts) to (find) the (fountain.) He (finally) died (after) (fighting) the Indians. (Unfortunately,) no one has ever (found) the (fountain) in (Florida) or the (formula) (for) eternal youth. However, the (fun) and sun in (Florida) are (enough) to attract (folks) (from) every (hemisphere) to this (famous) state.

Check Yourself 1, Page 185

1. B M (E)	(have)	6. B (M) E	(several)
2. B (M) E	(heavy)	7. B (M) E	(clever)
3. B (M) E	(over)	8. B M (E)	(love)
4. (B) M E	(victory)	9. (B) M E	(very)
5. B (M) E	(oven)	10. B (M) E	(television)

Check Yourself 2, Page 185

1. ((clever)/clover/cover)   **Van** is a _____ student.
2. (clever/clover/(cover))   I bought a **velvet** _____.
3. (berry/(very)/ferry)   **Vera** is _____ pretty.
4. (leaf/(leave)/live)   The train will _____ at **seven**.
5. (leaves/(loves)/lives)   **Vicky** _____ her sons, **Victor** and **Vance**.
6. (off/(of)/if)   My **vest** is made _____ leather.
7. (alive/(arrive)/live)   The plane will _____ at **five**.
8. (belief/(believe)/bereave)   I _____ **Vinny** will be **eleven** in **November**.
9. ((several)/severe/seventh)   **Eve** has _____ **TVs** in her living room.
10. (oven/(over)/overt)   He left before the **movie** was _____.

Check Yourself 3, Page 186

I (Never) Saw a Moor

Emily Dickenson

I (never) saw a moor
I (never) saw the sea;
Yet know I how the heather looks,
And what a (wave) must be.

I (never) spoke with God,
Nor (visited) in (Heaven;)
Yet certain am I (of) the spot
As if the chart were (given.)

Check Yourself 1, Page 188

(Ohio)　　　Michigan　　　(Oklahoma)　　　(Houston)

(Idaho)　　　Massachusetts　　　Washington　　　(New Hampshire)

Chicago　　　(Hartford)　　　(Hawaii)　　　(Tallahassee)

Check Yourself 2, Page 189

Helen: (Hi,) Mom. Welcome (home.)

Mother: (Hi) (honey.)

Helen: (How) was (Holland?)

Mother: Like a second (honeymoon!) I'm as (happy) as a lark. (How) are you?

Helen: Not so (hot!) (Henry) is in the (hospital) with a broken (hip.)

Mother: That's (horrible.) (How) did that (happen?)

Helen: (He) (heard) a noise outside. (He) went (behind) the (house) and fell over a (hose.)

Mother: (How) are my (handsome) grandsons?

Helen: They won't (behave.) And my (housekeeper) (had) to quit.

Mother: (Perhaps) you'd like me to (help) at (home.)

Helen: Oh, Mom, I was (hoping) you'd say that. (Hurry) to the (house) as soon as possible.

Mother: I guess the (honeymoon) is over. (Here) we go again!

Check Yourself 1, Page 193

(week)　　　(someone)　　　(queen)　　　write

(while)　　　who　　　wrong　　　(worry)

whose　　　(waiter)　　　(reward)　　　(square)

guilt　　　(unwilling)　　　saw　　　(worthy)

(west)　　　lawyer　　　(anywhere)　　　low

Check Yourself 2, Page 193

(Woodrow) (Wilson)

(Woodrow) (Wilson) (was) the (twenty)-fifth president of the United States. He (will) always be remembered for his (work) to establish (world) peace. (Wilson) (was) born in 1865 and later (went) to Princeton University. He became president in 1913 and stayed in the (White) House for two terms. His first (wife) died (while) he (was) in office, and he later married a (Washington) (widow.) (When) the United States entered (World) (War) (I) in 1917, (Wilson) (quickly) provided the needed (wisdom.) After the (war,) (Wilson) made a (nationwide) tour to (win) support for the League of Nations. (Wilson) (was) (awarded) the Nobel Prize for his (worthwhile) (work) for peace. He died in (1924.) (Everywhere) in the (world,) (Wilson) (was) thought of as a (wise) and (wonderful) leader.

1. If you **live** in **Dublin**, you **also live** in ___Ireland___ .
2. If you **live** in **London**, you **also live** in ___England___ .
3. If you **live** in **Lisbon**, you **also live** in ___Portugal___ .
4. If you **live** in **Lucerne**, you **also live** in ___Switzerland___ .
5. If you **live** in **Milan**, you **also live** in ___Italy___ .
6. If you **live** in **Baltimore**, you **also live** in ___Maryland___ .
7. If you **live** in **Brussels**, you **also live** in ___Belgium___ .
8. If you **live** in **Orlando**, you **also live** in ___Florida___ .
9. If you **live** in **Sâo Paulo**, you **also live** in ___Brazil___ .
10. If you **live** in **New Orleans**, you **also live** in ___Louisiana___ .

1. 1 ②   (rice   lice)
2. ① 2   (lake   rake)
3. ① 2   (belly   berry)
4. 1 ②   (rent   lent)
5. ① 2   (lime   rhyme)

6. ① 2   (look   rook)
7. ① 2   (collect   correct)
8. ① 2   (Ilene   Irene)
9. 1 ②   (arrive   alive)
10. ① 2   (lose   ruse)

(July)(11th)

(Linda,)

(Leon) and I had bad (luck.) — (Luggage) was (lost) (while) (traveling) from (La) Paz, (Bolivia,) to (Honolulu.) — (Airline) (personnel) were (all) very (helpful.) — They (told) (Leon) they (will) (certainly) (locate) (all,) (eventually,) if we're (lucky.) — It (looks) (like) the (luggage) (landed) in (Lima.) — At (least) we met (lots) of (lovely) (people.) — (Also,) we could (leave) on a (later) (flight.) — (I'll) (telephone) with new (flight) (schedule.) — We should be home for (lunch) with the (family) at twelve (o'clock.) — (Hopefully,) our (arrival) won't be (delayed.) — Talk to you (later) — (Love) you a (whole) (lot.) — (Lou)

1. rave   brave/crave/grave
2. right   bright/fright
3. rip   drip/trip
4. ream   dream/cream
5. row   crow/grow/brow

6. rain   brain/drain/train/grain
7. rash   trash/brash/crash
8. room   broom/groom
9. round   ground
10. race   brace/grace/trace

1. This **creature** has black and white **stripes**.
   This **creature** is a ___zebra___ .
2. This **forest creature** has long **ears** and is a **celebrity** at Easter.
   This **creature** is a ___rabbit___ .

3. This **creature** has **large antlers** and is **around** at **Christmas**.

   This **creature** is a __reindeer__ .

4. This **creature** has spots and a very long neck.

   This **creature** is a __giraffe__ .

5. This **creature** lives in the **arctic**, is **large**, and is very **hungry**.

   This **creature** is a **polar** __bear__ .

6. This **forest creature carries her** babies in a pouch.

   This **creature** is a _kangaroo_ .

7. This **friendly creature "croaks"** and says **"ribbi, ribbi."**

   This **creature** is a __frog__ .

8. This **forest creature** is a very talkative **bird**.

   This **colorful creature** is a __parrot__ .

9. This **fierce creature** has black and yellow **stripes**.

   This **ferocious creatur**e is a __tiger__ .

10. This **graceful creature started** as a caterpillar.

    This **pretty creature** is a _butterfly_ .

Check Yourself 3, Page 203

Robin Hood

The story of Robin Hood has been retold many times. Robin Hood was an outlaw who lived in Sherwood Forest. He lived there with Maid Marion, Friar Tuck, and others. Robin was really a hero rather than a criminal. He robbed the rich and gave to the poor. He was a remarkable marksman with his bow and arrow. The story of Robin Hood has been written about and dramatized since the eleventh century. Robin truly represents a righteous figure opposing cruelty and greed.

Check Yourself 1, Page 206

1. Don't step on the (glass / grass). [gl] [gr]
2. Please put this on your (list / wrist). [l] [r]
3. The entire family is (pleasant / present). [pl] [pr]
4. It was a terrible (climb / crime). [kl] [kr]
5. Look at the bright red (flame / frame). [fl] [fr]

6. He likes black (clothes / crows). [kl] [kr]
7. She has the (blues / bruise). [bl] [br]
8. That's a new (bloom / broom). [bl] [br]
9. I lost the (lock / rock). [l] [r]
10. We need new (tiles / tires). [l] [r]

Check Yourself 2, Page 207

1. __read__ (Did you **lead** the book?)
2. __bloom__ (The flowers are in **broom**.)
3. __lake__ (Take a swim in the **rake**.)
4. __lock__ (Be sure to **rock** the door.)
5. __correct__ (The answer is **collect**.)

1. The color of Halloween pumpkins is ___orange___.
2. I like bananas that are ripe and ___yellow___.
3. Caribbean waters are usually a bright ___blue___.
4. Emeralds should be a clear ___green___.
5. Fran's lipstick is a deep ___red___.
6. Formal attire requires ___black___ tie.
7. People frequently use color when their hair turns ___gray___.
8. "Brunette" describes someone with ___black___ or ___brown___ hair.
9. The color of orchids is often deep ___purple___ or ___lavender___.
10. Many models use lemon juice to give their hair ___blonde___ highlights.

Check Yourself 1, Page 211

1. course   count   (choose)   chorus
2. can't   can   (cent)   cone
3. Canada   Texas   Kansas   (Massachusetts)
4. key   keep   keen   (kneel)
5. (celery)   corn   carrots   cabbage
6. mix   box   explain   (xylophone)
7. (knee)   back   ankle   cheek
8. (Charles)   Carol   Chris   Michael
9. mechanic   (much)   chrome   Christmas
10. milk   (cider)   coffee   cream

Check Yourself 2, Page 212

The (American) (Cowboy)

(Americans) (created) the name (cowboy) for the men who (cared) for (cattle.) You might (recall) the (typical) singing (cowboy) in the movies. He was (kind), (courageous), and good-looking. He always (caught) the (cow), (colt), and of (course) the girl! But the real (cowboy) was a hard (worker) who had many (difficult) (tasks.) He had to (take) the (cattle) to (market.) These lonely (cattle) drives (took) many (weeks) through rough (country.) The (cowboy) had to (protect) the (cattle) and (keep) them from running off. In (fact) or (fiction,) the (cowboy) will (continue) to be a (likeable) (American) (character.) *Ride 'em* (cowboy)!

Check Yourself 1, Page 215

1. luggage   tag   forget
   Don't forget to ask for a luggage tag.
2. grow   garden   ground
   The garden will grow in the fertile ground.
3. dog   growl   bug
   The dog started to growl at the bug.
4. green   grass   log
   I tripped over a log in the green grass.
5. glad   gift   groom
   The groom was glad to receive a gift.

> *Breakfast*
>   (Grapefruit)   (Fried eggs)   (Grits)   Sausage
>
> *Lunch*
>   (Hamburgers)   (Grilled onions)   Gelatin   (Vinegar dressing)
>
> *Dinner*
>   Lasagna   (Leg of lamb)   (Green peas)   (Chicken gumbo)
>
> *Dessert*
>   Angel food cake   (Glazed doughnuts)   (Grapes)   (Figs)

Check Yourself 1, Page 219

1. ① 2 3   (clam clan clang)   4. ① 2 3   (team teen teen)
2. 1 ② 3   (ban bam bang)   5. 1 ② 3   (sun/son some/sum sung)
3. 1 2 ③   (rung run rum)

Check Yourself 2, Page 219

1. Marilyn Monroe   3. Margaret Mitchell
2. Micky Mantle   4. Mickey Mouse

Check Yourself 1, Page 222

1. S Ⓓ   (It's the **sane** thing. It's the **same** thing.)
2. Ⓢ D   (Pick up the **phone**. Pick up the **phone**.)
3. S Ⓓ   (He is my **kin**. He is my **king**.)
4. Ⓢ D   (This is **fun**. This is **fun**.)
5. S Ⓓ   (Please don't **sin**. Please don't **sing**.)

Check Yourself 2, Page 223

When **John** got home, his wife **Gwen** was _____in_____ the kitchen. She was _____on_____ the **phone** **again**. It was later ___than___ he realized; it was already **ten** o'clock! **John** was so tired he **went** to his bedroom. ___Then___ he sat ___down___ **on** his bed **and** took off his shoes ___and___ socks. "___Can't___ you get off that **phone**," he called to **Gwen**. "Yes, I _____can_____," she yelled back. But by the time **Gwen** walked ___into___ the room, **John** was fast asleep!

Check Yourself 1, Page 225

1. 1 ② (She's a sinner. She's a **singer**.) 4. ① 2 (I heard the **bang**. I heard the bam.)

2. ① 2 (It's not that **thing**. It's not that thin.) 5. 1 ② (They had rum. They had **rung**.)

3. 1 ② (It's just a whim. It's just a **wing**.)

Check Yourself 2, Page 225

1. (bring)	6. tangerine	11. (along)	16. engage
2. (anger)	7. (swing)	12. (talking)	17. (stinging)
3. (hang)	8. (tangle)	13. sponge	18. stingy
4. angel	9. danger	14. grin	19. lunch
5. (dancing)	10. (sink)	15. (running)	20. (bank)

Check Yourself I, Page 228

1. (thin)	thing	6. seem	(scene)
2. (ban)	bang	7. some	(sung)
3. sinner	(singer)	8. hammer	(hanger)
4. comb	(cone)	9. (ram)	rang
5. (rum)	run	10. (gone)	gong

Check Yourself 2, Page 228

1. **Jean** sat **in** the (sum /(sun)/ sung)

2. The bird hurt his (whim / win /(wing))

3. It is **fun** to (rum /(run)/ rung)

4. The **meat needs** to ((simmer)/ sinner / singer)

5. They **removed** the (bam /(ban)/ bang).

Check Yourself 3, Page 228

1. I'll call ((them)[m]/ then[n]).

2. He (ran[n] /(rang)[ŋ]) twice.

3. That (bun[n] /(bum)[m]) is old.

4. We got (some[m] /(sun)[n]) at the beach.

5. I heard a (bam[m] /(bang)[ŋ]).

6. You shouldn't ((sing)[ŋ]/ sin[n]).

7. The children like (swinging[ŋ] /(swimming)[m]).

8. It's a small (ping[ŋ] /(pin)[n]).

9. Get rid of the ((gum)[m]/ gun[n]).

10. Buy another (hammer[m] /(hanger)[ŋ]).

Announcer: Is your skin feeling dry? Are you finding new wrinkles and lines? Then you need Pom's Skin Cream. Men and women everywhere are talking about our cream. Listen to famous film star Molly Malone, who has been acting for a long, long time.

Molly: Hmmm. Of course, everyone knows I started making films when I was nine. But I've been using Pom's Cream for years and I think it's wonderful. Just put it on every morning and evening, and in one week you'll start seeing the difference. Your face will gleam and shine and you'll look just fine!

Announcer: And now for a limited time, you can get two jars for the price of one. Remember, use Pom's Skin Cream and you, too, can look like a film star.

Check Yourself 1, Page 233

1. _2_ hot	_1_ hog	_3_ hop	6. _2_ fade	_3_ fate	_1_ fake
2. _3_ wrote	_1_ rope	_2_ robe	7. _3_ wipe	_2_ white	_1_ wife
3. _1_ save	_2_ safe	_3_ same	8. _2_ peg	_3_ pen	_1_ pet
4. _2_ right	_1_ ride	_3_ ripe	9. _1_ prize	_2_ prime	_3_ pride
5. _2_ mad	_1_ mat	_3_ map	10. _2_ bid	_1_ big	_3_ bit

Check Yourself 2, Page 234

1. The key opens the _____. ((lock)/ log / lot)

2. The _____ is in the fire. (lock /(log)/ lot)

3. _____ the dirty dishes. ((Soak)/ Soap / Sole)

4. Wash your hands with _____. (soak /(soap)/ sole)

5. He _____ the letter. ((wrote)/ rose / rode)

6. He _____ the bicycle. (wrote / rose /(rode))

7. The _____ landed. (plague /(plane)/ plate)

8. The _____ is broken. (plague / plane /(plate))

9. Send a birthday _____. (cart /(card)/ carve)

10. The bags are in the _____. ((cart)/ card / carve)

Check Yourself 3, Page 234

1. I can't find the ((belt)/ bell).

2. My son is (five /(fine)).

3. I think he's ((dead)/ deaf).

4. Tim bought another (car /(card)).

5. The (guild /(guilt)) is ours.

6. The ((pack)/ pact) was sealed.

7. There's a (lake/ lane) near the house.   9. The (den / dent) is very small.

8. I (can / can't) go.   10. The (coal/ colt) is black.

Check Yourself 4, Page 234

Ann: Hi, Pam! How was your da_t_e last nigh_t_ with Pat?

Pam: Nothing went righ_t_ last nigh_t_. Pa_t_ had a fla_t_ tire and came la_t_e!

Ann: How was the foo_d_ at the Ol_d_ Inn?

Pam: It was ba_d_. The soup was col_d_. My stea_k_ was tough. They ra_n_ out of chocola_t_e ca_k_e.

Ann: What about the dinner Pa_t_ a_t_e?

Pam: His duc_k_ was overdo_n_e. His garli_c_ brea_d_ was sta_l_e!

Ann: Did it cos_t_ a lot of money?

Pam: Yes! And Pat didn't ha_v_e enough to pay the bi_ll_.

Ann: I guess you won'_t_ go ou_t_ with him agai_n_!

Pam: Why do you say tha_t_? We're going for a bi_k_e ri_d_e this afternoon. He's so handso_m_e!

Check Yourself 1, Page 238

1. [kt] [kst] [sks] [ks]   Sam **liked** to swim when he was young.
2. [kt] [kst] [sks] [ks]   Stella **walks** home from school.
3. [skr] [sk] [sks] [sk]   Please don't **scream**; I can hear you!
4. [skr] [kt] [ks] [sk]   Our teacher is very **stric**t.
5. [skr] [st] [sks] [sk]   My cat **scratched** me.
6. [spl] [spr] [str] [sts]   How did you **sprain** your ankle?
7. [skr] [sk] [sks] [sts]   Try not to take unnecessary **risks**.
8. [skr] [sk] [skt] [kt]   The firefighters **risked** their lives to save us.
9. [skr] [kst] [skt] [ks]   Bob washed and **waxed** his car.
10. [spr] [spl] [sp] [sl]   Many flowers bloom in the **spring**.

Check Yourself 2, Page 239

1. E A L S T
   It's a crime to _____steal_____.
2. I P R A S E
   To __praise__ someone is to pay them a compliment.
3. S K A
   To make a request is to _____ask_____.
4. S P W A
   A __wasp__ is an insect that stings.
5. S P I R E P E R
   To _perspire_ means to sweat.
6. P L M P U
   The opposite of skinny is __plump__.

7. U S T E R C L
Be sure to pronounce each consonant ___cluster___ clearly.

8. R P S H A
Be careful when using an object with a ___sharp___ point.

9. S T R A M E
The children went swimming in the ___stream___.

10. E A K S Q U S
Squeals, shrieks, screeches, and ___squeaks___ are all annoying sounds.

Check Yourself 3, Page 239

1. [spr] [spl] (skr) [str]   (**screwdriver**; I lost my **screwdriver**; **screwdriver**)

2. [spr] [spl] [skr] (str)   (**street**; I live on this **street**; **street**)

3. [spr] [spl] (skr) [str]   (**scrub**; The cook will **scrub** the pots; **scrub**)

4. [spr] (spl) [skr] [str]   (**split**; Let's **split** the cost; **split**)

5. [spr] [spl] (skw) [str]   (**squeeze**; **Squeeze** the toothpaste; **squeeze**)

6. [sps] [spt] [skt] (kst)   (**fixed**; He **fixed** the broken desk; **fixed**)

7. [sps] [spt] [skt] (rks)   (**parks**; The **parks** have trees; **parks**)

8. [sps] (spt) [skt] [sks]   (**grasped**; My son **grasped** my hand; **grasped**)

9. [sps] [spt] (kst) [sks]   (**mixed**; We **mixed** the batter for the cake; **mixed**)

10. [sps] [spt] (spl) [rks]   (**splendid**; The weather is **splendid**; **splendid**)

Check Yourself 1, Page 245

1. We ___danced___ the rumba and tango. [t]

2. She ___talked___ on the phone for an hour. [t]

3. Dad ___painted___ the fence green. [ɪd]

4. The student ___asked___ three questions. [t]

5. They ___waited___ fifteen minutes for the bus. [ɪd]

6. I've ___lived___ in the same house for four years [d].

7. My father ___mailed___ a letter. [d]

8. The man ___walked___ five miles. [t]

9. I ___deposited___ my check in the bank. [ɪd]

10. He ___washed___ his car with a hose. [t]

Check Yourself 2, Page 245

1. C (I)   (Yesterday, I **shine** my shoes.)

2. C (I)   (The children **watchid** [watʃɪd] TV.)

3. (C) I   (Dad **rented** a car.)

4. C (I)   (Who **call** you this morning?)

5. C (I)   (John **cleant** his room.)

1. (stopped) started stated
2. (finished) followed phoned
3. (loved) looked liked
4. tasted traded (taped)
5. cooked (cleaned) baked

6. packed (pasted) passed
7. ironed sewed (mended)
8. whispered (shouted) screamed
9. skipped hopped (lifted)
10. (pushed) pulled raised

Roberta: Karl, have you **started** [ɪd] your diet? I hope you haven't **gained** [d] any weight.

Karl: I **boiled** [d] eggs and **sliced** [t] celery for lunch.

Roberta: Have you **exercised** [d] at all?

Karl: I **walked** [t] five miles and **jogged** [d] in the park.

Roberta: Have you **cleaned** [d] the house? Calories can be **worked** [t] off that way.

Karl: I **washed** [t] and **waxed** [t] the floors. I even **painted** [ɪd] the bathroom.

Roberta: Who **baked** [t] this apple pie? Who **cooked** [t] this ham?

Karl: When I **finished** [t] cleaning, I was **starved** [d]. I **prepared** [d] this food for dinner.

Roberta: Oh, no! I'll take this food home so you won't be **tempted** [ɪd].

I really **enjoyed** [d] being with you. Your diet is great!

Karl: What **happened** [d]? Somehow, I **missed** [t] out on all the fun.

1. The men cut the (tree /(trees)).
2. He repaired the ((watch)/ watches).
3. The (book /(book's)) cover is red.

4. Did they finally make ((peace)/ peas)?
5. Did you see the little (cups /(cubs))?

1. talks walks (runs)
2. dishes (gates) pages
3. pears apples (oranges)
4. eyes (noses) toes
5. (saves) makes cooks

6. newspapers magazines (books)
7. dogs birds (cats)
8. tables chairs (couches)
9. (dentists) doctors lawyers
10. lunches beaches (chimes)

From (As) *You Like It*

All the (world's) a stage,

And all the men and women merely (players;)

They have their (exits) and their (entrances;)

And one man in his time (plays) many (parts,)

His (acts) being seven (ages.)

From *Othello*

Good name in man and woman, dear my lord,

Is the immediate jewel of their (souls;)

Who (steals) my purse (steals) trash; 'tis something, nothing;

'Twas mine, 'tis his, and has been slave to (thousands;)

But he that (filches) from me my good name

(Robs) me of that which not (enriches) him

And (makes) me poor indeed.

From *The Merchant of Venice*

Hath not a Jew eyes?

Hath not a Jew (hands), (organs), (dimensions), (senses), (affections), (passions?)

Fed with the same food,

Hurt with the same (weapons,)

Subject to the same (diseases,)

Healed by the same (means,)

Warmed and cooled by the same winter and summer, as a Christian is?

[s]	[z]	[ɪz]
exits	world's	entrances
parts	players	ages
acts	plays	filches
makes	souls	enriches
	steals	senses
	thousands	diseases
	robs	
	eyes	
	hands	
	organs	
	dimensions	
	affections	
	passions	
	weapons	
	means	

English Pronunciation Made Simple

Student CD Tracking Guide

CD 1

TRACK	ACTIVITY	PAGE
1	Audio Program Introduction	
2	Audio Program Instructions	
3	Lesson 2, Check Yourself	8
4	Lesson 2, Check Yourself	11
5	Lesson 2, Check Yourself 1	12
6	Lesson 2, Check Yourself 2	13
7	Lesson 2, Check Yourself 3	13
8	Lesson 3, Check Yourself 2	17
9	Lesson 4, Check Yourself 1	21
10	Lesson 4, Check Yourself 2	21
11	Lesson 5, Check Yourself 1	24
12	Lesson 5, Check Yourself 2	25
13	Lesson 6, Check Yourself 1	29
14	Lesson 6, Check Yourself 2	29
15	Lesson 8, Check Yourself	36
16	Lesson 8, Check Yourself	38
17	Lesson 8, Check Yourself 2	41
18	Lesson 9, Check Yourself 1	45
19	Lesson 9, Check Yourself 2	46
20	Lesson 9, Check Yourself 3	46
21	Lesson 10, Check Yourself 1	50
22	Lesson 11, Check Yourself 1	54
23	Lesson 11, Check Yourself 2	54
24	Lesson 13, Check Yourself 1	59
25	Lesson 19, Check Yourself 2	88
26	Lesson 19, Check Yourself 3	88
27	Lesson 22, Check Yourself 1	109
28	Lesson 24, Check Yourself	119
29	Lesson 24, Check Yourself	122
30	Lesson 24, Check Yourself 1	125
31	Lesson 24, Check Yourself 3	126
32	Lesson 24, Check Yourself 4	126

CD 2

TRACK	ACTIVITY	PAGE
1	Audio Program Introduction	
2	Audio Program Instructions	
3	Lesson 26, Check Yourself 1	133
4	Lesson 27, Check Yourself 1	137
5	Lesson 28, Check Yourself 2	141
6	Lesson 30, Check Yourself	146
7	Lesson 30, Check Yourself	149
8	Lesson 30, Check Yourself 1	151
9	Lesson 30, Check Yourself 3	152
10	Lesson 32, Check Yourself 1	157
11	Lesson 32, Check Yourself 2	158
12	Lesson 32, Check Yourself 3	158
13	Lesson 33, Check Yourself 2	162
14	Lesson 33, Check Yourself 2	165
15	Lesson 33, Check Yourself 1	167
16	Lesson 33, Check Yourself 2	167
17	Lesson 36, Check Yourself 2	174
18	Lesson 39, Check Yourself 1	185
19	Lesson 41, Check Yourself 1	193
20	Lesson 42, Check Yourself 2	198
21	Lesson 44, Check Yourself 1	206
22	Lesson 44, Check Yourself 2	207
23	Lesson 47, Check Yourself 1	219
24	Lesson 48, Check Yourself 1	222
25	Lesson 49, Check Yourself 1	225
26	Lesson 49, Check Yourself 2	225
27	Lesson 50, Check Yourself 1	228
28	Lesson 50, Check Yourself 3	228
29	Lesson 51, Check Yourself 1	233
30	Lesson 51, Check Yourself 3	234
31	Lesson 52, Check Yourself 1	238
32	Lesson 52, Check Yourself 3	239
33	Lesson 53, Check Yourself 2	245
34	Lesson 53, Check Yourself 3	246
35	Lesson 54, Check Yourself 1	252
36	Lesson 54, Check Yourself 2	252